America's Natural Places

Regional Volumes in *America's Natural Places*

East and Northeast, Donelle Nicole Dreese

Pacific and West, Methea Kathleen Sapp

Rocky Mountains and Great Plains, Kelly Enright

South and Southeast, Stacy Kowtko

The Midwest, Jason Ney and Terri Nichols

AMERICA'S NATURAL PLACES

SOUTH AND SOUTHEAST

Stacy Kowtko

Stacy Kowtko, General Editor

GREENWOOD PRESS
An Imprint of ABC-CLIO, LLC

A B C ☰ C L I O

Santa Barbara, California • Denver, Colorado • Oxford, England

Copyright 2010 by Stacy Kowtko

Library of Congress Cataloging-in-Publication Data

Kowtko, Stacy.
    America's natural places. South and Southeast / Stacy Kowtko.
      p. cm. — (Regional volumes in America's natural places)
    Includes bibliographical references and index.
    ISBN 978-0-313-35088-7 (set hardcover : alk. paper) — ISBN 978-0-313-35089-4 (set ebook) —
ISBN 978-0-313-35269-0 (alk. paper) — ISBN 978-0-313-35270-6 (ebook)
  1. Protected areas—Southern States.   2. Endangered ecosystems—Southern States.   I. Title.
    S932.S84K69   2010
    333.720975—dc22   2009032382

14 13 12 11 10   1 2 3 4 5

This book is also available on the World Wide Web as an eBook.
Visit www.abc-clio.com for details.

ABC-CLIO, LLC
130 Cremona Drive, P.O. Box 1911
Santa Barbara, California 93116-1911

This book is printed on acid-free paper (∞)
Manufactured in the United States of America

CONTENTS

Series Foreword

The United States possesses within its borders some of the most diverse and beautiful natural wonders and resources of any country on earth. Many of these valuable natural places exist under a constant threat of damage from environmental pollution, climatic change, and encroaching civilization, just to name a few of the more destructive forces. Some natural areas enjoy the care and protection of neighboring human societies, but some have fallen to the wayside of concern. This series of reference volumes represents a collection of distinct areas of preservation concern in the following five geographical divisions of the United States: the East and Northeast, the Pacific and West, the Rocky Mountains and Great Plains, the South and Southeast, and the Midwest. The goal is to present representative challenges faced across the country, providing information on historical and ongoing preservation efforts through the process of identifying specific sites that representatively define the United States as an environmental entity. Individual entries were chosen based on the following criteria: biodiversity, ecology, rare or endangered species habitats, or unique environmental character. Many of the entries are nature preserves, state or national parks, wildlife habitats, or scenic vistas. Each selection focuses on a particular area and describes the site's importance, resident flora and fauna, and threats to the area's survival, along with historical and current information on preservation efforts. For sites that are physically accessible, there is information on location, access methods, and visiting tips. Although each volume is organized by state, many natural places cross state borders, and so the larger focus is on environmental ecosystem representation rather than state definition. The goals are to inform readers about the wide variety of natural places across the country as well as portray these natural places as more than just an exercise in academic study. The reality of natural preservation in the United States has an immediate impact on everyone.

Each volume contains a short introduction to the geographical region, including specific information on the states' natural environments and regionally specific concerns of restoration and preservation. Content entries represent one or more of the following criteria: ecological uniqueness; biodiversity; rare or endangered species habitat; exceptional natural beauty; or aging, fragile, or disappearing natural environs. By reading the various entries in each volume, readers will gain understanding concerning environmental issues of consequence as demonstrated by the representative entry choices. The audiences especially suited to benefit from this series are high school and undergraduate students as well as hobbyists and nature enthusiasts. Readers with an interest in local, regional, and environmental health will find easily accessible, useable information throughout the series. The following paragraphs offer short excerpts from the introductions of the regional volumes in *America's Natural Places*.

The East and Northeast United States is a corridor, a doorway to America that has facilitated movement and migration into the continent. The subject of corridors is revisited frequently in the East and Northeast volume as it covers natural areas beginning as far west as Kentucky, as far south as Virginia, and voyages up the coast to Maine. Smaller corridors are described here as well, because many of the places featured in this book have their own respective passageways, some more wild than others. This volume is also about larger corridors—those that connect the past to the present and the present to the future. These natural areas are storytellers chronicling the narratives of cultural and ecological histories that not only have much to tell about the region's past, but also are microcosmic indicators of the earth's current global health. They are corridors into our future as they tell us where our planet is going—toward the loss of countless native species, archeological treasures, and ecosystems that are vital for a sustainable planet. These natural areas are themselves guided paths, passageways into a healthier future as they teach us what is happening within their fragile ecological significance before their lessons are lost forever.

The American Pacific and West is a place of legendary proportions; its natural resources have beckoned to entrepreneurs, prospectors, immigrants, adventurers, naturalists, writers, and photographers, thereby deeply embedding the region into U.S. history, culture, commerce, and art. J. S. Holliday wrote. "I think that the West is the most powerful reality in the history of this country. It's always had a power, a presence, an attraction that differentiated it from the rest of the United States. Whether the West was a place to be conquered, or the West as it is today, a place to be protected and nurtured. It is the regenerative force of America." Over the course of its history, the ecosystems of the Pacific and West have been subject to a variety of forces, both restorative and destructive. Individual entries in the Pacific and West volume seek to not only detail the effects of these forces but to describe the flora, fauna, and topography that make each entry unique. As a cumulative effect, the volume offers an inclusive depiction of the region as a whole while echoing the famous call to "Go West."

"The western landscape is of the wildest variety," Wallace Stegner wrote of his homeland. "There is nothing in the East," he continued, "like the granite horns of Grand Teton or Teewinot, nothing like the volcanic neck of Devil's Tower, nothing like the travertine terraces of Mammoth Hot Springs." Consisting of deserts, grasslands, alpine mountains, plateaus, canyons, cliffs, and geyser basins, the Rocky Mountains and Great Plains is a region of great biodiversity and natural beauty. From the 100th meridian over the peaks of the Rocky Mountains, this landscape has been the source of frontier legends, central to the nation's geography as well as its identity. Home to the world's first national park and some of the most extractive industries in the nation, this landscape displays the best and worst of human interactions with the natural world. Fossils in Colorado are evidence of ancient inland seas. Tall-grass prairies reveal pre-Anglo American ecology. This volume teaches students to read natural landscapes as products of interacting dynamics between culture and nature. People of many backgrounds, ethnicities, and cultures have contributed to the current state of the environment, giving readers a strong, provocative look at the dynamics of this ever-changing landscape.

"The American South is a geographical entity, a historical fact, a place in the imagination, and the homeland for an array of Americans who consider themselves southerners. The region is often shrouded in romance and myth, but its realities are as intriguing, as intricate as its legends." So states Bill Ferris. This volume explores the variable, dynamic South and Southeast through the details of its ecoregions and distinct areas of preservation. Individual entries provide the elements necessary for examining and understanding the threats, challenges, and promises inherent to this region. State partitions serve as geographical divisions for regional treatment, but the overall goal of this work is to present representative examples of the varying ecosystems across the area rather than focusing on the environmental character of individual states. When combined, the sections present a total picture of the South and Southeast through careful selections that portray not only the coastal wetlands and piedmont areas characteristic of the region but also the plateaus, mountains, highlands, plains, and woodlands that define the inland South and Southeast. The goal is to produce a comprehensive picture of the South and Southeast natural environs as they combine to present a unique character and quality that shapes Southern reality today.

The Midwest stands historically as the crossroads of America, the gateway to the West. The region is incredibly diverse, long shaped by geological forces such as the advance and retreat of glaciers. It is a transitional region, where the eastern temperate forests meet the Great Plains of the West and where the southern extent of the northern forests transitions from the mixed-wood plains to the Ozark forests and southeastern plains of the South. Human presence and interaction, however, have greatly reduced and currently threaten this diversity. The Midwest's rich soils and forests, along with its abundant lakes and streams, make this region's natural resources some of the county's most desirable for farming, logging, and development. As a result, little of the once-vast prairies, forests, and wetlands remains. Nonetheless, many efforts, both public and private, are underway to restore and protect the diversity of the Midwest. By taking a holistic approach, individual entries in this volume exemplify the varied ecosystems of the region with the volume as a whole covering all the major Midwest ecoregions. As readers explore the various entries, a comprehensive understanding of the natural systems of the Midwest will emerge, grounded in the region's natural and cultural history and shaped by its current and future challenges.

PREFACE

Traveling across the South and Southeast United States presents unparalleled opportunities for visitors to experience some of the most beautiful and most endangered natural habitats in the country. If Anthony Robbins is correct in saying "it's never the environment, it's never the events of our lives, but the meaning we attach to [them], how we interpret them, that shapes who we are today and who we'll become tomorrow," then this region of the country has both unique resources and unique challenges in defining itself through the meaning it attaches to its natural environs. The "meaning" of the South and Southeast as a region, then, is characterized by a constant struggle to find the balance between a state of environmental health, the need for economic stability, and the inevitability of damaging climatic forces. Environmental systems across the area have long sat on the receiving end of change initiated both by humans and by natural forces. What that leaves today is a mixed legacy of restoration and preservation needs. This volume attempts to define those needs across the vast diversity of ecosystems that make up the southern-central and eastern portions of the United States as well as explore efforts in motion that hope to restore and preserve the environmental glory that was once abundant across the region.

The process of selecting natural sites to represent larger regional issues involved consideration of several factors. First, great care was taken to choose only one or two sites that represent each type of ecosystem found in the South and Southeast when it was possible to limit using this criterion. Another issue addressed was characterizing restoration and preservation efforts. This condition means that some environment types have a higher representation percentage in order to present as many different plans of action as possible. Some of the most important characteristics considered when choosing entries for this volume include the numbers and types of endangered species, the site's ability to represent common southern and southeastern environments, the uniqueness of a preserve's action plan, and the human and natural history of a discrete area. For each state, there are also sites included that represent singular instances of these criteria in that no other preserve in the state exhibits similar characteristics, making the area unique not only to the state but often to the country as a whole. The goal was to create an accessible collection of both representative and distinctive environments that, when combined, produce an environmental portfolio of sorts that helps readers gain a better understanding of the challenges faced not only by each site but by each state as a whole. Through judicious entry inclusion, this collection should provide a comprehensive natural personality of the American South and Southeast.

This book should appeal to a general audience and to those with specific environmental interests, such as photographers, hikers, campers, conservationists, and visitors. High school and undergraduate students will find this volume and series useful as well because of its representative approach to regional environmental representation. Students writing research papers, working on class projects, and familiarizing themselves with common environmental issues across the region will find this work informative. Although it is not meant to function as a textbook or a technical guide to environmental science, this volume of *America's Natural Places* offers a summary overview of the most important conservation sites and preservation issues in the South and Southeast. Environmental education is the path to widespread sustainability, and this resource is focused on broadening the common knowledge base and hopefully fueling an interest in readers to dig deeper, learn more, and ultimately participate in efforts to strengthen local environments and the importance of responsible stewardship.

SOUTH AND SOUTHEAST

500 mi
500 km

CANADA

Lake Superior

Lake Huron

Lake Ontario

Lake Michigan

Lake Erie

N

Greensboro ★ Raleigh

★ Nashville

NORTH CAROLINA

TENNESSEE

Charlotte

Memphis

Little Rock ★

Columbia

SOUTH CAROLINA

ARKANSAS

Atlanta ★

Birmingham

MISSISSIPPI

Montgomery ★

Dallas

Atlantic Ocean

LOUISIANA

Jackson

ALABAMA

GEORGIA

TEXAS

Austin ★

Baton Rouge ★

Tallahassee ★

Jacksonville

Houston

San Antonio

New Orleans

Orlando

Tampa

FLORIDA

West Palm Beach

BAHAMAS

Gulf of Mexico

Miami

MEXICO

INTRODUCTION

"The American South is a geographical entity, a historical fact, a place in the imagination, and the homeland for an array of Americans who consider themselves southerners. The region is often shrouded in romance and myth, but its realities are as intriguing, as intricate as its legends." So states Bill Ferris. This volume explores the variable, dynamic South and Southeast through the details of its ecoregions, ecosystems, and distinct areas of preservation. Individual entries provide the elements necessary for examining and understanding the threats, challenges, and promises inherent to this region. State partitions serve as geographical divisions for regional treatment, but the overall goal of this work is to present representative examples of the varying ecosystems across the area rather than focusing on the environmental character of individual states. When combined, the sections present a total picture of the South and Southeast through careful selections that portray not only the coastal wetlands and piedmont areas characteristic of the region but also the plateaus, mountains, highlands, plains, and woodlands that define the inland South and Southeast. The goal is to produce a comprehensive picture of the South and Southeast natural environs as they combine to present a unique character and quality that shapes Southern reality today.

Ecosystem designations allow scientists to define areas of commonality based on similarities in geology, vegetation, soils, climate, wildlife, water properties, and land use. Based on both living and nonliving elements in an environment, for example, the level system the United States Environmental Protection Agency uses emerged from John Omernik's work concerning the definition and characterization of specific ecoregions within the United States. The purpose of this kind of research is to provide a foundation for classification, investigation, and understanding of ecosystems and their components in the effort to better preserve, manage, and perhaps restore valuable natural environments. By using a common language, specialists can better communicate about their understanding and study of the challenges faced in environmental preservation. Several other hierarchy classification systems exist and each serves its own important purpose for understanding and studying natural environments. Eight federal agencies currently collaborate to refine and perfect regional environmental understanding using these various systems. By promoting focus on the total landscape rather than a single resource, single field of study, or single agency perspective, the agency teams work together to ensure consistency and quality of regional descriptions.

Each region of the United States exhibits characteristics that make it unique to the continent, and the South and Southeast are no exception. While there are many historical, cultural, and environmental connections between the South and Southeast, there are many differences as well. Climatic zones include everything from temperate to subtropical and tropical and across the spectrum to arid. The diversity of flora and fauna found across the region defines the South and Southeast as separate and unique from other regions of the country, and, within the regions, that diversity defines environmental areas even more.

Consider the Appalachia and Ozark regions, for example. Although often coupled in geographical study, these adjacent ecoregions are distinct, unique entities. Appalachia contains three significant belts lying parallel to each other. The first and farthest to the east is the Blue Ridge belt. This is the most mountainous part of Appalachia, despite the fact that this belt is also severely eroded. Next to the Blue Ridge sits some of the richest farming land in Appalachia. This ridge and valley combination houses the Great Valley of Appalachia. Although called a valley, it is rather hilly and has served historically as a pathway for movement and migration to, from, and within Appalachia. Then, in western Appalachia sits the Appalachian Plateau into which years of stream erosion carved a ragged pattern of landscape. Adjacent to Appalachia are the Ozark-Ouachita uplands, with the Ouachita Mountains comprised of folded ridges and valleys separated from the Ozarks by the Arkansas River valley. Human interaction and development in this region has a long history. One of the largest development projects in U.S. history accomplished modification of the Tennessee River for navigation through the Tennessee River Valley Authority. When humans meet nature, monumental changes take place—some for the better and some for the worse.

Take, for example, the greater everglades ecosystem of south Florida. It spans from the middle of Florida at Orlando all the way down through the Florida Keys coral reef. The larger system includes conservation sites such as the Everglades and Biscayne National Parks, Big Cypress National Preserve, and the Florida Keys National Marine Sanctuary. Today the Florida Bay exhibits significant evidence of environmental damage due to human development. Large algae blooms, dangerously high salinity, and dying beds of sea grass all testify to the damage caused by flood control and water redirection for agriculture and urban development. Not only is the natural environment in danger of becoming irreparable, the human communities of southern Florida are suffering as a result. The proposed plan of action is to enact a comprehensive ecosystem restoration program that will take longer than 20 years to complete, cost $8 billion, and utilizes over

60 individual restoration components. The ultimate goal is to "get the water right," and 6 federal departments, 7 Florida state agencies, 16 counties, 2 Native American tribes, and various businesses and interest groups have committed to making it happen.

One area that has seen great strides in repair and restoration is the Lower Savannah River Environmental Restoration Project, which was completed in June 2003. Environmental restoration is defined by the Southern Regional Water Program as "the reestablishment of the general structure, function, and dynamic self-sustaining behavior of a disturbed ecosystem." Engineering efforts modified the Lower Savannah River basin in Georgia with a series of navigation cuts. The restoration project involved building an 80-foot diversion structure at Navigation Cut 3 that forced water back through a bypassed oxbow. In conjunction with this construction, the contractor also opened a channel to adjacent Bear Creek and realigned the mouths of Bear and Mill Creeks. The original goal in creating the cuts was to facilitate barge travel in a straight line. Eventually, though, willows grew and sediment accumulated around the bends, isolating them from the river and reducing vital water levels in surrounding lands. Many plant and animal species depend on reliable water levels in the Lower Savannah River basin for survival, and the 40 years of drain-off following cut construction threatened their environments. Ultimately, everyone benefits from this project. The city of Savannah is now saving more than $200,000 a year from reduced water treatment costs. The treatment plants also have less silt and organic materials as their workload reduces. The Georgia Department of Natural Resources and the U.S. Fish and Wildlife Service now have an easier job maintaining wetland habitats for local endangered species. When restoration of a natural habitat benefits both human and natural communities, a sustainable environmental future is then one step closer.

By choosing representative examples from a variety of framework systems, *America's Natural Places: South and Southeast* will explore this variable, dynamic region through the details of its ecoregions. Although not every state will be covered with an equal quantity of representation, select natural areas from each state will illuminate the predominant environmental characteristics. When combined, the chapters present a total picture of the South and Southeast through a careful selection of sites across the region to best define it as a whole. The goal is a better understanding of the South and Southeast natural environments as they combine to present a unique character and quality that is the South and Southeast.

ALABAMA

Alabama is a state that holds a surprising array of diverse natural environments. Although not normally the first example of aquatic biodiversity to come to mind, Alabama exhibits some of the best examples of large freshwater economic systems in the country. The widespread river systems and watersheds house more species of freshwater fish, mussels, turtles, snails, and crayfish than any other state. In northern Alabama, the majesty of the southern Appalachian Mountains dominates the landscape, which contains forests, streams, and waterfalls in abundance. At the end of the Appalachian range, Piedmont hills give way to the Black Belt, where the state's cotton industry once flourished. Further south, pine forests and hardwood groves characterize the countryside that eventually ends in the marshes on the shores of the Gulf of Mexico. According to the Audubon Society, Alabama ranks second only to California in its physiographic diversity. Sitting between the magnificence of the Appalachians and the splendor of the Gulf Coast is a state holding some of the rarest environmental treasures of North America. The timber industry and intensive agriculture made their mark on the Alabama landscape, and now preservation and reclamation projects work to protect valuable natural treasures across the state.

Between the 1960s and today, Alabama has made great strides in environmental restoration, protection, and monitoring. The Alabama Environmental Council, founded in 1967, signaled the beginning of efforts across the state that would ultimately result in significant environmental gains, including the drastic reduction of urban particulate matter air pollution, the formation of over 100 state environmental organizations, and the designation of protected natural areas throughout the region. Education is widely available on the unique natural treasures and environmental challenges in Alabama. In 1989, the Environmental Education Association of Alabama formed as a group of educators, agencies, business members, and industry representatives interested in teaching about Alabama's unique environmental character. Now offering workshops, an annual conference, excursions, an awards program, and grants, the association has made great changes the realm of environmental education in Alabama for more than two decades. The Alabama Clean Water Partnership, for example, celebrated the 30th anniversary of the Clean Water Act with publication of its initiatives and participation in the 2002 World Watershed Summit in Washington, DC. Costal Wonders functions as a nonprofit residential camp experience for Alabama youth, offering everything from Estuary Studies to Happenin' Herps and Team Initiatives to Night Mysteries for the perpetuation of earth stewardship in the hearts and minds of local youth.

According to the Alabama Department of Archives and History, many involved in environmental preservation think of the state as a "sacrifice zone," which suggests that the state does not enjoy the best reputation for enacting and enforcing federal environmental regulations. The gains made in preservation, however, do not fully support that assumption. The only city in Alabama that has experienced significant air pollution issues is Birmingham, and the particulate air matter concentration there has been significantly reduced over the last two decades. The preservation of coastal sand dune ecosystems has served a dual purpose in protecting not only what remains of a once much larger sand dune system but also preserving a unique habitat that is home to many creatures such as the endangered beach mouse. Of the original 100 miles of coastline, 22 are left to the surviving beach mouse populations, and environmental groups are working continuously to strengthen this fragile system. Unfortunately, in the 1980s, several sites in Alabama became hazardous waste dumping areas for other states. Although environmental awareness and activism has increased, it is this type of threat (among many others) that keeps Alabama from realizing its full preservation potential. Many local, state, and federal organizations are working in concert to prevent the spread of environmental damage and, when possible, reverse degradation that has taken hold. To protect and restore Alabama's unique biodiversity takes the efforts of many, and the state is making great strides toward restoring its unique environmental glory.

Coosa Bog

Coosa Bog, the first Alabama acquisition for the state's chapter of the Nature Conservancy, was attained in order to focus on restoration efforts, including prescribed burning and exotic and aggressive species control. A colony of green pitcher plants, one of fewer than 40 that currently exist, calls the bog home. The bog also shelters other fragile and rare species like the grass-leaf loosestrife. Located in Cherokee County, it is a small preserve—just under four acres—and, due to the area's delicate natural balance, visitation is extremely limited. The resident flora populations, once spread over several states, have been significantly negatively affected by human habitation. Also, the suppression of naturally occurring fires has harmed the rejuvenation ability of these once abundant species. By limiting public access and closely monitoring the balance of naturally occurring species and foreign aggressive incursion, Coosa Bog provides a small but valuable haven in Cherokee County, Alabama.

One of the rarest plants in Coosa Bog is the green pitcher plant. The plant's main food source are the insects that get trapped by falling into the tubular leaves. The leaves are topped with a hood covering the widened ends that keeps insects from escaping. The liquid enzymes contained within then digest the hapless creatures in preparation for absorption. The life cycle of these amazing plants begins with a flowering from mid-April to early June, after which the pitchers die off to be replaced by small, curved leaves that nourish and protect the root system until the next spring. Because of the plant's ability to extract proteins and other nutrients from the insects it traps, the shallow soils are sufficient for the health of this rare colony of green pitcher plants. The grass-leaf loosestrife prefers the drier, well-drained soils surrounding the bog, with stream banks and dry creek beds being the areas of choice. Even the smallest of areas, like Coosa Bog, can be valuable environs for preserving unique, threatened species native to northern Alabama.

Further Reading
Camilleri, Tony. *Carnivorous Plants*. Pymble, Australia: Kangaroo Press, 1999.
"Carnivorous Plants." www.cc.utah.edu/~jsg16/cp.htm.
McPherson, Stewart. *Pitcher Plants of the Americas*. Blacksburg, VA: McDonald & Woodward, 2006.

DRY CREEK

Dry Creek Preserve provides one example of a preserve dedicated to saving and restoring the population of one endangered species. The Alabama leather flower is currently known to exist in five natural populations. Dry Creek Preserve's goal is to monitor this population to determine what management strategies will be necessary for long-term propagation and preservation. In addition to this endangered species, the upland rose gentian, prairie dock, and other native plants reside along the banks of Dry Creek, mixed in with oak and hickory forests, as well as bottomland hardwoods. In addition to these floral colonies, Dry Creek hosts a resident beaver population and functions as an important environment for migratory and nesting songbirds. Although focused on the monitoring and preservation of the Alabama leather flower, the entire ecosystem balance benefits from the Nature Conservancy's presence in this delicate location. As the key to the survival of the Alabama leather flower, physical access to this preserve is tightly controlled and only available by prior arrangement with the Nature Conservancy of Alabama.

Dry Creek Preserve is a unique collection of flora and fauna that functions together to provide a safe haven for the Alabama leather flower. Glades such as the Dry Creek Preserve allow for wetter soils in the winter and into spring that dry considerably through summer and into the fall. Within these glades, flat areas along the floodplains of the stream bed provide the perfect habitat for wildflowers such as the upland rose gentian.

These moist to slightly drier conditions encourage hardy flora such as the prairie dock to take hold as well. The oak-hickory forest stands support and protect Dry Creek from erosion of the relatively shallow soils. Oak-hickory forests are the most widespread and the most diverse forests in the United States. They are a hardy foundation for many microenvironments across the biological spectrum. Dry Creek, like many microenvironments across the East and Southeast, benefits from the stability and protection that oak-hickory forests provide.

Another stabilizing factor for Dry Creek is its resident beaver population. Beaver presence contributes to strong healthy natural environments for many creatures, such as fish, frogs, ducks, frogs, and birds. Not only do beavers create animal-friendly environments, they contribute to the botanical health of their surroundings as well. The dams they build help prevent erosion, raise the water table, and act as a filter for waterways. In many areas of the country, beavers were trapped to the brink of extinction, and, by the beginning of the 20th century, the beaver had disappeared from many areas of natural habitat. Draining waterways for agricultural purposes did not help beaver population numbers, and today scientists estimate that population numbers are barely five percent of what they were when Europeans began populating North America in the 16th century. Because they breed only once per year, require healthy water environments, and the young leave at the age of two to establish their own territories, beaver numbers remain small in localized areas. Additionally, there are many predators of the beaver, as well as manmade dangers such as roadways that threaten populations. One colony or family of beavers can require up to a half mile of stream habitat, and all of these factors combined result in relatively small and extremely manageable population numbers. Dry Creek beavers contribute to the health of the preserve and, as a result, the protection of preserve's main focus, the Alabama leather flower.

The Alabama leather flower is a perennial herb found in only five sites in northeast Alabama and one in northwest Georgia. Each of these sites has been affected by human presence, either by being turned into highways or pasture land or being logged for timber products. The soil best suited for this species is of silt clay alluvial character and often naturally coexists with prairie flora. Pre-European prairie environments are most likely this species' natural habitat, and the loss of these natural environments is the main threat to the survival of the Alabama leather flower. Additionally, it is not a very competitive plant, and so aggressive species have little trouble in overtaking the alluvial soils necessary for leather flower growth. Active management of the population at Dry Creek includes maintaining an open canopy to meet the plant's sunlight needs and reducing competition from more aggressive species. Prescribed burns and selective logging have been successful management tools as well. Local landowners and preservation organizations such as the Nature Conservancy contribute to active efforts at restoring and protecting Dry Creek as a haven for the Alabama leather flower.

Further Reading

Bailey, H.A., and A.W. Bailey. *Fire Ecology: United States and Southern Canada.* New York: John Wiley and Sons. 1982.

Boyd, R.S., and C.D. Hilton. "Ecologic Studies of the Endangered Species *Clematis socialis*." *Castanea* 59 (1982): 31–40.

Center for Plant Conservation. http://www.centerforplantconservation.org/ASP/CPC_ViewProfile.asp?CPCNum=1004.

GRAND BAY SAVANNA

The Grand Bay Savanna Landscape Conservation Area, managed by the Nature Conservancy of Alabama and Mississippi, is an intact mosaic of natural environments that historically characterized the southern coastal plain of the United States. Three significant microtypes stand out: wet pine savanna, coastal maritime forest, and shore estuarine communities. The significance of Grand Bay is the immense level of biodiversity in the different subcommunities and the ecological processes that sustain each microenvironment. Environmental stressors plague Grand Bay, many of which are a result of the growing human population in the area. Although destruction of natural habitat is an obvious threat, the more subtle danger comes in the form of environmental degradation. The disintegration of these environments often takes place slowly over long periods of time, making monitoring and restoration activities harder to enact. The side effects that come with changes in water quality, the spread of non-native aggressive flora and fauna, and the disappearance of natural ecological processes are difficult to measure and happen much more slowly than outright habitat devastation; as a result, they are more difficult to mediate and correct. The Nature Conservancy works with conservation groups and resource agencies to maintain the current level of biodiversity and restore self-regulating natural mechanisms of environmental system management.

Located 20 miles southwest of Mobile, within this collection of environments, there are at least 20 distinct communities that collectively host more than 70 rare plant and animal species. The total area of all Grand Bay Savanna areas of preservation and restoration action in Mississippi and Alabama is approximately 150,000 acres, which necessitates cooperation between public groups, environmental organizations, government agencies, and private interests. A wide variety of animals depend on the many different habitats in the Grand Bay Savanna mosaic. Spotted sea trout, red drum, blue crab, brown shrimp, and oysters call the coastal waters home. The gopher tortoise and the endangered Mississippi sandhill crane inhabit the area's shores. Some of these species' habitats are important for human commercial purposes, and some are important simply in the light of natural balance, but all play a role in restoring and maintaining the health of Grand Bay areas.

Taking one species out of an ecological system can drastically alter its ecological health, and the gopher tortoise is part of that cycle. One of the ecological roles the tortoise plays is providing homes for other land animals through its abandoned burrows or by sharing the burrow with other tortoises. As one of the few areas of Alabama to host the burrowing gopher tortoise, Grand Bay also depends on these grazing animals for the spreading of seeds. Another integral piece of the ecological puzzle that is Grand Bay is the endangered Mississippi sandhill crane. There are approximately 100 individuals remaining in the wild and only about 20 breeding pairs. These cranes are about four feet tall and carry a six-foot wingspan. Their coloring is dark gray, and they sport a red crown, white cheek patches, and black legs. Wet pine savanna is the only habitat to support this rare bird. There are 15 species of crane worldwide, and, of those 15, 11 species are considered at risk of extinction. Sandhill cranes and whooping cranes are the only species found in North America. The Mississippi sandhill crane was designated a sandhill crane subspecies in 1972. Their loud, rattling bugle call can be heard over the savanna when visitors stop along the roadside of the preserve today, but without aggressive protection, this increasingly rare resident may disappear from Grand Bay.

Further Reading

Coastal America. "Project Summary: Mon Louis Island/Grand Bay Savanna, AL." www.coastalamerica.gov/text/regions/gm/monlouis.html.

U.S. Fish and Wildlife Service. "The Alabama Coastal Birding Trail." www.fws.gov/southeast/pubs/facts/al_bird_trail.pdf.

U.S. Fish and Wildlife Service. "Mississippi Sandhill Crane National Wildlife Refuge." www.fws.gov/mississippisandhillcrane/index.html.

Yaffee, Steven, Ali Phillips, Irene Frentz, Paul Hardy, Sussane Maleki, and Barbara Thorpe. *Ecosystem Management in the United States: An Assessment of Current Experience*. Washington, DC: Island Press, 1996.

GULF CREEK CANYON PRESERVE

Gulf Creek Canyon Preserve sits on Chandler Mountain in central Alabama's St. Clair County. The Nature Conservancy of Alabama, charged with preservation of this site, says that the preserve offers one of the most scenic views in the state. Striking cliffs dominate the landscape, and many types of raptors and vultures call the canyon skies home. Gulf Creek runs through the preserve at the bottom of the canyon, offering a myriad of recreation opportunities. This area does receive heavy rains at times, which can create a dangerously swift current in the creek. Additionally, the fast-moving waters eat into the surrounding sandstone layers, increasing the risk of rock slides. These heavy rains, though, also enhance waterfalls along the tributaries of Gulf Creek, creating beautiful seasonal scenery. As a natural area of preservation and recreation, Gulf Creek Canyon offers much. Visits should be coordinated through site staff. The Nature

Conservancy works to maintain trails and monitor the resident flora and fauna populations so that visitors can safely enjoy the beauty and serenity of the area.

Some of the natural populations include mature hardwood forest stands as well as blooms of Cumberland azalea and decumbent trillium. The Cumberland azalea provides an especially beautiful addition the Gulf Creek Canyon fauna. Its orange-red blooms stand out against the deep green foliage of its leaves. Its blossom cycle is later in the season, so its presence extends seasonal coloring and beauty that flowering plants provide the preserve, often into midsummer. The decumbent trillium, also known as trailing toadshade, found in the area grows in colonies that lie close to the ground with flat leaves and dark maroon blossoms that extend up from the center. Its flowering season is earlier than the native azaleas, spanning from mid-March to April. A variety of other leafy plants characteristic of Gulf Creek Canyon complement these species, creating a natural environment suited for the more mountainous areas of central and north-central Alabama. Gulf Creek Canyon provides a perfect location for the protection of these native flowering plants found few other places in the United States.

Ovenbirds, scarlet tanagers, and yellow-billed cuckoos call these forests home as well. Ovenbirds are a small, floor-dwelling species of warbler with a wing span of 7 to 10 inches. Their distinctive call of "cher, tea-cher, tea-cher" can be heard in Gulf Creek Canyon throughout the summer. Ovenbirds coexist well with other warbler species, for example, by dividing up the forest environment for living and breeding purposes with related species creating something of a territorial-like existence. Its name comes from the shape of its nest, which is domed with a side entrance, resembling a Dutch oven. Studies of this species suggest that at least half of all adult ovenbirds die each year, creating a significant rotation in living populations, and, with only the forests of northeast Alabama to call home, Gulf Creek Canyon provides an important habitat for ovenbird populations. Coexisting within this environment are scarlet tanagers. They prefer the forest canopy as well, and, despite their striking red color, they are not easy to spot due to their secretive nature. Cornell's *All about Birds*, the institution's online guide to bird watching, describes this bird's song as "reminiscent of a robin with a sore throat." While the scarlet tanager's living and breeding grounds cover much of the U.S. East and Northeast, this species is sensitive to the disturbance and fragmentation of it natural forest habitats. Gulf Creek Canyon provides one haven for species such as this to thrive and grow.

Further Reading

Cornell Lab of Ornithology. "All about Birds." http://www.allaboutbirds.org/NetCommunity/Page.aspx?pid=1189.

The Nature Conservancy. "Places We Protect." www.nature.org/northamerica/states/alabama/preserves.

Porter, John Jr. *A Birder's Guide to Alabama*. Birmingham: University of Alabama Press, 2001.

Towe, L. C. *American Azaleas*. Portland, OR: Timber Press, 2004.

LITTLE RIVER CANYON

Little River is unique among Alabama rivers because most of its length sits on top of a mountain, and, as a result, it offers varied locales for recreation and enjoyment such as waterfalls, forests, canyons, and cliffs. As an important part of the southern Appalachians, Little River Canyon National Preserve is protected by the National Park Service for its natural resources and is utilized for its recreation opportunities. The climate of the site is generally mild with four distinct seasons. An array of fall colors graces the 11-mile scenic drive through the park beginning in October. By late December, the brilliant colors are gone, replaced by delicate frost and icicles. Temperatures hover in the 30s for most of the winter but rarely dip below freezing. Because the park receives more precipitation in the winter, water levels rise enough for kayakers to run the river. These higher water levels last through the spring and into the summer, when the preserve experiences relatively warm days and slightly cooler nights, and, although the water levels are a little too low for kayaks and canoes, they are just right for wading, swimming, and diving.

The mains reasons many people come to Little River Canyon are for the backcountry access, the beautiful scenic drive, and the kayaking opportunities. The backcountry areas are especially suited for horseback and all-terrain vehicle riding, four-wheel drive access, and primitive camping. There are 23 miles of primitive roads that lead visitors into the prime backcountry areas located north of the canyon. Because there are more than 100 rare, endangered, and threatened plant and animal species, it is important that visitors keep all vehicles on the roads. Hunting is also allowed in some areas of the park during specified dates and times, and the opportunity to gather berries and nuts is available, although there is a limit of one five-gallon bucket per day for personal use. A myriad of activities await the adventurous guest ready and willing to rough it a bit to get into the less-traveled areas of the park.

On the western side of the park, visitors can enjoy the 11-mile scenic drive along Highway 176, off of Highway 35. The purpose of the drive is to provide a series of overlooks from which to enjoy the canyon's natural beauty. Each overlook has a pull-out, and, in this area of the park, little walking is required to enjoy the amazing vistas. While access to this area is free, the drive is only open during daylight hours. The views awe inspiring, and careful observers can spot many endangered species of flora and fauna along the way. Lynn Overlook, for example, hosts eight rare species. The small elf orphine grows close to the ground and flowers at the first sign of spring rains. The Little River onion is an extremely rare perennial herb currently a candidate for government protection. Growing among sandstone boulders and ledges is the Nuttall's rayless goldenrod, which sports flat-topped yellow flowers, complementing the trees, shrubs, and lichen that call these rocky outcrops home. At Hawks Glide Overlook, brilliant red trumpet honeysuckle graces the undergrowth. At the final overlook, Eberhart Point, a dirt trail takes hikers down to the bottom of the canyon. Although the trail is only three-quarters of a mile long, the hike is moderately difficult, and hiking back out of the canyon can be a difficult experience.

DeSoto State Park is located within the National Preserve boundaries, offering more organized and developed opportunities for recreation.

Little River Canyon National Preserve plays an important natural role in the ecology of northeastern Alabama. When the spring thaws start in the mountains, kayakers can brave the resulting class V white-water rush. The forested uplands of the Appalachian Plateau sit serenely above the canyon rim, framing the gorge with natural beauty. Rising 1,800 feet above sea level at the highest point all the way down to 500 feet at the east gulf coastal plain juncture, the Appalachian (or Cumberland) Plateau reaches northward all the way to New York. This area has held human interest for some time due to the coal fields that lie underneath. The plateau was formed during the shifts that created the Appalachian Mountains; however, the resulting bulges were less severe than the bordering range. Valleys sporadically break into the plateau landscape, and natural forces have accented the landscape over time by exposing limestone and shale along the surrounding crests. Mining is, by far, the most common and profitable human activity in the area, but sites such as the Little River Canyon Preserve protect natural habitats and landscape important to the local ecology as well as human communities that also inhabit the land.

Further Reading
DeSoto State Park. "Home of Mother Nature." www.desotostatepark.com.
National Park Service. "Little River Canyon." http://www.nps.gov/liri/index.htm.
Walker, Sue. *In the Realm of Rivers*. Montgomery, AL: NewSouth Books, 2005.

NATCHEZ TRACE

The 32-mile section of the Natchez Trace Parkway that passes through Alabama offers motorists an opportunity to see some of Alabama's finest scenery, natural environments, and historical spots. It is the middle leg of a parkway that runs the entire length of the Natchez Trace. The earliest use of the Natchez Trace was Native Americans following animal migration paths. After European arrival, the trail was used by Spanish explorers, British troops, and frontier settlers. This historic trail runs close to the parkway in most areas and is maintained by the National Park Service. The first stop along the path, after entering Alabama from Mississippi on the Natchez Trace Parkway, is Freedom Hills Overlook. A rather steep quarter-mile trail leads to the highest vista point along Alabama's section of the parkway and offers stunning views of the surrounding terrain. The next stop on the path is a trail that leads to Buzzard's Roost Spring, where visitors can learn the story of Chickasaw Chief Levi Colbert. Continuing north along the road leads to Colbert Ferry, where George Colbert operated a stand and ferry stop. Legend has it that Colbert charged Andrew Jackson $75,000 to ferry his army across the river. After crossing the Tennessee River, the last stop on the parkway in Alabama is Rock Spring, which offers a self-guided trail along Colbert Creek only 10 miles from the Alabama-Tennessee border.

Freedom Hills Overlook, as the highest point along the Alabama leg of the Natchez Trace Parkway, is one of the awe-inspiring stops along this road through the wilderness. A paved walkway leads to the overlook, providing a short but steep quarter-mile hike from the parking area. This particular spot is approximately 800 miles above sea level, making it one of the highest points in the area—in fact, higher than any point in Mississippi, which is just over 10 miles to the west. Continuing north along the parkway leads to the valley that contains the Tennessee River. Lush forests lure visitors, providing a natural peace along a path comfortably worn by centuries of use.

Buzzard's Roost Spring, the second stop on Alabama's section of the parkway, offers a short trail that has exhibits concerning the history of Chickasaw Chief Levi Colbert, who owned a nearby stand. Also known as Itawamba Minco, or bench chief, he served as translator in attempted compromises with President Andrew Jackson involving the movement west of the Mississippi River by the Chickasaw people. Only when Colbert was indisposed by illness was the U.S. government able to push through the signing of a treaty that would relocate the Chickasaw people to lands west of the Mississippi. The pay for their tracts of lands was reduced by half in Colbert's absence to a mere 25 cents an acre. Being one of the most celebrated of Chickasaw chiefs, he was an influential, intelligent, and respected man. Had Colbert been present, it is likely that the Chickasaw people would not have suffered as dearly at the hands of U.S. treaty negotiators, who deftly took advantage of the great chief's absence. The area around Buzzard's Roost Spring was one of several places the chief and his people called home until the treaty was signed.

Next along the parkway, Colbert Ferry offers both natural and historical treasures. In the late 1700s, George Colbert operated a ferry that crossed the Tennessee River. The section of the river that flows through Colbert County was called Muscle Shoals, both because of the strength of the river and the several species of freshwater mussels found there. The ferry no longer runs, but there is a boat launch and ranger station. The National Park Service has set up a couple of hike-in, primitive campsites that offer visitors overnight access to the river and its environs. A site with more hospitable offerings is Rock Spring and Colbert Creek. As the last site that provides access to the Tennessee River in Alabama, this is a great place to stop and enjoy the natural and historical treasure of the Natchez Trace before heading into the beautiful state of Tennessee.

Further Reading

Manning, Russ. *The Historic Cumberland Plateau: An Explorer's Guide*. Knoxville: University of Tennessee Press, 1999.

Mississippi Genealogical & Historical Research. "Chickasaw Chiefs and Prominent Men." www.natchezbelle.org/ahgp-ms/chiefs/chiefs2.htm.

Prairie Grove Glades

Prairie Grove Glades contains the largest cedar glade of this type in the entire state of Alabama. The wildflower variety is stunning when the glade is in bloom. Home to at least 12 rare plant species, the glade is comprised of flat limestone areas with shallow soil distributed among cedar and other hardwood stands. The vegetation areas of the glade house rare flora species such as Harper's umbrella plant and the Alabama larkspur, with yellow and white Alabama glade cress covering the more rocky areas. Several other species of flowering plants populate the glade, and, during springtime, watery seeps support beautiful croppings of quillwort and sunnybells. The glade also houses lyrate bladderpod, a small annual mustard that is federally designated as threatened. Currently under the protection of Alabama's Nature Conservancy, the organization works to prevent dumping and all-terrain vehicle damage to the area and strives to build more nature trails and continue restoration efforts. Controlled burning is an important part of the restoration process in this delicate preserve. The preserve is open to the public during the day and can be accessed by following an old road into the glade complex. In respect of the unique collection of rare plants, visitors are asked to stay on the provided paths.

Some of the plant species hosted in the Prairie Grove Glades include rare and threatened varieties. Harper's umbrella plant—also known as Harper's buckwheat—is found only in the shale soils of Alabama, Tennessee, and Kentucky. It lives in a nonflowering state for up to four years, then develops a long flowering stalk before dying. Prairie Grove Glades is one of only a handful of sites where this rare species has a foothold. Found with Harper's buckwheat are other rare flora, including Alabama gladecress. Common among natural rock outcroppings, the ground in these areas is usually wetter in the spring and then drier through the summer. The gladecress takes advantage of these conditions by flowering in March, which is a bit earlier than its neighbors, and then spreading its seeds in May and June before other plants can establish a presence. Alabama larkspur and glade quillwort also top the list of endangered inhabitants of this area. Larkspur bloom from late spring through late summer and add to the health of the glades by attracting butterflies and hummingbirds to assist with natural pollination. Quillwort and yellow sunnybells thrive in the wetter soils of spring as well. Prairie Grove Glades, with its nutrient-poor shale soils, provides the perfect ground foundation for these and other delicate and rare species to thrive.

Further Reading

Baskin, J.M., and C.C. Baskin. *Cedar Glades of the Southeastern United States*. Cambridge, England: Cambridge University Press, 1999.

Gardener's Network. "How to Grow Larkspur Flowers." www.gardenersnet.com/flower/larkspur.htm.

Quarterman, E., M.P. Burbanck, and D.J. Shure. *Rock Outcrop Communities: Limestone, Sandstone, and Granite*. New York: John Wiley & Sons, 1993.

RABBIT ISLAND

Rabbit Island, Alabama, a mere 26 acres off the coast of Ono Island in Baldwin County, is a unique example of a coastal marsh island that was donated to the state's Nature Conservancy. The Conservancy's main goal is to protect a habitat that hosts the nesting sites of a variety of migrating shorebirds. Part of this protection plan involves limiting human presence on the island; to make sure nesting populations are not disturbed, the preserve can be visited only by prior arrangement through the Alabama Nature Conservancy. Communities of marsh rabbits, salt marsh water snakes, and diamondback terrapins also call the preserve home. These populations combine to create a unique marsh island community at risk of pollution damage and natural threats. As severe hurricanes become more and more common in the Gulf of Mexico, Rabbit Island feels nature's fury much more often than it has in the past. These valuable species require protection from human encroachment and natural threats alike to ensure the safety of this valuable natural habitat.

One of the integral species residing on Rabbit Island is the marsh rabbit, for which the island gets its name. The marsh rabbit is a darker relative of the more common cottontail rabbit and exhibits some unique behavioral characteristics. When threatened, these rabbits will use standing water as a refuge, floating with only its eyes and nose periscoping above the waterline. It is more suited to water escapes, because its short legs make it less agile on land than most other rabbits. Short hind legs, however, do allow it to walk using only its hind limbs which is an unusual characteristic. Great horned owls and northern harriers are its most dangerous predators, with larger snakes running a close third. They are herbivores and important primary consumers of vegetation in the areas they inhabit.

The diamondback terrapin is the only species of turtle in North America that lives in brackish water. In many areas of the eastern United States, these turtles are threatened by the destruction of nesting beaches and accidental trapping in crab pots. Commercial harvesting for their meat also plays a role in their survival. They were once considered a delicacy and were hunted almost to extinction. Although it holds no federal endangered status, it is considered a species of concern by the state of Alabama. Because turtles often feed on decaying animal and plant matter, they function as cleaners in their environments, helping maintain the natural health of their habitat. These residents of Rabbit Island, along with many other species, create a unique marsh community along the coast of Alabama.

Further Reading

Thompson, Leah, and Stephen Frost. University of Michigan Museum of Zoology, Animal Diversity Web. "Sylvilagus Palustris (Marsh Rabbit)." http://animaldiversity.ummz.umich.edu/site/accounts/information/Sylvilagus_palustris.html.

Roberta Case Pine Hills Preserve

The Roberta Case Pine Hills Preserve, at more than 350 acres, sits in the foothills of central Alabama. It contains one of the largest populations of the Alabama canebrake pitcher plant, which is designated a federally endangered species. The best environments for the canebrake pitcher plant are isolated seepage areas, where water seeps up out of the ground, found throughout the area's pine forests. Additionally, this preserve supports a large population of the rare Harper's heartleaf and, along with the canebrake pitcher plant, is found nowhere else in the world. Through the removal of aggressive woody vegetation and prescribed burning, the controlling agency, the Nature Conservancy, works to maintain and restore the longleaf pine forests and seepage areas necessary to the healthy preservation of this natural environment.

One of the methods used to encourage a healthy, self-sustaining environment in the Roberta Case Pine Hills is prescribed burning. More than half of the preserves managed by the Nature Conservancy of Alabama contain fire-dependent ecosystems. Reproduction, growth, and survival of many native plants and animals in the area require periodic burns. Fire suppression efforts over the last three decades have greatly harmed these areas. The reintroduction of fire to these environments is just one step of many along the path to restoration and long-term preservation. The Roberta Case Pine Hills Preserve benefits from prescribed burns, because longleaf pine ecosystems are now on the road to a healthier status, and rare species like the Alabama canebrake pitcher plant are gaining more of a foothold with every controlled fire. Like all pitcher plant species, the Alabama canebrake is carnivorous. It traps and consumes insects in its tubular leaf body. Although the plant grows in wetter areas and seeps, it is sun loving, so periodic fires that clear woody brush from its habitat are essential. The plants also depend on moist soil conditions, so the construction of fire lines and harvesting activity can be detrimental. First described by Fred and Roberta Case (hence the preserve's name), this rare plant is found in only three counties in Alabama and nowhere else in the world. The Cases spent a great deal of time searching for and then monitoring almost 30 colonies and advocated for site protection. It was their tireless efforts that resulted in the founding and naming of this preserve in their honor.

Further Reading
Gaddy, L. L. "A Review of the Taxonomy and Biogeography of *Hexastylis*." *Castanea* 52 (1987): 186–96.
U.S. Fish and Wildlife Service, Division of Endangered Species. "Species Accounts: Alabama Canebrake Pitcher-Plant." http://sciences.aum.edu/bi/BI4543/saru.html.

RUSSELL CAVE NATIONAL MONUMENT

Evidence suggests that, for more than 10,000 years, prehistoric people have lived in Russell Cave, located in the northeast corner of Alabama, just south of the Tennessee border. A visit to Russell Cave National Monument offers the opportunity to explore ancient North American human history as well as experience the unique natural beauty of the cave and its surrounding environment. The National Geographic Society purchased the 300 acres that surround the cave shelter and then donated the land to the American people. In 1961, President John F. Kennedy designated the donation a national monument. Its name comes from the Russell family, who owned the land at the turn of the 20th century, when the area was first mapped out in detail. The main attraction for this national preserve is the long history of human habitation. A museum at the site offers artifacts along with reproductions of items found in the cave. Through the museum experience, people can learn about the history of those who lived there as well as the history of the archaeology that has taken place at the site. Some of the educational activities include demonstrations by interpretive rangers that show the use of weapons and tools common to ancient Russell Cave communities. The bookstore offers specialized literature on ancient native peoples and their way of life as well as works about the local ecology. Adding to the rich human history of the area, every year in spring, Russell Cave hosts a Native American festival for the enjoyment of its patrons and offers demonstrations of Native American cultural practices.

The many artifacts excavated from the cave environment offer clues about life in the caves before European contact. Most of the pottery found in Russell Cave, for example, is not more than 2,500 years old, providing evidence to both pre- and post-Contact Native societies, while limiting understanding to only the most recent centuries of ancient American history. Some of the pottery types used by natives survived for generations, while some seemed to have only been in use for a few years. The most recent pottery in the cave system was broken sometime between 1500 and 1650 c.e., according to scientific dating techniques. Artifact study suggests that atlatls were commonly used by these residents, as well. The atlatl is a spear-throwing device that is used as an extension of the arm and greatly increases the range of thrown weapons. During the growing season, the site supports a garden with the plants that would have been commonly used by the cave's inhabitants. Evidence suggests that the local flora remained unchanged for thousands of years, until the arrival of Europeans and the introduction of new and often aggressive species, forever altering the surrounding ecology. Cave staff work diligently year-round to ensure the preservation of these valuable sources of human history and change over time in northeast Alabama.

Some of the oldest natural history of the area dates back to 350 million years ago, when the area was part of a vast sea. Fossils of brachiopods and corals have been found in the limestone rocks in and around the cave. Today, North Alabama Birding Trail Site 44 runs through the cave's lands and offers hikers the opportunity to observe some of the more than 100 resident avian species. The Alabama Birding Trail as a whole is not a trail in the traditional sense but rather a collection of 50 sites located across 11 counties that are known for exceptional bird-watching opportunities. This area is most known for the occurrence of summer tanagers, scarlet tanagers, and endangered yellow-billed cuckoos. The path at Russell Cave that offers the best birding vistas is partially paved but often presents steep terrain along its 1.2-mile loop. Picnic areas are scattered throughout the oak-hickory forest stands found around Russell Cave, but there are no camping facilities, making the monument a day-use area only. In the past, caving was a popular attraction because the system offers over seven miles of mapped passageways, but the discovery of rare species—for example, a type of scorpion that lives nowhere else in the world—has curtailed public access to and use of the cave system in order to preserve the valuable natural legacy in addition to the detailed human historical record.

Further Reading

Laymon, S. D., and M. D. Halterman. "Can the Western Subspecies of the Yellow-billed Cuckoo Be Saved from Extinction?" *Western Birds* 18 (1987): 19–25.

Rogers, William. *Alabama: The History of a Deep South State*. Birmingham: University of Alabama Press, 1994.

Terres, John K. *Audubon Society Encyclopedia of North American Birds*. New York: Knopf. 1995.

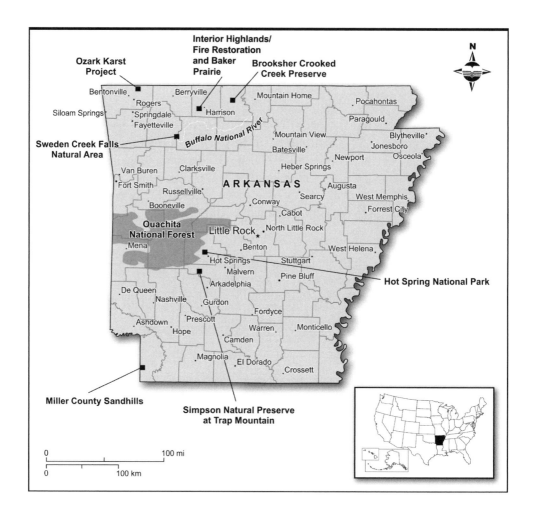

Brooksher Crooked Creek Preserve, 18

Buffalo National River, 19

Hot Springs National Park, 21

Interior Highlands/Fire Restoration and Baker Prairie, 22

Miller County Sandhills, 24

Ouachita National Forest, 25

Ozark Karst Project, 27

Simpson Natural Preserve at Trap Mountain, 29

Sweden Creek Falls Natural Area, 30

ARKANSAS

Arkansas presents a unique mix of mountainous regions and river valleys with the alluvial plains of the Mississippi River in the east and gulf coastal plains to the south. Rugged hills and deep forested valleys fill the Ozark Plateau, which is shaped by swiftly flowing streams. Separating the Ozark Plateau in the north and the Ouachita Mountains in the south is the Arkansas River and its valley. As one of the two major ranges in the United States that run east to west, the Ouachita Mountains hold vast timber resources, mineral deposits, and hot springs. The Mississippi Alluvial Plain of the Mississippi River covers the entire eastern third of Arkansas. This delta region is covered with nutrient-rich soils carried by the river and its tributaries, creating valuable agricultural lands. The west gulf coastal plain is a lowland area of pine forests and farmland punctuated by important natural resources, including natural gas, petroleum deposits, and bromine flats. A long history of human habitation in Arkansas and interest in the bountiful natural resources provides the backdrop for what today are ongoing restoration and preservation efforts across the state.

Arkansas's history of environmental concern and action stretches back more than 50 years. In 1949, the Arkansas General Assembly created the Arkansas Water Pollution Control Commission as a branch of the state health department. It took almost 20 years to become the Arkansas Pollution Control Commission, which formed to address both water and air pollution concerns as an independent state agency. The 1970s brought more reorganization and a new focus on open-cut mining, expanding the state's interests and authority once again. Today the department includes the Commission Directors of Forestry, Game and Fish, Geology, Health, Natural Resources, and Oil and Gas combined with the service of seven private citizens appointed by the governor. Functioning as the environmental policymaking body for the entire state, the commission administers programs, sets operational guidelines, and functions as a body of appeal. Working with the commission is the Department of Environmental Quality, which is responsible for the day-to-day regulation and administration of many environmental programs. Water and air pollution control, solid waste disposal, surface mining, and hazardous waste disposal are divisions that all fall within the department's jurisdiction. In addition, there are public outreach and assistance and environmental preservation divisions focused on education and preservation. Overall, the state organization and oversight of environmental issues and concerns has evolved and expanded greatly over the last few decades to emerge as a force of change in Arkansas aimed at balancing the needs of natural preservation and human habitation in a resource-rich land.

Today some of the biggest concerns for the Arkansas natural environment include protection of fragile wetland environments and improper waste disposal, especially in natural waterways. Other concerns include outreach programs involved in teaching children about the dangers of low-lying ozone concentrations, especially during hot Arkansas summers. The Arkansas Department of Environmental Quality provides an air quality index for public awareness and education on the side effects of poor air quality, including descriptions of what to look for to determine whether levels of air pollution warrant staying indoors. Educational programs also aim to reduce the harmful effects of landscaping and gardening as well as household chemicals by educating Arkansas residents on efficient, safe procedures for use and disposal of common chemicals in and around the home. One program—Environmental Protection Begins in Your Own Backyard—offers chemical alternative suggestions, composting process education, environmental landscaping plans, and other citizen action options that empower Arkansas residents to take preservation into their own hands, helping to ensure future generations of environmental commitment.

Brooksher Crooked Creek Preserve

As part of the Ozark Mountain river system, Crooked Creek is considered one of the best smallmouth bass fisheries in the United States. Additionally, the preserve through which Crooked Creek runs hosts bluff-top glades and savanna plant communities with a variety of Arkansas wildflowers. Located in Marion County on more than 100 acres of land, the preserve features a half mile of riverside environment and several large bluffs that overlook the creek. Visitors can access the river by foot, but there are no maintained or marked trails. Currently, there are no camping sites either, although a primitive camping area for the Broosher Preserve is in the planning stages.

The preserve has been under the Nature Conservancy's control since 2001, when the organization received the land as two separate gifts. The preserve is part of a larger project that includes a wildlife management area under the control of the Arkansas Game and Fish Commission and a privately owned site under a conservation plan. The most important concerns of the project plan include the restoration of native plant communities and the stabilization of stream banks. Much of the lowlands and streamside areas have been converted to pasture, allowing for the overpopulation of non-native species. Among the native species that remain, plants of special conservation concern include Ashe's juniper and purple beardtongue. Visitors can identify Ashe's juniper by its dark blue berries with whitish blooms. To identify purple beardtongue, spotting tubular flowers that range in color from violet to deep purple with a hairy lower lip is the key. A fifth stamen protrudes noticeably from the middle of the flower and is covered in hair as well, giving the flower its common name. In addition to these plant species, Crooked Creek is also home to many aquatic animals found only in the Ozark Mountains. The checkered madtom, a native miniature catfish, and the Arkansas saddled darter are of concern in protection efforts because of the limited range of their environment. Additionally, observant visitors can spot a Cooper's hawk or a red-shouldered hawk, both of which are considered rare in Arkansas. Without the protection offered by the partnership in charge of Brooksher Crooked Creek Preserve, these unique species of flora and fauna would have a much smaller chance of successful survival.

Further Reading

Ernst, Tim, and Pam Ernst. *Arkansas Nature Lover's Guidebook: How to Find 101 Scenic Areas in the Natural State*. Pettigrew, AR: Cloudland.net Publishers, 2006.

Henshaw, Julia W. *Mountain Wild Flowers of America: A Simple and Popular Guide to the Names and Descriptions of the Flowers that Bloom above the Clouds*. Boston, MA: Ginn, 1906.

BUFFALO NATIONAL RIVER

As one of the few rivers in the 48 contiguous states that remains undammed, the Buffalo flows down its unfettered 150-mile length over raging rapids as well as lazy stretches through the Arkansas Ozarks and finally into the White River. The banks of this wild river host unique natural environmental, pre-Contact Native American artifacts, and pioneer homestead evidence, creating a national recreation area with much to offer. Over 30 years ago, the Buffalo River was established as the first national river "for the purposes of conserving and interpreting an area containing unique scenic and scientific features, and preserving as a free-flowing stream an important segment of the Buffalo River in Arkansas for the benefit and enjoyment of present and future generations." The National Park Service is currently developing a management plan that addresses resources, preservation, development, and visitor use for the next two decades, and it encourages public participation through the Web site in the planning process. In addition to the multitude of both land- and water-based recreational activities, historical preservation plays a major role in the park's mission, offering visitors the chance to experience Native American bluff-dwelling remains, pioneer settlements, and mining communities. Few national forests offer as much diversity in experiential opportunities as Buffalo National Forest.

The upper river section is the largest of three major districts, stretching from the Upper Buffalo Wilderness to Mount Hersey. This region contains two wilderness areas and some of the most rugged park terrain. Although it offers the most river access points, this area also offers some of the roughest water. Additionally, most of the hiking trails in the park are located in the Upper River area. Trails lead to waterfalls, caves, and historic log houses, providing much of the heaviest-used trail land in the park. The middle River section offers some of the river's smoothest waters. The Tyler Bend Visitor Center, located in the Middle River district, hosts an exhibit area and auditorium for the enjoyment and education of park visitors. The largest wilderness area is in the Lower River district. Much of the park's camping activity takes places in this area, and two popular attractions are the Indian Rockhouse Trail and the Rush Historic District, which in times past was a zinc mining community. Combined, these three districts house amazingly diverse wild environments carefully managed for human recreational use and enjoyment.

The seasons at Buffalo River are a special experience for park visitors. Each exhibits its own unique character. Summer is arguably the least comfortable time to visit the river, when heat, humidity, and insects can be uncomfortable. Water recreation, though, offers a welcome respite from the summer extremes. Fishing opportunities abound in this catch-and-release area, and the deep pools that line the river host waders seeking relief in the hottest months. Fall is a study in color contrasts, when the changing of leaves in the largely deciduous forests rivals the more popular East Coast color viewing. Scenic Highway 7, in particular, offers unparalleled views of the changing foliage. Maintained trails provide opportunities to hike into the forests, and trails such as the Buffalo River Trail and the Old Horse Trial alternately take hikers to scenic vistas and river crossings interspersed throughout the blazing autumn forest. One or two weeks during winter offer landscapes covered by a gentle layer of snow, a rarity for Buffalo River. The hollows where waterfalls normally flow then freeze over with ice formations, creating stark winter scenery. The temperatures, however, are unpredictable, but when the conditions are right, Buffalo River transforms into a winter wonderland worth the visit. The spring months of April and May offer a variety of wildflowers, green foliage, scenic creeks, and rushing waterfalls. The age of the ancient Ozarks has allowed the elements to carve into the natural landscape, creating many waterfalls across the area, some carving their way through rock walls to fall to the pools below, like Dismal Creek. Camping, canoeing, swimming, fishing, and nature photography opportunities draw many visitors during the spring, which is the season commonly agreed to be the best time to visit.

A unique feature of Buffalo National River's mission is an artist-in-residence program that allows professional artists to explore their particular art form surrounded by the natural beauty and majesty of the Buffalo River. All visual artists, writers, composers, and performers are welcome to apply, and three positions are granted each year—one each in the spring, summer, and fall. The park provides up to three weeks of housing, and the artist is required to submit a piece of work that represents their stay at the river. The park can then display the work submitted for public enjoyment. While in residence, the artist might speak to visitors about their experience, sharing through demonstration, lecture, or some other means. Such an untamed area lends itself well to creative inspiration, and the artist-in-residence program provides a perfect outlet for inspired artistic creation.

Further Reading
National Park Service. "Buffalo National Forest Currents." http://www.nps.gov/buff/planyourvisit/upload/FinalCurrents2007ReducedSize.pdf.

HOT SPRINGS NATIONAL PARK

Hot Springs National Park has stood witness to a long history of human activity. Prior to the arrival of Europeans on the shores of the New World, Native Americans quarried novaculite for weapons and tool construction. In the early 1800s, Thomas Jefferson ordered exploratory expeditions of the area as part of the Louisiana Purchase. Based on the beliefs surrounding the health benefits of hot springs, a busy town quickly grew with the hot springs as the centerpiece to support a health spa industry. By the 1930s, there was a store and log cabins constructed to support the budding tourism industry. Forty years before the establishment of Yellowstone National Park, President Andrew Jackson signed legislation that designated "four sections of land including said springs, reserved for the future disposal of the United States shall not be entered, located, or appropriated, for any other purpose whatsoever." Hot Springs National Park contends that this legislation, by creating a natural reservation of the hot springs area, makes the park the oldest in the country. After surviving a conflict over competing claims by private citizens, by 1878, the springs and the surrounding mountains were permanently set aside as Hot Springs Reservation, formally and forever under government control and protection.

Although the hot springs are the primary natural feature of the park, preservation of the springs as natural phenomena has not been the main focus. Public use and access is the main concern of park efforts at conservation, with the mountains around the area managed to preserve the water system that feeds the hot springs. Many small mammals call the park home, and the mild climate ensures a wide variety of bird species, including songbirds, wild turkey, and raptors. Although no rare or endangered animal species are found in the park, the springs and mountains provide valuable natural habitat for the many flora and fauna species typical of the region. The forests are a mix of oak, hickory, and pine trees interspersed with wildflowers and blooming trees to add to the biological diversity, some of which are considered rare and endangered. *Castanea ozarkensis*, a rare local chinquapin species of flowering chestnut tree, grows in the park, as well as the rare Graves' spleenwort, named as such because the plant was thought to treat spleen disorders. The park also hosts many mosses, algae, and liverworts. The rare blue-green algae *Phormidium treleasei* grows in areas where hot spring waters meet light and air. The presence of hot springs creates an environment unlike any other in the Ozark Mountain range, which allows for the occurrence of rare species like *P. treleasei*.

The hot springs are a result of complex geological forces originating from a small range within the Ouachita Mountain system. Rain percolates through surface soil, creating carbonic acid as it reacts with carbon dioxide. As the acidic water continues to work its way through the ground, it absorbs other minerals as well. The deeper the water travels, the more its temperature rises, and scientists believe that somewhere between 6,000 and 8,000 feet below the surface, the water converges into underground streams. Cracks in the earth's crust allow for fast escape routes, where the water emerges as the hot springs humans have utilized and enjoyed for centuries.

One of the environmental concerns of preservation is human habitation close to park boundaries. Much of the park sits next to roads and homes, exposing the forests to air pollution, nonnative incursion of plant and animal species, and litter accumulation. In a concerted effort at constructive conservation education, the park provides literature on the hot springs, local flora and fauna, and a program called How Long Does It Last? that teaches local youth about the impact of human presence and waste on the natural environment of the park. The main focus of the education program is to teach how long different types of human trash remain in the environment before decomposing. Paper lasts two to four weeks, and a plastic six-pack ringed holder lasts as long as a century. People might expect items such as an aluminum can to rival plastic, but many would be surprised to know that an orange or banana peel has a trash life of up to two years. The importance of understanding not only the decomposition process itself but also the impact of human presence cannot be underestimated, because the long-term health of the springs and the water system that supports them is one of the most immediate preservation concerns for Hot Springs National Park.

Further Reading

Hanor, Jeffrey S. *Fire in Folded Rocks*. Hot Springs, AR: Eastern National Parks and Monuments Association, 2003.

Shugart, Sharon. "Hot Springs National Park." *The Encyclopedia of Arkansas History & Culture*. http://www.encyclopediaofarkansas.net/encyclopedia/entry-detail. aspx?entryID=2547.

Interior Highlands/Fire Restoration and Baker Prairie

The Ozark Highlands and the Ouachita Mountains are characteristically beautiful examples of Arkansas scenery. The woodlands and savannas of these two regions are remnants of an environment type that once stretched from Oklahoma to the Appalachian Mountains and the eastern seaboard. Now known as the Interior Highlands, these mountains and valleys hold the headwaters for several major river systems and host a wide variety of natural habitats brimming with unique species of flora and fauna. According to the Nature Conservancy of Arkansas, the Ouachita Mountains are home to almost 50 species found nowhere else on the planet. During the last 100 years, the forests were heavily utilized for lumber and paper production. In the mid-20th century, people became concerned that tree cutting was taking too heavy a toll, and they began to take what seemed to be logical measures of allowing forests to regrow and suppressing fires. In the mid-1990s, the U.S. Forest Service, the Arkansas Game and Fish Commission, and the Nature Conservancy partnered to evaluate the health of the forests in the Interior Highlands. One result of this partnership was a plan to reintroduce fire as part of the natural processes in a healthy forest ecosystem, something that for decades people suppressed out of the mistaken belief that fire only damages woodlands. Without natural fires in forest undergrowth, the number of trees increases greatly, by at least three times as many trees as the forests supported historically. Trees compete strongly for water and nutrients, and this competition weakens the forest system as a whole. Drought, disease, and pest infestation pose significant problems in weakened systems. The red oak borer, for example, has eaten its way through more than one million acres, leaving multitudes of oaks dead and dying. In their place rises species of maple, ash and elm, causing major upset in the natural balance of flora and fauna in the forest environments. Additionally, the tree-crowded natural stands increase the danger of large-scale, intense wildfires that burn much farther and much faster than undergrowth fires, ultimately hurting rather than helping the Interior Highland forests.

One example of prairie lands in the Interior Highlands is the Baker Prairie Preserve. Baker Prairie is all that remains of what once was a 5,000-acre tall-grass prairie that stretched across northwest Arkansas. It is located in Harrison and is a mere 71 acres. By taking Industrial Park Road in Harrison, visitors come to Goblin Drive, which takes them into the preserve. Spring is an especially colorful time to visit, with Indian paintbrush, wild hyacinth, and orange puccoon in bloom. More delicate flora of special concern include the royal catchfly, prairie violets, downy gentian, and silky aster. Many unique species of animal call the prairie home as well. The prairie mole cricket is one of the largest insects in all of North America. A digging species, males come out from the soil to dig tunnels in early spring. After sunset, the mating male's call can be heard more than a quarter of a mile away because of the amplification effects of their tunnel homes. The ornate box turtle lives in unplowed grasslands as well, so Baker Prairie provides a perfect environment for their survival. Widespread habitat destruction through the building of highways, for example, is responsible for the decline in numbers of these rare species. This prairie provides a special haven of protection within the growing human population of Harrison. Fence row and woody vegetation removal, along with prescribed burning and control of nonnative plant species, work together to preserve this dwindling yet valuable Arkansas prairie environment.

Further Reading
Benke, Arthur C., and Colbert E. Cushing. *Rivers of North America*. New York: Academic Press, 2005.

Cooley, Gary. "The Simple Art of Ozark Flower Hunting." Ozark Mountains Web site. www.ozarkmtns.com/spring/images/springblooms/article1.htm.

Ford, Gary D. "School Days for Baker Prairie." *Southern Living*, May 2006, 64.

MILLER COUNTY SANDHILLS

Named for its deposits of ancient marine sand, Miller County Sandhills is one of the few remaining sites of its kind in Arkansas. The forests that grow here are more open because the sands create a difficult growing environment. As one of the few of its kind, Miller County Sandhills hosts several rare flora species that are especially adapted to the sandy soils. The Arkansas Natural Heritage Commission and the Nature Conservancy administer the site, which encompasses 184 acres that consist mostly of open woodlands with gentle rolling hills. There are no marked or maintained trails for visitor use, but a trip into the area in late May and early June offers trekkers a blossoming wildflower treat. Twenty-one plants of special concern have been documented in the area, and four of them—climbing milkweed, little-leaved prairie clover, tragia, and hairy grama—are found nowhere else in Arkansas. Although the sandhills historically have suffered environmental degradation, active management strategies have started the process of recovery, and today natural residents such as bluejack and margaretta oaks can be found in abundance, scattered among an understory that is typical of sandhill natural communities.

The climbing milkweed, one of the typical sandhill community residents, prefers drier, rockier soils than some of the milkweed family. Little-leaved prairie clover shares this love of sandy soils and thrives in the Miller County Sandhills. With a high drought tolerance and a penchant for coarse soil, the hairy grama joins the collection of sandhill plants as a well-adapted companion. Tragia, while found in several states in the United States, is found nowhere else in Arkansas except Miller County Sandhills. Another player in this natural habitat is the bluejack oak with its characteristic blue-hued leaves. The acorns of this tree are valuable to natural wildlife such as deer, raccoons, quail, and squirrels. It seems that wildlife prefer the bluejack oak acorn to other acorns, suggesting that either the taste or the nutritional value of these acorns is of a higher quality than other oaks. Without this sandhill preserve—one of only three intact sandhill areas in Arkansas—an important ecosystem would be in danger of disappearing. Miller County Sandhills provides a haven for this interdependent, delicately balanced natural environment.

Further Reading

Jones, Stephen R. *The Last Prairie: A Sandhills Journal.* New York: International Marine/ Ragged Mountain Press, 2000.

U.S. Environmental Protection Agency. "Midwest Oak Ecosystems Recovery Plan: A Call to Action." *Great Lakes Ecosystems: 1995 Midwest Oak Savanna and Woodland Ecosystems Conferences.* www.epa.gov/ecopage/upland/oak/oak95/status. html#ARKANSAS.

OUACHITA NATIONAL FOREST

The Ouachita National Forest covers just under two million acres and stretches across central Arkansas and southeastern Oklahoma. Timber and wood production, watershed improvement and protection, habitat management for local flora and fauna, wilderness area control, mineral resource leasing, and outdoor recreation all play a role in the management of this valuable natural region. Headquartered in Hot Springs, Arkansas, management authorities work to educate the public on Ouachita National Forest's important role in the state's natural health, resource economy, and recreation opportunities. The Forest Service aims high with a mission statement that says it will "sustain the ecological health and productivity of lands and waters entrusted to [its] care and provide for human uses compatible to that goal." The Forest Service's vision for the Ouachita National Forest includes cultivating a healthy forest that hosts a full complement of native plant and animal species, creating a cooperative effort between staff and citizens that works to develop appropriate management programs, and offering a competent and diverse workforce dedicated to the forest and the public it serves. It is the oldest and largest national forest in the South, first being named the Arkansas National Forest in 1907 by Theodore Roosevelt and receiving its current name, which means "good hunting ground," in 1926.

The natural composition of the forest is largely a pine-hickory mix. It contains more than 700 miles of recreational trails, allowing for access to some of its deepest and wildest areas. Additionally, visitors can enjoy scenic areas, float camps, shooting ranges, historical sites, and wilderness areas during the months of April through September. Some access points, though, stay open longer, allowing visitors to experience the vast beauty of changing seasons between the third week in October and the middle of November. Passes must be purchased for entry and use of the forest lands. Maps and brochures are available on the forest's Web site and through the mail by contacting the forest headquarters. Prepared visitors can find every natural recreation activity available through a bit of advanced planning and preparation.

One of the important actions underway in the national forest is the Pine-Bluestem Project. This program enacted by the U.S. Forest Service aims to restore through a process of ecosystem renewal over 150,000 acres of public forest land to conditions found in the region historically. Some of the first travelers to this region prior to European settlement described the Ouachita Mountain forests as dominated by hardwood, pine, and mixed oak.

Common animals were elk, bison, and white-tailed deer. Today's mountain slopes are still dominated by forests, but the forests themselves have changed drastically. For example, the density of trees per acre has increased from 170 to 250 due to fire suppression efforts, yet the mean diameter of each tree is smaller by two inches. Grasses used to dominate the understory, but now woody underbrush rules. The composition of animal species has changed, with elk and bison being completely eliminated and a variety of other species now considered endangered. Commercial exploitation has reduced natural habitat greatly and endangered the survival of a wide variety of plants and animals that historically have called the Ouachita Mountain forests home. Between the early 1900s and 1940, much of the virgin forest cover was exploited by the wood and lumber industry. Following this came an era of management through fire suppression, which created the higher density of trees per acre and the aggressive overtaking of the understory by woody plants.

Ecosystem management using prescribed burns and species-specific planning is now the plan of choice in the Pine-Bluestem Project. Increasing the use of prescribed burns coupled with tree cutting that simulated natural disturbance is a centerpiece of action. There is also a modified control strategy in place when battling wildfires that allows for the natural process of burn and regeneration to have necessary and needed positive effects of pruning forest plants through natural fire selection. An important part of this plan

Ouachita National Forest. (Brian Cormack)

includes replacing nonnative species as well as developing and maintaining natural connections between mature forest habitats. With all of this action aimed at restoration and maintenance, an important element is recognizing that humans are an important part of the system. The public is not restricted in its use of the Pine-Bluestem lands, while close monitoring of the restoration efforts is constantly taking place in a cooperative relationship between university experts and forest service scientists. To measure success of the program, experts use biodiversity, recreation opportunities, and timber supplies as yardsticks of progress. Balancing the natural needs of the ecosystem with human demands is a constant process, and a successful program is able to address all needs equally.

One measure of ecosystem health is the successful reintroduction of extirpated species to the forest lands. Elk have been successfully reintroduced to nearby habitats, but reintroduction into the Pine-Bluestem area failed due to brainworm infestations. Moist, high-tree-density environments host a snail that carries brainworm, which limits efforts to bring the forests back to a state of historical natural health. Despite this and other setbacks, ecosystem management and restoration is possible, as demonstrated by the Pine-Bluestem Project. Landscape ecology, restoration efforts, and species recovery can work hand in hand with recreation access and the timber industry, and this project blazes a successful trail for future efforts to balance the needs of nature with the demands of society.

Further Reading

Davis, Richard. "National Forests of the United States." Forest History Society. http://www.foresthistory.org/Research/usfscoll/places/National%20Forests%20of%20the%20U.S.pdf.

Mohlenbrock, Robert. *This Land: A Guide to Eastern National Forests*. Berkeley: University of California Press, 2006.

Ozark Karst Project

The Ozark karst ecosystem is the underground foundation of the Ozark Plateaus and is comprised of caves, springs, and aquifers. Karst terrain is a type of geography that results from the breakdown of dissolvable bedrock over time. As water takes on carbon dioxide while passing through surrounding soils, it becomes acidic, and it is this acidity that produces karst features. Reaching all the way from northern Arkansas and southern Missouri to eastern Oklahoma, this phenomenal underground system houses a wide variety of animal species, including types of bats, fish, crustaceans, and many others. Included in this array of underground life are at least 60 species that are found nowhere else. Because the natural habitats of these species are so limited, many animals of karst systems are considered globally imperiled, and the Endangered Species Act protects eight of them. Additionally, the system is an important source of groundwater for human communities, so protecting this area is important for both natural environment concerns and human community interests.

The history of preservation efforts prior to 1950 is sparse. Because the area was largely rural, little effort was expended, or needed for that matter, except to keep out unwanted visitors and vandals. During the 1950s, however, agricultural activity, human habitation, and industrial presence expanded, putting more pressure on the karst system. As human activity in the area continued to grow and awareness of the karst system's central role in the surrounding natural environment increased, efforts at protection and preservation grew. Beginning in the late 1970s, the Nature Conservancy started acquiring caves, repairing existing gates, installing new ones, and removing accumulated debris. Additionally, the porous nature of the surrounding lands lends itself to pollution. As a result, runoff from rain enters groundwater quickly, along with any pollutants carried along the way. Growing human presence continues to threaten as residential and industrial developments are often built directly over these fragile underground ecosystems. Agricultural chemical pollutants are another source of danger and, combined with the other threats posed by human presence and interaction, create the necessity for preservation and restoration intervention.

The Ozark karst project involves a great deal of effort directed toward species habitat preservation. Understanding the nature of cave locations commonly used by resident species, limiting human presence in the environments, and protecting surrounding lands from habitat loss due to development all top the list of important concerns. Establishing buffer zones around caves and sinkholes that are part of the karst system is an important part of the environment protection process. Accurate mapping of the inhabited cave systems is also extremely important. Sediment control and erosion plans are also vital pieces of the preservation puzzle. While preventing the spread of human presence is practically impossible, mediating the impact that presence has on local habitat is not. By fully understanding the interaction of above-ground environments with subterranean systems, areas like the Ozark Karst Project can be protected for future use and benefit as natural habitats for endangered species and groundwater resource areas for local human communities.

Further Reading

Elliot, William R., and Thomas J. Aley. "Karst Conservation in the Ozarks: Forty Years at Tumbling Creek Cave." *2005 National Cave and Karst Management Symposium*. http://www.utexas.edu/tmm/sponsored_sites/biospeleology/pdf/2006%20tumbling%20creek%20cave.pdf.

Turner, Ellen. "Ozark Karst: A Fragile Landform." http://www.cals.lib.ar.us/butler center/lesson_plans/lesson%20plans/Lesson%20plans-retained/Ozark%20karst.pdf.

U.S. Fish and Wildlife Service. "Recommendations for Proposed Activities in the Ozark Highlands." http://www.fws.gov/southwest/es/Oklahoma/Documents/Enclosures/BMP%20for%20Karst%20Features%201.23.2007%20dbf.pdf.

Simpson Natural Preserve at Trap Mountain

S tarting at the base of Trap Mountain and reaching all the way up to the steep slopes and ridgelines, this tract of land contains fantastic examples of Arkansas's natural biodiversity. As part of the Ouachita Mountains, Simpson Natural Preserve encompasses four general types of habitats. Glades exist on ridgelines, as well as both north- and south-facing slopes. Post oak and bluejack oak are characteristic tree residents of these forests, and the rare Arkansas cabbage grows in the understory of these areas. The woodland slopes of the preserve host shortleaf pine, hickory, and oak trees that support shrubs, wildflowers, and grasses in the understory there. The riparian forest that runs along the creeks and moist lower slopes supports flowering dogwood, a variety of fern species, and the dwarf iris. Wooded seeps add to the biodiversity, with their most characteristic contribution being orchids. The mixture of animal life that resides in this preserve adds to the overall diversity. Nearly two dozen species of butterflies, including the rare Diana fritillary, more than 60 avian species, white-tailed deer, black bears, and more create an interesting natural community. This wide range of unique environments and residents creates a preserve unlike any other in the state.

A major component of this area is the riparian forest that grows in the lower elevations. Riparian forests are wooded areas adjacent to a body of water. The term *riparian* specifically refers to areas adjacent to flowing water, such as rivers, streams, and estuaries, as well as still bodies of water, such as ponds, lakes, and reservoirs. The roles that the forests play in their ecological systems include helping control sediment, reducing the damaging effects of flooding, and aiding in the stabilization of stream banks. Riparian forests are different from uplands forest because of their characteristic plant communities, soils, hydrology, and topography. Because of their proximity to wetlands, both plant and wildlife communities are more diverse than drier, upland forests. Additionally, these forests help improve the quality of adjacent bodies of water. They are well suited to work as filters, removing excess nitrogen, sediments, and phosphorus, ultimately functioning as buffers for the environment. These benefits are valuable, but, most importantly, riparian forests absorb and store nutrients for the surrounding environment in their woody material. Flood control, natural habitat provision, and stream stability also benefit from these natural buffer zones, making their importance to the local ecology unmatched.

Wooded seeps play an important ecological role, as well. Often appearing as a slope community, they are generally found in lower elevations very near to smaller mountain streams. When calcium-rich water flows out of limestone bedrock and soaks the soil of these wooded areas, the perfect nutrient-rich seep conditions are created that support herbaceous plant growth and shrubs and trees. Seeps function within their environs something like a filter. Wetlands store excess water and slowly release the water back into the surrounding environment. The root systems of the woody plants help filter the water as it seeps back into the water system, sending back cleaner water than what was originally put into it. This function alone makes seeps one of the most valuable types of wetlands in the lower elevations. The protection of seep areas at Simpson Natural Preserve is one of its most important roles for this reason.

The rare Diana fritillary butterfly benefits greatly from the protection the preserve offers. As the official state butterfly of Arkansas, it is considered one of the most beautiful of the more than 130 butterfly species found across the state. This large species is named Diana for the mythological goddess of the moon and hunting and fritillary, derived from the word *fritillus*, meaning "dice box," which references the distinctive pattern of spots on the wings. In the mid-1990s, scientists searching for colonies found diminishing habitats as a result of fire suppression and urban development. They are now a designated species of concern. The best habitats for Diana fritillaries are moist mountain slopes that offer forest cover, unlike many butterfly species, which usually prefer open spaces. The chances of this butterfly being spotted by humans are high, mainly because they are rather large and their adult life span is up to five months. Another danger lies in the use of BT-based (*Bacillus thuringiensis*) sprays that utilize bacteria to control gypsy moths. Although it is a natural insecticide, Diana fritillary larvae are particularly susceptible. Some recent studies, though, show populations over a wider geographical range than first suspected, and it is possible that populations are more stable in Arkansas than previously believed. Overall, habitat conservation action can only strengthen the place of Diana fritillary in the natural scheme of environments like Simpson Natural Preserve.

Further Reading

Llewellyn, Jean. "The Importance of Riparian Forests." Tobyhanna Creek/Tunkhannock Creek Watershed Association. www.tctcwa.org/html/body_riparian_forests.html.

Opler, P. A., and V. Malikul. *A Field Guide to Eastern Butterflies*. Baltimore, MD: Johns Hopkins University Press, 1998.

SWEDEN CREEK FALLS NATURAL AREA

Sweden Creek Falls Natural Area is located in the Boston Mountains of the Ozarks. Protected by the Arkansas Natural Heritage Commission, the land holdings focus on areas of importance to the state's biodiversity and natural health. Each natural area under the jurisdiction of the commission has an individualized management plan formed and executed by staff and contractors. The management plans include five general categories of activity: grounds maintenance, prescribed burning, invasive species management, natural environment restoration, and research. According to the commission's Web site, "many of Arkansas' natural areas exist as 'islands' in a sea of disturbed land." This means that what happens to adjacent lands affects the managed natural areas. It is the commission's job through direct management plans and cooperative partnerships to make sure that human activity on the adjacent land tracts has as little impact as possible on the managed natural areas.

Sweden Creek Falls Natural Area is a combination of mesic woodlands, forests, dry glades, and native pastureland. On the dry slopes, pine and oak woodlands characterize the environment, and on the lower west- and east-facing slopes, the natural community is dominated by oak. The major waterfall is approximately 80 feet tall and helps maintain a moist environment that supports a thriving fern community. Additionally, sandstone glades on the ridgetop house the rare small-headed pipewort. This pipewort depends on wet, open glade environments like the one supported by the water system at Sweden Creek Falls. Because it is not naturally a competitive species, prescribed burns that eliminate aggressive plants are an important part of its ecology. It is found in only four areas on the planet: Arkansas, Oklahoma, Texas, and Georgia. By protecting this unique, delicately balanced environment, Sweden Creek Falls Natural Area helps ensure the survival of this and other endangered and important natural species.

Further Reading

Kavanagh, James, and Raymond Leung. *Arkansas Trees and Wildflowers: An Introduction to Familiar Species*. Guilford, CT: Globe Pequot Press, 2008.

Warriner, Michael. "Arkansas System of Natural Areas." *The Encyclopedia of Arkansas History & Culture*. http://encyclopediaofarkansas.net/encyclopedia/entry-detail. aspx?entryID=2626.

Big Cypress National Preserve, 34

Biscayne National Park, 36

Blowing Rocks Preserve, 39

Disney Wilderness Preserve, 40

Everglades, 41

Florida Keys, 43

Indian River Lagoon, 45

Machaba Balu Preserve, 48

FLORIDA

F lorida exhibits more unusual ecosystems than any other state in the country. From coral reefs, marshes, swamps, and mangrove forests to dunes, hardwood hammocks, pinelands, and scrubs, Florida holds some of the most interesting and unusual habitats in North America. More than 30 different kinds of corals can be found off of Florida's shores along coral reefs that are the habitats for thousands of plant and animal species. Freshwater marshes are grassy wetlands characterized by year-round standing water, and the marsh grasses act as a natural filter for water that passes through. Freshwater swamps not only have standing water, but they also host a variety of trees, plants, and animals that thrive on the rising and falling water levels. Of all of the mangrove species on the planet, three are native to Florida. Red mangroves grow along water edges, black mangroves grow in higher elevations, and white mangroves inhabit more upland areas. Regardless of their location, the need for brackish water is common to all mangrove glades. Hardwood hammocks are small, thick stands of hardwood trees that can grow in marshes, mangrove swamps, and pinelands. The pinelands, however, are the most common ecosystem found in Florida, and the plants of this ecosystem grow well on level land and porous limestone. Scrubs are found in these areas as well; this ecosystem contains thick undergrowth of oaks and palmetto. These plants grow best in nutrient-poor, sandy soil, of which Florida has plenty. The many sand dunes along Florida's beaches are important nesting sites for sea turtles and shorebirds. These brief descriptions of Florida's major ecosystems only scratch the surface of the immense natural variety in native habitats across the state.

Environmental preservation and restoration in Florida has a history nearly as unique as its natural diversity. Because of the distinctive challenges posed by Florida's ecosystems, especially concerning water quality, environmental interest and action have been in the forefront of public policy for some time. As a collection of largely water-dominated ecosystems, Florida offers unique and often groundbreaking answers to difficult preservation and restoration questions. The Florida Department of Environmental Protection's Division of Law Enforcement, for example, is Florida's oldest state law enforcement agency. The state legislature created a shellfish commission in 1913 to supervise a growing commercial fishing industry. By the early 1940s, the Florida Sewerage and Industrial Waste Association came into being to address issues of waste water management and pollution control. Today known as the Florida Water Environment Association, its mission brings together water quality professionals to formulate and provide education programs, professional development, and public policy aimed at preserving and restoring Florida's valuable water resources. Many organizations and agencies have formed over the last few decades in direct response to the unique needs of Florida's extensive water ecosystems, because the largest environmental threats to Florida all involve water-based bionetworks.

Some of the unique solutions embraced by Florida's environmental agencies and professionals include an agro-ecology program based at the Florida Center for Environmental Studies, a coalition of 10 state universities and four private higher education institutions. This program focuses on the boundary between agriculture and natural ecosystems across Florida. Land stewardship, sustainable agricultural practices, and multiple use models for public lands all figure into the agro-ecology program. The Department of Environmental Protection administers the Florida Coastal Management Program, which functions as a network of agencies implementing and enforcing current statutes to protect natural coastal resources. On the restoration front, the Everglades Restoration initiative focuses on restoring both natural and manmade environments to create a sustainable balance and is arguably the longest projected, and perhaps most complex, restoration program in the United States. Human presence and natural damage to the original four million acres that was the Everglades is potentially reversible, and with time, dedication, money, and man power, some of the country's most important natural treasures are slowly being restored. Research and application of innovative environmental policies characterize Florida's bold and valiant efforts toward self-repair and sustainability.

BIG CYPRESS NATIONAL PRESERVE

Located about 45 miles west of Miami, Big Cypress National Preserve encompasses a large freshwater swamp that is essential to the health of the neighboring Everglades. In many ways, Florida is one big network of interdependent water systems that rely on each other for their mutual benefit. Protecting more than 700,000 acres that house a mixture of tropical and temperate natural communities, the preserve was created in 1974 to enact conservation measures important to restoring and maintaining water quality, natural resources, and the ecological health of this important system. Three of the most integral programs work toward Florida panther restoration, hydrologic improvement, and understanding the role of fire in vegetation regeneration. Burns play a significant role in maintaining the health of this natural area. During the period between winter and summer, frequent lightning historically started natural fires in the area. Over many years, these fires created fire-dependent communities, and today, as part of a managed maintenance program, the National Park Service initiates controlled burns. There was a time when the Park Service put out all fires under the misguided impression that all fires have overwhelmingly negative effects. Now only fires that threaten people and property are put out, and naturally started fires are allowed to burn under the watchful eyes of experts.

The fire management plan for Big Cypress includes several important objectives that aim to enhance the ecological health of the preserve. One concern is the accumulation of fire fuel sources around structures and roadways along with the protection of cultural and natural resources that could be severely harmed or destroyed by fire. Habitat management for game animals, as well as protected and rare species, is also important. Part of the management plan involves research into the role of fire in the Big Cypress ecosystem, such as the function of clearing and controlling the spread of invasive and exotic plant species. Finally, prescribed burns in certain areas help keep scenic vistas clear of debris while providing the natural regenerative benefits of burning. Many seeds, for example, thrive best just after a fire has taken place, because important nutrients necessary for growth are released by the heat. Although wildfires could play the same role, human interests are often threatened when fires are allowed to freely burn, so the control exerted in prescribed burning allows for all of the benefits while the risks are mitigated.

The natural habitat of this wet cypress forest hosts an extremely diverse collection of flora and fauna species. Some of the commonly found animals include alligators, cottonmouths, eastern diamondback rattlesnakes, and the elusive Florida panther. The Florida panther now inhabits only a fraction of the range that once hosted this majestic animal. Southern Florida's tropical savanna climate with hot, wet summers and mild, dry winters sustains the panther's climatic needs. To survive and reproduce, however, the panther must have adequate shelter and food sources. The biggest threat to the survival of the remaining panther populations is the degradation and loss of natural habitat. Other threats include disease, lack of large prey, environmental contaminants, and inbreeding. Florida's human population grew by almost five million between 1935 and 1990, and this phenomenal growth presents the most immediate threat to panther populations because of human impact on the environment. Degradation and fragmentation of natural habitat, along with domestic feline disease and the reduction of large prey sources, greatly impacts the dwindling Florida panther population.

Several other endangered species reside here, as well, including the West Indian manatee, the eastern indigo snake, and the Florida sandhill crane. West Indian manatees are large, gray aquatic mammals with oval-shaped bodies that taper to paddle-like tails. Estuaries are prime habitats for manatees, making Big Cypress a perfect home for these amazing animals. Manatees spend their winters in Florida but during the summer months can range as far west as Texas and as far north as Virginia. As completely herbivorous animals, when not traveling, most of their time is spent relaxing or eating. Due to the threats endangering their natural habitats, there is a Florida Manatee Recovery Plan in action coordinated by the U.S. Fish and Wildlife Service. The enforcement of speed restrictions for boats in certain areas is a key component of Florida's protection plan. Other conservation issues include scientific research that deals with the biology, mortality, distribution, behavior, and habitat concerns, as well as education and public awareness programs, all of which are important ongoing efforts at developing sustainable maintenance programs for manatee habitat protection.

Originally envisioned as a buffer between humanity and the Everglades, Big Cypress has become a preserve of importance in its own right. The Florida panther and the West Indian manatee are only two of the many species that call this estuary home. The preserve operates under some unusual guidelines, however, with some parts of the area approved for hunting, cattle grazing, oil exploration, and off-road vehicle use. One additional unique element of Big Cypress is its position as the southernmost end of the Florida National Scenic Trail. Submerged under water most of the time, this portion of the trail provides visitors with one of the most unusual hiking experiences in the United States. The 1,100-mile trail ends in the middle of Big Cypress, and the Big Cypress stretch is approximately 40 miles long. Not only does the almost continuous underwater submersion make the hike difficult, heavy rains and wind often destroy any trailblazing attempts. When hiking this part of the trail, many bring their own collapsible seating and sleeping hammock to have places to sit and sleep outside of the standing water. Few other places in North America offer such a unique hiking experience, and those seeking alternative outdoor experiences will be richly rewarded in this unusual natural area.

Further Reading

Florida Panther Net. "Panther Handbook." http://myfwc.com/panther/handbook/index. html.

McPherson, Benjamin F., and Robert Halley. "The South Florida Environment: A Region under Stress." *U.S. Geological Survey Circular 1134.* http://sofia.usgs.gov/publications/circular/1134/Circular1134.pdf.

Ripple, Jeffrey S. *Southwest Florida's Wetland Wilderness: Big Cypress Swamp and the Ten Thousand Islands.* Gainesville: University Press of Florida, 1996.

BISCAYNE NATIONAL PARK

Situated along the southeast edge of the Florida peninsula and about 20 miles east of Everglades National Park is Biscayne National Park. Established as a national monument in 1968 and enlarged and designated a national park in 1980, Biscayne National Park protects a rare combination of flora and fauna, both on land and in the sea. Within the park, visitors can wander along the mangrove shoreline, wade in crystal clear waters, explore pristine islands, and dive to living coral reefs. Reachable by boat or car, the park attracts more than half a million visitors per year to its almost 200,000 acres. One facet that makes this park so unique is that the vast majority of the area is submerged, making water recreation and preservation the main focus. Human populations have been part of Biscayne National Park's landscape for some time. Native Americans, tree cutters, settlers, pirates, fortune hunters, bootleggers, artists, millionaires, and presidents have used Biscayne Bay and its keys for recreation, financial gain, or both. The beauty and the majesty of the area have called many to its shores, offering adventure and escape to those who seek a different path.

Although the past may have witnessed treasures in Biscayne Bay of the material kind, today the park's wealth is measured in natural terms. Some of the earliest residents of the keys were known as "wreckers" because of their efforts at plundering the many sunken ships in the bay waters. By the early 20th century, wrecking had become less profitable due to efforts by the U.S. government at making the waters safer for ship passage, and so local residents turned to a different kind of plunder in order to make a living. Turtles and sponges proved to be valuable harvests, but, by 1905, disease had taken its toll on the sponge population, and today the scarcity of sponges is much higher than in previous years. Turtles were hunted heavily for decades—so much so that, by the 1960s, they were named on the federal endangered species list. Others have been drawn to this area because of the coral reefs and their amazingly clear waters. One natural feature, the mangrove shoreline, was for many years misunderstood and undervalued. Today the role that mangrove stands play in the health of the bay and its residents makes the mangroves an important piece to protect. Additionally, many species of bird call the bay area home, adding to the vast biodiversity that comprises Biscayne National Park.

As a bird sanctuary, this area is difficult to rival. A wide variety of avian species is drawn to the bay. Brown pelicans, for example, find the bay great for fishing. The brown pelican is unique among pelicans in that it is the only dark pelican and the only one that dives in midflight into the water to catch its prey. During the first half of the 20th century, pelican populations were greatly reduced by hunters in search of their feathers, as well as by those who felt it necessary to protect fishing areas. Pesticide poisoning took its toll as well, causing the brown pelican to be added to the federal endangered list in 1970. A ban on DDT, one of the biggest pesticide threats to bird populations, helped existing numbers grow, and, by 1985, the numbers stabilized, resulting in the removal of the species from the endangered list. Another Biscayne resident, the white ibis, patrols mudflats in search of small fish and crustaceans. Standing approximately two feet tall, this wading bird is often spotted in shallow water areas looking for large insects to eat. The Arsenicker Keys of Biscayne National Park host many colonies of wading birds such as the white ibis during the winter, largely because the shallow waters around these mangrove islands are perfect for foraging.

The forests of the park are jungle-like in appearance, characterized not only by stands of mangrove, but also hardwood hammocks. These hammocks are dense stands of broad-leafed trees that are home to many tropical species of tree, such as gumbo limbo, cocoplum, and mahogany, which grow alongside the more common live oak and red maple trees. These stands tend to grow in slightly elevated areas, so the forests rarely flood. Additionally, acids from decaying plants dissolve surrounding limestone, creating a natural moat that helps protect these forests from fire. Inside the forests, the tall, shady trees create a protected area for undergrowth that hosts ferns and other plants that thrive in the moist environment. Although the tallest trees rarely reach above 50 feet, mature hammocks form dense canopies that shade lower-growing plants from direct sunlight, and the resulting high humidity means that ferns and mosses thrive near the ground. While the location, natural moat, and resident humidity mean that hardwood hammocks are generally protected from fire damage, there are some conditions under which fires can threaten this type of forest. If there is a drought, fire becomes an important concern, because it can take several decades for a hardwood hammock to recover from significant fire damage.

When looking at the flora of Biscayne National Park, several species stand out as typical of these subtropical forests. Wild tamarind trees and the gumbo limbo grow together, arching high overhead to form a dense canopy that provides a protective cover for ferns and mosses. Bromeliads and orchids grow along the trunks and branches of the trees that comprise the hammock environment. The midstory is populated by smaller versions of the canopy trees along with smaller species, such as the white stopper and cinnamon bark. The lower understory hosts saplings along with shrubs such as wild coffee and white indigo berry. Woody shrubs and vines are also found here, but, due to the lack of adequate sunlight, ground cover generally remains sparse. The outer edges are dense with vegetation that requires, in comparison, a great deal of sunlight. The thick growth along the edges allows for a higher humidity and lower temperature inside the understory than would otherwise be possible. Bahama strongbark, saw palmetto, sweet acacia, and poisonwood all grow in these dense areas of the hardwood hammocks. These plants are characteristic of hardwood hammock environments and comprise a large percentage of the natural growth around the forest edges. A typical species of flora is the sweet acacia, which sports little yellow flowers that smell sweet and grape-like. Bahama strongbark, a hardy neighbor to the acacia, is a slow-growing, drought tolerant addition to the hardwood hammock fringe areas. The fragrant flowers attract pollinators, and birds are often seen enjoying the brightly colored fruits of the shrub. The saw palmetto provides fruit for consumption by bears, hogs, and deer but received its name from the sharp-edged leaves that help protect the plant from rampant foraging. Poisonwood, another important inhabitant, is a relative of poison sumac and poison oak and, like these sometimes-irritating cousins, causes serious skin irritation after contact. Combined, these species create a unique environment that thrives in the warm, humid climate of the Florida Keys. Biscayne National Park protects this delicate environment as a valuable natural habitat of the larger keys ecosystem.

Further Reading

Florida Museum of Natural History. "South Florida Aquatic Environments" http://www.flmnh.ufl.edu/FISH/southflorida/sitemap.html.

Williams, Joy, and Robert Carawan. *The Florida Keys: A History & Guide*. New York: Random House, 2003.

BLOWING ROCKS PRESERVE

Blowing Rocks Preserve is a barrier island site in Florida under the direction and control of the Nature Conservancy. Several natural habitats are protected on the 70 acres of preserve land. Beach dune, coastal strand, mangrove wetlands, oak hammock, and tropical hammock combine to make up this small but significant site. The rocky limestone shoreline is the largest of its kind on the Atlantic coast, and the preserve is named for the 50-foot tall plumes of seawater created by storm activity and high tides that crash waves up against the coastal limestone formations. Sitting just 30 miles north of West Palm Beach at the tip of Jupiter Island, the preserve is accessible to the public daily. For a small beach access fee, visitors can enjoy a boardwalk that runs along the Indian River Lagoon, a beachside nature trail, and a butterfly garden. For a relatively small preserve, Blowing Rocks provides valuable protection for fragile habitats and unrivaled opportunities for experiencing its unique environs.

In the late 1960s, Jupiter Island residents initiated this preservation project by donating the land to the Nature Conservancy. Today, the preserve is a model of successful native plant restoration, sea turtle protection, and ecosystem management. Indian River Lagoon, the tip of which is home to Blowing Rocks Preserve, is arguably the most diverse estuary in North America. Fall is the best time of year to visit this unique area for both its wildlife viewing opportunities and its nature walk prospects. As fall sets in, a variety of migrating birds pass through the region, including hawks, falcons, and warblers. A walk along the dune path reveals a variety of native flora that temporarily host migrating bird populations. The gumbo limbo tree, sea grape, and palm populations provide temporary homes for the influx of avian residents. The gumbo limbo is a native Floridian tree that has peeling red-brown bark, giving it the nickname of tourist tree because the bark resembles a peeling sunburn. The sabal palm is Florida's state tree, as well as the state's most abundant. Sea grapes abound as well, and fall is the perfect time for harvesting their edible fruit. As part of the larger estuary of Indian River Lagoon, Blowing Rocks Preserve provides public enjoyment of the protected fragile barrier island habitats.

Further Reading

Davis, S. M., and J. C. Ogden, eds. *Everglades: The Ecosystem and Its Restoration.* Delray Beach, FL: St. Lucie Press, 1994.

McPherson, Benjamin, and Robert Halley. "The South Florida Environment: A Region under Stress." *U.S. Geological Survey Circular 1134.* http://sofia.usgs.gov/publications/circular/1134/Circular1134.pdf.

DISNEY WILDERNESS PRESERVE

The Disney Wilderness Preserve is one of several protected sites under the control of Florida's chapter of the Nature Conservancy. Located south of Orlando and encompassing the headwaters of the Everglades ecosystem, this 12,000-acre preserve is a fantastic model of restoration as well as one of the largest wetlands mitigation projects of its kind in the United States. Bordered by Lake Russell, one of the last undeveloped Florida lakes, the preserve is generally accessible by the public during the week, offering a shorter one-mile hike to Lake Russell along with a longer 2.5-mile loop that offers a closer look at the preserve's natural communities. Entrance fees are low for this beautiful, unique natural area that is home to rare and endangered species of flora and fauna. Bald eagles, Florida scrub-jays, sandhill cranes, and gopher tortoises reside here, protected by the restoration and preservation actions of the Florida Conservancy.

The history of preservation dates back to 1993, when the Walt Disney Company and the Florida Department of Environmental Regulation, along with the Nature Conservancy and five other organizations, formed a partnership to establish the preserve on an original expanse of 8,500 acres of land to the south of Walt Disney World. Master planning for Walt Disney World Resort involved efforts at mitigation through the creation of wetlands equal in size to any destroyed in the development process. Artificially created wetlands, however, rarely survive and are rarely successfully integrated into the larger ecosystem. Instead, the company, functioning within a partnership, enacted a large-scale restoration and enhancement plan that placed the land under permanent protection, guaranteeing that the wetlands in the area would remain in their natural state. Because the lands were originally part of a working ranch, the preserve was used heavily for logging and grazing during the 1940s. By researching and implementing procedures to restore original environmental characteristics and restoring natural water flow patterns, the Disney Wilderness Preserve has become something of a living laboratory where visitors can learn firsthand about the natural systems being preserved.

This preserve offers visitors a special opportunity to contribute to the preservation efforts underway at the site. An organized volunteer program focuses on recruiting service time in scientific and restoration projects that include wildlife monitoring and invasive species removal. Volunteers can also participate in the maintenance of gardens and other landscaped areas and trail, ground, and building maintenance. There is even the opportunity to help with operations management and educational outreach programs. Support for special events, library maintenance, hike guidance, and the leading of buggy tours are among the many services volunteers provide. Visitor involvement, however, does not have to be this extensive for people to learn from and enjoy the rich natural resources and beauty the preserve houses. Today, the health of this "shallow river of grass," as it was described by author Marjorie Douglas, affects much of the land and waterways south of the preserve. The restoration of these wetlands has played a significant role in helping maintain the health of the lands it feeds and established a legacy of conservation action in this valuable natural area.

Further Reading

Hogan, Linda, and Brenda Peterson. *The Sweet Breathing of Plants: Women Writing on the Green World*. New York: Farrar, Strauss, and Giroux, 2002.

Stoneman, Marjorie Douglas. *Everglades River of Grass, 60th Anniversary Edition*. Sarasota, FL: Pineapple Press, 2007.

EVERGLADES

Everglades National Park has grown over the last 60 years to encompass more than a million and a half acres of land. The ecosystem is a delicate balance of interdependent flora and fauna and sits at the juncture between temperate and subtropical climates, the result of which is a level of biodiversity that is not easily matched anywhere else. The layout of the land is such that a broad, flat sheet of water flows over and through the limestone as it makes its way to the sea during the wet season; when it is dry in the winter, these freshwater sources dwindle to only a few spots that become quickly crowded with wildlife competing for precious fresh water. Among those species who call this unique area home are more than 20 threatened or endangered animals, 25 orchid varieties, more than 1,000 kinds of seed-bearing plants, 120 tree species, and more than 300 types of birds. Initially, it was concern over commercial encroachment into the avian rookery natural environment that was the impetus behind the establishment of the park, and, although it has been impossible to restore and maintain historic population numbers, today tens of thousands of birds nest in the area, providing unique opportunities for both casual viewing and scientific study.

Not only does the United States recognize the importance of preserving the Everglades, it is also designated an International Biosphere Reserve, a UN World Heritage Site, and a Ramsar Wetland of International Importance. The Man and Biosphere program of UNESCO (the United Nations Educational, Scientific, and Cultural Organization) protects prime examples of major ecosystems through the International Biosphere Reserve program as standards by which to measure the impact of human use and presence on natural areas around the planet, as well as to predict the impact humans will have on unprotected areas. UNESCO also recognizes the area as a site of heritage importance under the Convention Concerning the Protection of the World Cultural and Natural Heritage due to its unique blend of natural and cultural history and importance. Finally, the Ramsar Convention on Wetlands, signed in Ramsar, Iran, in 1971 helps protect the area under an intergovernmental treaty that provides foundational guidance on the conservation and use of wetlands. The multitude of protection efforts that are aimed at Everglades National Park testifies to its significance as a representative wetland, and its health and survival is an important piece of international environmental understanding and preservation.

The ecosystem is unique in many ways. Relatively speaking, the Everglades is very young; the foundational limestone bedrock is barely 8,000 years old. No part of the park rises more than eight feet above sea level, and what is seen today has only emerged since the last ice age. Within this short time period, however, human presence has had a significant impact on the Everglades system. Canals and levees now redirect the Everglades' only water source—the rain that falls on it—away from the Everglades and the natural habitats that are either home to or a stopping area for many migratory bird species. Many species are specially adapted to utilize ecosystems that have distinct wet and dry seasons like the Everglades. When human interference comes into play, natural feeding and nesting cycles fall victim to the side effects of that interference. If human disruption of natural water resources breaks the natural patterns of water supply and flow, then traditional feeding and nesting grounds are detrimentally disrupted, often leading to the loss of generations of rare and valuable plant and animal species. Alligators, for example, build their nests just above the highest reach of natural water levels. If humans alter the natural cycle and create situations where flooding occurs, nests are drowned and a new generation is destroyed. A set of species affected by artificially altered water levels is the aquatic apple snail and the snail kite bird. The endangered snail kite bird feeds on the apple snails that lay their eggs just above the wet season water line. Both drought and flood conditions have the potential to wipe out apple snail populations, and, as a result, the snail kite bird populations suffer. In addition to human water management concerns, human presence also introduces foreign, exotic species to the natural mix, which are often more competitive than the naturally occurring species. It is difficult to imagine that such a large ecosystem could be so detrimentally affected in a short period of time, but the last half century of human interference has taken its toll, making the Everglades the focus of one of the largest natural preservation and restoration projects in the world.

Housed within the park are protected populations of both large and small animals. Rare turtles and sparrows exist with manatees and crocodiles in a natural mosaic of diversity. Wetland drainage, alteration of water pathways, and hunting have all had a significant impact on population numbers. The American crocodile, once common across the South and Southeast, has been severely affected by human presence and interference. Historically, there were many more than the current population levels; today, in Florida, crocodile numbers barely reach 1,000. Growing anywhere from 7 to 15 feet long and living over 60 years in the best of scenarios, they live in brackish and saltwater areas. They are easily distinguished from their alligator cousins by their longer, narrower snout and their lower teeth, which are visible even when the crocodile's mouth is closed. They are shy and rather reclusive, which has helped protect them from hunting and human aggression. Although hunting has long been the historical danger, human development, illegal killing (without the underlying purpose of hunting), and roadway dangers are the biggest threats to remaining populations.

Also found in the Everglades is the Atlantic leatherback turtle. Listed as endangered in 1970, the leatherback is the largest, deepest diving, and widest ranging of all sea turtles. An adult can reach a length of eight feet and weigh as much as 2,000 pounds. Although the leatherback can be found in the Atlantic, Pacific, and Indian Oceans with a range as far north as the British Isles and as far south as Australia, recent estimates place the nesting female population at only 23,000 to 46,000 compared to the 115,000 estimated in 1980. Mexico's nesting leatherback population has suffered the most, declining from an estimated 65 percent of the total world population to barely 1 percent of that number today. The Everglades now hosts one of only a handful of populations left in the world, and it is the smallest of all. The crash in population numbers is due to a variety of influences, including harvesting, degradation of nesting habitat, and even the disorienting effects of beachfront lighting on hatchlings. Because leatherbacks have such a large migratory range, long-term international cooperation is necessary to maintain the existing population numbers. Everglades National Park is a prime example of what international efforts can produce when preservation entities coordinate and direct their efforts at ecosystem management and cooperation: a safe haven of immeasurable natural value.

Further Reading

Grunwald, Michael. *The Swamp: The Everglades, Florida, and the Politics of Paradise*. New York: Simon & Schuster, 2006.

Lutz, P. L., and J. A. Musick, eds. *The Biology of Sea Turtles*. Boca Raton, FL: CRC Press, 1997.

FLORIDA KEYS

The Florida Keys encompasses several zones that combine to create the Florida Keys National Marine Sanctuary. Education and preservation efforts revolve around two major categories of human activity: recreation and industry. The coral reef that comprises a major part of the Florida Keys system is the largest in North America and the third largest in the world. Coral reefs form when marine organisms use calcium carbonate to construct either internal or external skeletons. These skeletons form reef systems that provide shelter and sustenance to a wide variety of marine animals and plants. Generally, coral reefs are found only in latitudes between the Tropic of Cancer and the Tropic of Capricorn. The conditions provided by these tropic waters—warm, stable temperatures and consistent salinity—offer the perfect physical environments for coral reef establishment and maintenance. The Florida Keys is an example of warm currents establishing these conditions north of the tropics. The presence of the Gulf Stream significantly expands the range of coral reef existence. The rigid nature of the reef helps protect its shoreline from some of the destructive power of storm waves. Additionally, hundreds of plant and animal species call the reef home, many of which have human commercial applications. Recreational activities such as fishing, snorkeling, and scuba diving are a predominant foundation for the economy of the keys. The coral reefs that surround the keys are an important part of both the natural and human environments that depend on a healthy reef system.

To a certain extent, natural forces create some of the threat experienced by the keys' coral reefs. The vast majority of threats, however, come from both direct and indirect human contact. Visiting patterns show that more than three million people visit the keys every year. Eighty thousand people call the area their permanent home. This significant human presence means that the keys' environments, including the coral reef, are drastically affected by human activity, both intentional and unintentional. Boat groundings, swimmers standing on corals, propellers, anchor use, and damaging fishing methods have all taken their toll on the health of the reef system. Additionally, a variety of nutrient sources add to the problems of this valuable natural environment. Sewage treatment plants, cesspools, septic tanks, and marinas all contribute damaging by-products, putting native species at risk. Several threat management and mitigation programs are in place, but the damage caused by human presence cannot be negated; it can only be supervised and, to a certain extent, moderated. With so much leisure and economy activity dependent on a healthy reef system in the keys, restoration and preservation takes priority in conservation efforts.

Reef Relief is a grassroots organization dedicated to the protection of and restoration of coral reef environments. It is dedicated to preserving and protecting living coral reef systems through local, regional, and international efforts. Public awareness, scientific understanding, grassroots protection, program development and implementation, and ecotourism support all play vital roles in Reef Relief activities. The three main program areas that Reef Relief focuses on are an environmental education and policy guidance campaign, a coral photo monitoring survey and online coral archive centered on Key

Saturday morning sunrise on an Islamorada bonefish flat. (Angie Chestnut)

West, and an international survey and buoy program involving the Bahamas. As part of its educational efforts, a coral reef ecology course offers important education geared toward raising awareness of the fragility and importance of the keys' coral reef system and reducing the human impact in the Florida Keys. Public and private efforts involving education and preservation such as the valiant efforts of Reef Relief play indispensible roles in restoring and preserving the health of natural water systems in the United States and around the world.

In addition to underwater reef communities, four interrelated wetlands make up the natural environment of the Florida Keys. Salt marsh, buttonwood, mangrove, and freshwater wetlands function as wildlife habitats, pollutant filters, and storm-water storage. Salt marsh wetlands share ocean environment characteristics and provide important natural support for coral reefs and sea grass beds. They are less frequently flooded than mangrove areas and provide storm-water storage and natural habitats while functioning to maintain and increase resident water quality. Buttonwood wetlands house the same environment as salt marsh wetlands, with the addition of green buttonwood trees. Mangrove wetlands are closest to the sea, and, as a result, daily tidal activity floods these areas. Coastal protection and animal habitats comprise the mangrove wetlands that ring the keys. In contrast to these shoreline communities, inland salt ponds provide avian areas for wading birds, waterfowl, and shorebirds. The Florida Keys Advanced Identification Project identifies and maps the different wetlands found across the keys and assesses the health of each area. The wetlands form an interdependent ecosystem that needs monitoring and protection in order to fulfill its vital role in the natural health of the keys as a whole.

Further Reading

Davis, Jack E., and Raymond Arsenault. *Paradise Lost? The Environmental History of Florida.* Gainesville: University Press of Florida, 2005.
Odum, Howard T., Elisabeth C. Odum, and Mark T. Brown. *Environment and Society in Florida.* Philadelphia: Taylor & Francis, 1997.
Reef Relief. www.reefrelief.org.

INDIAN RIVER LAGOON

Indian River Lagoon is situated on the boundary between temperate and subtropical zones in Florida and is hailed as one of the most biologically diverse estuary systems in the continental United States. More than 3,000 plant and animal species call the lagoon home, and, as a result, the area has enjoyed the protection of the Environmental Protection Agency for nearly two decades as an estuary of national significance. A lagoon, by definition, is a shallow coastal body of water that is separated from the ocean by barrier islands running parallel to the shoreline. Tidal currents bring water in and out of a lagoon through inlets cut into the islands. There are three main types of lagoons: leaky, choked, and restricted, the last of which characterizes Indian River Lagoon. The system consists of multiple channels that function as a water exchange between the lagoon and the ocean. Wind patterns contribute to the current system by facilitating the transportation of water, increasing the exchange capacity. Both vertical and lateral water mixing occurs as a result. This means there is little change in salinity when measuring vertically, but horizontally salinity does decrease as the water increases its distance from the ocean. This well-mixed lagoon contains three subbasins with differing tidal amplitudes, excursion lengths, and current speeds. The resulting biodiversity is virtually unmatched anywhere in continental North America.

Encompassing just over 150 miles of Florida's east coast, the lagoon is managed by the St. Johns River Water Management District under the Indian River Lagoon National Estuary Program. In 1987, the Surface Water Improvement and Management Act designated the area as a water body with a priority need for protection and restoration. Some of the main problems that led to this focus include the loss or degradation of more than 75 percent of the resident salt marsh and mangrove wetlands, an increase in freshwater mixing due to both natural forces and human activity, and pollution as a result of waste and storm-water drainage into the lagoon. Shellfish habitat and sea grass beds proved to be especially vulnerable to these threats, and, by 1991, the lagoon became an official part of the National Estuary Program. One of the main focuses has been improving water and sediment quality to encourage restoration of sea grass beds and mangrove areas so that they can better perform their natural functions of protection and filtration.

Water quality, flooding issues, water supply management, landscaping, and other concerns all play into environmental issues that form the core of problems addressed by preservation and restoration activities at Indian River Lagoon. The multitude of resident species are extremely affected by the changes, both natural and human induced, that the lagoon experiences. Housing one of the most diverse avian populations in the United States and nearly one-third of North America's manatee population, the focus on protecting the lagoon's natural environment has wide-ranging effects. The beaches provide major nesting areas for sea turtles, hosting one of the densest populations in the Western Hemisphere. The lagoon's importance as a recreation destination cannot be ignored either. Boaters and anglers frequent its waters while contributing millions of dollars to Florida's economy in the process. The southern end of the lagoon is of special concern, because frequent freshwater discharges into the lagoon's waters decrease the salinity required for many plant and animal species to thrive. Additionally, waste water that is heavily laden with fertilizers has caused significant, damaging algae blooms that are overrunning delicate natural habitats. Private activists and public servants continue the fight to find appropriate balance between the flourishing of natural environments and the needs and demands of human presence. One of these efforts included the building of a sediment trap called a baffle box in a drainage area along a developed section of the shoreline. The estimated amount of sediment in its almost two decades of existence is approximately four tons. The success of this initial construction has resulted in the building of several more baffle boxes in an expanded program throughout the lagoon.

This relatively simple technology promises to help the estuary maintain a cleaner natural environment.

In addition to the large variety of plant and animal species resident at Indian River Lagoon, naturally occurring marine fungi and protists comprise an important part of the living environment. Ascomycota and basidiomycota make up the fungi population while phylum ciliophora, chrysophyta, dinoflagellata, and rhizopoda encompass the protists' inhabitants. Combined, the result is a delicate balance of necessary elements that are all foundational to a healthy estuary environment. The American alligator is one of the most majestic of the species found in the lagoon and is listed on the federal threatened species list. The American alligator is one of two living species of alligator and is native only to the southeastern United States. It resides almost exclusively in wetland areas in an interdependent relationship that benefits the wetlands by controlling rodent and other animal populations that could potentially overtax natural vegetation levels. The alligator's greatest contribution to wetland environments, however, is the creation of gator holes. By using its mouth and claws to dig and its body and tail to deepen, gator holes store much-needed water during the dry season and through the winter. Many animal species besides the alligator obtain water from these valuable storage areas when there is little natural water available.

As a vital part of the lagoon's environment, alligator population numbers have suffered from human encroachment and activity. Hunting and habitat loss are the two biggest culprits. As recently as the 1970s, many believed the number of remaining alligators to be beyond recovery. The U.S. Fish and Wildlife Service, state wildlife agencies, and the establishment of alligator farms have all contributed to a miraculous revival in numbers. One of the biggest contributors to this success was the placement of the American alligator on the endangered species list, which resulted in the outlawing of alligator hunting. By 1987, the U.S. Fish and Wildlife Service designated the alligator as a fully recovered species and no longer endangered. The limited nature of the alligator's natural range keeps the animal on the threatened list, and the reduction of its habitat means that population numbers, while strong in many areas of the Southeast, are still potentially in danger. The maintenance and protection of Indian River Lagoon is one of many projects helping to ensure the survival and flourishing of this amazing creature.

Further Reading

Ainsley, Amy W., Johnnie D. Ainsley, Derek S. Busby, Robert A. Day, Katherine A. Recore, and Troy B. Rice Adams. *Indian River Lagoon Comprehensive Conservation and Management Plan*. Tallahassee, FL: Indian River Natural Estuary Press, 1996.

Dybas, C. L. "Florida's Indian River Lagoon: An Estuary in Transition." *BioScience* 52, no. 7 (2002): 554–59.

Smithsonian Marine Station at Fort Pierce. "The Indian River Lagoon Species Inventory." http://www.sms.si.edu/irLspec/index.htm.

MACHABA BALU PRESERVE

Florida's Machaba Balu Preserve differs very little today from what settling Europeans found at this location more than 500 years ago. According to the Nature Conservancy's Web site, as part of the St. Marys River and Sea Islands conservation project, the site hosts approximately 10,000 acres of tidal salt marsh and 77 islands. Other protected lands surround the preserve, and it sits next to the Great Florida Birding Trail. The preserve offers canoeing and kayaking, and recreation areas are easily accessible. The conservancy selected this site because of its important role as a fish hatchery and spawning area for commercial and recreational fish species. Wading birds and shorebirds utilize the area for both feeding and breeding, adding to its environmental significance. Coastal development along Florida's northeast shoreline threatens the health of this important preserve that houses several threatened and endangered species.

Tidal creeks and backwaters around the preserve host manatees, turtles, dolphins, and terrapins. Roseate spoonbills, snowy egrets, and great blue herons are some of the shorebirds and wading birds that nest in the region. Additionally, bald eagles and ospreys call its hardwood stands home. Situated between the St. Johns River and Nassau Sound

Machaba Balu Preserve. (Haley A. Wilhite)

in northeast Florida, Machaba Balu Preserve represents a concerted effort between the Florida chapter of the Nature Conservancy, the National Park Service, and various state agencies at management and restoration of this threatened coastal area. Coastal estuaries and tidal marshes function as the meeting ground between ocean and land. In addition to providing important habitat sites for many plant and animal species, the preserve functions as a source of flood control and storm surge protection. Also, marshes provide a natural filtration system for pollution that would normally flow from inland areas to the sea. Unfortunately for the marshes, however, this means that pollution levels in the water and soil are often high, creating a dangerous threat to the natural health of the preserve. The proximity of Jacksonville means that the pollution risk is not going away anytime soon; intelligent management of the resources and health of Machaba Balu can help preserve and protect the area's important functions and contributions to Florida's northeast coast.

Further Reading

The Nature Conservancy. "Machaba Balu Preserve." http://www.nature.org/wherewe work/northamerica/states/florida/preserves/art10617.html.

Silliman, Brian R., Mark D. Bertness, and Edwin D. Grosholz. *Human Impacts on Salt Marshes: A Global Perspective*. Berkeley: University of California Press, 2009.

Appalachian National Scenic Trail

Marshall Forest Preserve

Springer Mountain

Camp Meeting Rock

Chattahoochee Fall Line

Dalton

Calhoun

Dahlonega
Cornelia
Hartwell
Rome
Etowah River
Gainesville
Marietta
Roswell
Athens
Atlanta
Decatur
Bremen
Forest Park
Carrollton
Covington
Newnan
McDonough
Eatonton
Griffin
Milledgeville
La Grange
Macon
Fort Valley
Dublin
Swainsboro
Columbus
GEORGIA
Statesboro
Vidalia
Americus
Cordele
Fort Stewart
Cuthbert
Savannah
Albany
Jesup
Blakely
Tifton
Moultrie
Waycross
Brunswick
Bainbridge
Valdosta
Thomasville

Heggie's Rock

Martinez
Augusta
Wrens

Ohoopee Dunes

0   100 mi
0   100 km

Appalachian National Scenic Trail, 52
Camp Meeting Rock, 53
Chattahoochee Fall Line, 54
Etowah River, 55
Heggie's Rock, 57
Marshall Forest Preserve, 58
Ohoopee Dunes, 59

GEORGIA

Most of Georgia's landscape is dominated by three major types of ecosystems: transitional piedmont, irregular plains, and southern coastal plains. Although the southern coastal plains are mostly flat lands, this area also contains barrier islands, lagoons, marshes, and lowland swamps. Lower in elevation with damper soils than the irregular plains to the northwest, the southern coastal plains enjoy longer growing seasons than other coastal areas. The inland plains of Georgia are a patchwork of crops, pasture, woodlands, and forests. Higher in general elevation than the coastal plains, longleaf pine, hickory, and oak forests dominate the still-forested areas. Higher still in elevation is the piedmont area of northwestern Georgia. Rocky landscape, plains, and foothills intermingle, creating a transition zone between the Appalachian Mountains and lower plains. Although this region was used for crop cultivation for some time, today it is largely used for human habitation and is dotted with pine and hardwood forests. With a wealth of natural resources spread throughout the state, Georgia has traditionally offered fertile ground for successful and profitable human settlement, sometimes at the expense of the local environment.

Environmental reforms in Georgia are a direct reflection of two major changes in the state's natural history: the inspiration of conservation efforts in the face of soil and timber reduction and the reversion of barren lands back into woodlands. With conservation and protection on everyone's minds, Georgia joined the national park bandwagon in the 1920s and 1930s by establishing many parks and preserves across the state. Also in the 1930s, new chemical practices developed at the University of Georgia revolutionized the paper industry and land use in Georgia by perfecting the process of turning young pines into paper. Through these actions, a partially wooded landscape began to reemerge. Some of the more recent major environmental restoration and preservation efforts are the actions of the Georgia Conservancy. Founded in 1967, some of its early successes include protection of Cumberland Island, the Okefenokee Swamp, and the Chattahoochee River National Recreation Area. Air and water pollution regulations became increasingly important through the 1960s and 1970s as the population doubled and urbanization spread. By the 1990s, species preservation began to play a more important role in regulation, and, in 2000, the Georgia Community Greenspace Program was inaugurated by the Georgia legislature, encouraging counties to set aside 20 percent of their land and water holdings as "permanently protected land and water, including agricultural and forestry land." Once the land has been designated a green space, the only uses and activities involving the preserved land must include protection of water quality, flood management, wetlands defense, soil erosion reduction, natural habitat preservation, scenery conservation, historic resource protection, and informal recreation. This program, by being based on local interest and concern, has proven successful over the few years of its existence and has set the stage for further environmental conservation as Georgia's human and natural landscape continues to change.

Along with rapid changes in population come the inevitable air and water pollution issues, and programs such as Mothers and Others for Clean Air and Water Footprint serve as education and action programs aimed at reducing the ever-enlarging human footprint on the soils and waters of Georgia. The Georgia Conservancy also offers Blueprints for Successful Communities, an "assistance program . . . designed to facilitate community-based planning efforts across the state" (www.georgiaconservancy.org/SmartGrowth/Blueprints_Home.asp). Many counties have benefited from the foundations laid by this groundbreaking program. Currently with 67 plant and animal species on the federal endangered and threatened lists, careful planning and growth execution could not be more important. Additionally, major drinking water sources are at risk because of saltwater intrusion in the wake of freshwater usage. While sweeping solutions are still in the works, research and intelligent development lead the way in the efforts to solve imminent clean water issues. As the fourth fastest growing state in the country, Georgia constantly endeavors to protect and conserve its valuable environmental treasures and resources.

APPALACHIAN NATIONAL SCENIC TRAIL

Known as the People's Path, the nation's first national scenic trail spans a multistate area beginning in Georgia and ending in Maine. The 2,175-mile trail was first envisioned in 1921 but not completed until 1937. The Trail Management Principles suggest that "the body of the Trail is provided by the lands it traverses, and its soul is in the living stewardship of the volunteers and workers of the Appalachian Trail community." This extremely long footpath is enjoyed by more than four million visitors every year, who engage in short jaunts, day trips, and long-distance backpacking excursions depending on their adventuring interests. Two-thirds of the population of the United States lives within a day's drive of the trail, making it one of the most accessible outdoor resources in the eastern United States. The original plan focused on preserving the Appalachians as a wilderness belt that could function as an easily accessible retreat from urban life. Today, the Appalachian Trail Conservancy is a volunteer organization that manages the entirety of the Appalachian National Scenic Trail. The natural and cultural resources associated with the trail and the educational opportunities all fall under the privy of the Appalachian Trail Conservancy as the preservation authority in charge. The result is a coordinated effort of nearly 40,000 members dedicated to preserving the trail for public use, enjoyment, and education.

The Georgia portion of the trail offers rugged hiking opportunities intersected by highway access points that sit roughly a day's walk apart. Although there are many steep areas along the trail, the average altitude is lower in Georgia than in the other southern states through which it crosses. The southern Appalachian Mountains remain today much as they were long before glacial movement transformed the lands to the north. Many rivers drain to the south, which provided a safe haven for many species during ice ages, and, as a result, the southern Appalachians contain a wide variety of freshwater animals. In an interconnected network of natural areas, the trail's protected corridor functions as an anchor for the nation's eastern forest lands, ultimately playing an important ecological and socioeconomic role.

Along the trail, no matter which part is hiked, there are many unique species of plant and animals to see. Between April and June, many species of trillium can be found along the way. It is one of the easiest spring wildflowers to spot, each species sporting three petals, three sepals, and three leaves. Also along the way is the Dutchman's britches flower blooming upside down with yellow-tipped white blossoms for which the plant is named. Late spring is the best time to see azalea in bloom as many species of this flowering shrub can be found throughout the southern Appalachian portion of the trail. Lucky hikers will spot the bald eagle, which now lives all along the trail. Successful reintroduction and preservation efforts have helped restore resident populations. With more than 2,000 threatened, endangered, or rare plant and animal species along its length, the Appalachian Trail offers unparalleled opportunities for experiencing nature up close and personal.

Further Reading

Appalachian Trail Conservancy. http://www.appalachiantrail.org.

Bryson, Bill. *A Walk in the Woods: Rediscovering America on the Appalachian Trail.* New York: Bantam Books, 1999.

CAMP MEETING ROCK

In addition to the Nature Conservancy of Georgia, the Georgia Land Trust works to preserve valuable landscape areas that play an important role in recreation, economy, or scenic experiences. Camp Meeting Rock is one area of conservation easement where the conservancy and the land trust have combined efforts to protect the 100 acres of granite outcropping that make up the area. Outcrops of this type occur in other areas of the Southeast, but over 90 percent of the total areas are in Georgia. Camp Meeting Rock is one of the largest in the region, and the preserve only encompasses a small part of a larger granite configuration.

The Nature Conservancy of Georgia notes that several plant species found few other places in the world flourish in this small preserve. The endangered black-spored quillwort is found in only six counties in Georgia, and one of those locations is Camp Meeting Rock. It grows in small, relatively wet granite depressions that Camp Meeting Rock has in abundance. The threatened pool sprite lives in the rock's vernal pools, even though for much of the year the pools are dry. The seed's ability to lie dormant for several seasons is the key to this inhabitant's survival. The hardy pool sprite simply lies dormant until the rains come. Additionally, the preserve is home to the rare longleaf flower, the stonecrop plant, and the dwarf granite stonecrop or puck opine. These are only a few of the many rare species at Camp Meeting Rock.

Further Reading
Alabama Land Trust and Georgia Land Trust. "About Us." http://www.galandtrust.org/ Aboutus.htm.

Chattahoochee Fall Line

The headwaters of the Chattahoochee River start their journey southward in the Blue Ridge Mountains of northern Georgia and travel for more than 400 miles before combining with the Flint River at the Florida border. Prior to the construction of dams along the river, it made a rapid and dramatically beautiful descent over the fall line along the Georgia-Alabama border. The length of the Chattahoochee runs through three distinct regions: the Blue Ridge Mountains, the Piedmont region, and the southern coastal plains. The most common forests found along its course are mixed oak, hickory, and pine areas. The upper canopy includes loblolly, northern red oak, and eastern red cedar trees, while the lower canopy hosts flowering dogwood, sumacs, and gum varieties. In recognition of the fall line's important natural resources, several interested groups and organizations have combined efforts to restore and maintain the nature health of the fall line.

The Chattahoochee River, at the point where it crosses the fall line near Columbus, Georgia, is the focus of Nature Conservancy activity aimed at safeguarding the valuable natural environment of this quickly changing region. A fall line is a narrow geological boundary situated between uplands and plains that is characterized by falls and rapids. The river crosses sandhills and rocky shoals that comprise the fall line, and then the Chattahoochee River and its tributaries flow through fire-dependant longleaf pine forests and floodplain hardwood stands. While history has seen a rich diversity of fish and wildlife populations, today many of the systems in the area are in danger. Diverted waterways, fractured forests, paved lands, and reduced wildlife populations characterize an area that once teemed with ecological variety. The spread of human populations and business development have negatively affected what was once a treasure house of natural resources. The Department of Defense, the Nature Conservancy, private landowners, and local businesses work together to strike a balance between human development and natural heritage protection of this valuable area.

The restoration and expansion of the areas' ecosystems are the focus of conservation efforts. Army land management and the conservancy, for example, combine their efforts to manage and monitor the natural habitats of Fort Benning so that preservation efforts and military interests are both fairly represented. In the fall line area, concerted work with local landowners has extended habitat protection efforts, resulting in improved regional conservation management. Local communities participate in the management and preservation of areas valued for their recreational opportunities and scenic beauty. Thousands of acres of land around the fall line have been inventoried for rare and endangered species. Without these efforts, the Chattahoochee Fall Line would stand little chance at surviving the demands of an ever-expanding human population.

Fall line streams, seepage bogs, and other wetlands in the area are of special concern to the Nature Conservancy and its preservation partners. In 2007, Congress approved the Water Resources Development Act (WRDA), which included a provision directing the secretary of the army to study and restore the aquatic-based ecosystem of the Chattahoochee Fall Line. This project will study the restoration of fish habitats through the possible removal of two dams located at Columbus, Georgia, and Phenix City, Alabama. Flood control, navigation, and environmental restoration will all play a role in the larger WRDA fall line project. The scope of projects such as this one testifies to the importance placed on the Chattahoochee River and its fall line region from both a human use and natural diversity perspective.

Further Reading

Brown, Fred, and Sherri M. L. Smith. *The Riverkeeper's Guide to the Chattahoochee River.* Birmingham, AL: Menasha Ridge Press, 1997.

Rivers of Alabama. "Chattahoochee Watershed." http://www.riversofalabama.org/ Chattahoochee/chattahoochee.htm.

ETOWAH RIVER

The Etowah River is the northernmost part of a waterway that begins in northern Georgia and stretches all the way to Mobile Bay in Alabama. It is a major headwater tributary of the Coosa River system, which spans this large geographical area. Located approximately one hour north of Atlanta, the Etowah River watershed is home to a relatively intact, diverse aquatic environment. Estimates suggest that the river is home to more endangered species of aquatic animals and plants than any other river of its size in the Southeast. The biggest threat to the watershed is expanding human development. The Nature Conservancy works with local organizations such as the Upper Etowah River Alliance to ensure that the needs of the environment are addressed in conjunction with the demands of urban expansion in the effort to preserve and protect the natural wealth of ecological diversity in the Etowah River watershed.

Ten imperiled aquatic species inhabit the Etowah River basin. Five species, all mussels, are believed to be extirpated, or locally extinct. One member of this diverse community is the Etowah darter, which calls the river home and is on the endangered species list. It is a slender fish that is just two to three inches long. The Etowah darter is endemic to the Etowah River basin and is found nowhere else in the world. Its range includes the river itself and eight of its tributaries. Despite this larger range, it is extremely rare and its environments of preference are small rapids and riffles. While other species of darter are often found in large numbers, the Etowah darter is found only as small collections of very few individuals. The health of the Etowah River and its tributaries is directly responsible for the maintenance of these rare fish. Many species found in the Etowah were once more widespread, but due to the many reservoirs spread along the length of the Coosa, original habitat ranges are now much more limited. Even the Etowah is split by a major reservoir, Lake Allatoona, and, as a result, endangered species are found only above the lake's location.

Several small stream fish that make their home in the basin are on the decline. The Etowah basin sits on the northern edge of the Atlanta metropolitan area. The counties that make up the lower portion of the basin have been some of the fastest growing counties in the nation for more than a decade. Over the course of the 1990s, the Atlanta metropolitan population grew more than any other area in the United States except Los Angeles. Agricultural lands and forests are being converted to accommodate this growth. Important vegetation responsible for stabilizing stream banks and maintaining high water quality is being removed; runoff from higher areas has increased; and stream location and flow is being altered by filling, piping, and other manmade modifications. One of the major results is increased erosion, which covers streambeds with silt, reducing foraging areas and spawning success for native aquatic species. The population of many of the native species is relatively stable, but the Allatoona Dam has limited their range drastically. Unmanaged development and population growth threatens to destabilize these areas already affected by human presence and can further jeopardize already imperiled species and their environmental needs.

Further Reading
Etowah Aquatic Habitat Conservation Plan. http://www.etowahhcp.org/index.htm.

HEGGIE'S ROCK

Heggie's Rock, one of the finest examples of Piedmont flat rock, is a unique outcropping like others in various areas across the eastern United States. Heggie's Rock Preserve is a small 100-acre piece of land that hosts an amazing biological diversity, both on the rock face itself and in the dish gardens found on the outcropping. Twelve of the 18 species considered endemic to granite flat rock thrive on Heggie's Rock, including the state threatened granite stone crop and the rare glad windflower. The preserve's fauna population is equally as diverse and interesting. Beavers and otters inhabit a stream that runs along one of the area's boundaries, and deer, turkeys, and lizards live on and near the rock formation. Many endemic species of spiders and insects can also be found here, with some of them found nowhere else in the world.

One of the threats to the outcropping's natural balance is the presence and encroachment of nonnative plant species. Japanese honeysuckle and Chinese wisteria threaten the delicate natural environments of the rock faces. Originally introduced as an ornamental plant during the 1800s, Japanese honeysuckle vines crowd out native plant species wherever they can get a foothold. It can strangle small saplings by twining around the delicate trunks, and, when found in the overstory, dense mats can form, shading everything below. Chinese wisteria can dislocate native species, which are often less aggressive. It has a tendency to girdle trees and shrubs with woody vines and choke them. The plant was first introduced to the United States in the early 1800s, and today invasions usually occur around previous ornamental plantings. Invasive species are a more subtle yet still extremely environmentally dangerous element present in these habitats only because of human introduction.

The presence of beavers and otters adds an interesting element of natural diversity to an already unique environment. Beavers, as a result of their dam building, often create rich habitats for other animals. Beavers maintain wetlands that can act as sponges for floodwaters, prevent erosion, and purify the water table. Waters downstream of beaver dams are cleaner because of the dams' natural filtration abilities. Because they breed only once per year, require unique stream habitats, and leave home at the age of two to establish new territory, beaver populations rarely overpopulate the areas they call home. If there is a risk of habitat burden, beavers will self-regulate their reproduction to mediate any negative effects their presence might have. By the early 1900s, beavers were almost extinct in North America due to trapping and the negative effects of agricultural draining. As an important element of helping maintain stream environments, the presence of beavers must be protected. The benefits of their natural contributions to local habitats cannot be matched any other way.

Heggie's Rock offers the unique opportunity to study these and a variety of other species and their native habitats. The Nature Conservancy calls the site a "natural laboratory for research and education," and the diversity inherent in the area proves this statement true. The public does have limited access to the site, but the Nature Conservancy must be contacted regarding all visits. Additionally, hikers of the region are asked to be careful where they step due to the delicate nature of the dish garden along the rock face. Periodic guided tours are sometimes available and given by volunteers. As a unique and fine example of granite outcropping, Heggie's Rock is a valuable habitat for its native flora and fauna species.

Further Reading

Invasive and Exotic Species. www.invasive.org.

Muller-Schwarze, Dietland, and Lixing Sun. *The Beaver: Natural History of a Wetlands Engineer*. Ithaca, NY: Cornell University Press, 2003.

MARSHALL FOREST PRESERVE

Marshall Forest is hailed as the only virgin forest in the United State that is within the confines of city limits. Rome, Georgia, is that city. Maclean Marshall, a naturalist and philanthropist, inherited the forest from his family, who purchased the land in 1880 and preserved it for "preservation's sake." A large percentage of the forest is old-growth and has never been cut by humans. It houses more than 300 species of plants along with many different animals. In 1976, Marshall gave the forest land to the Nature Conservancy to ensure its protection. It is approximately 300 acres total, with 75 acres having been farmed at one point in the past. Seventy acres of the preserve were added in 1985 and were not part of the original Marshall land grant. A little less than 100 acres still stands as old-growth, uncut forest. Friends of the Marshall Forest partner with the Georgia chapter of the Nature Conservancy to manage the land and provide tour access for the public. There are also self-guided nature trails that cross the preserve and a Braille Trail as well on the southwest side of the forest. Plant identification tags and station plaques guide visitors along the half-hour walks. Marshall Forest is an outstandingly rare example of flourishing nature within the boundaries of a city, something that is difficult to find—much less maintain—in the United States today.

Marshall Forest houses an unusual combination of pine-oak, chestnut oak, and mixed hardwood forest, which are both northern and southern tree species. More than 50 distinct tree varieties exist within the preserve. The Nature Conservancy, as the major managing entity, notes that it is unusual that Marshall Forest, as an old-growth habitat in a late stage of ecological succession, is not dominated by one plant community. Instead, sporadic areas are characterized by a combination of pines and hardwoods. Ice storms and occasional nature fires have created this environment by facilitating the presence of openings in the hardwood canopy through which pines are allowed to grow. From an endangered species perspective, the forest hosts the largest population of large-flowered skullcap in the state of Georgia. The preserve's specimens are the subject of study by scientists interested in better understanding the plant's life history. Additionally, there are a myriad of nonthreatened or endangered species that live in the forest. Marshall Forest's importance continues to grow as many natural areas in northwest Georgia are developed for human use. Although the land is self-maintaining and its designation as a national natural landmark protects it from human development, the monitoring of invasive, non-native species is always a concern in protecting this valuable natural example for future study and enjoyment.

Further Reading
Davis, Mary Byrd, ed. *Eastern Old-Growth Forests: Prospects for Rediscovery and Recovery.* Washington, DC: Island Press, 1996.

Ohoopee Dunes

The Ohoopee Dunes Natural Area is one of the most outstanding areas of natural beauty and preservation action in Georgia. Five tracts of land combine to form the expanse of the preserve, with the Georgia Department of Natural Resources cooperating in the preservation of one owned by the Nature Conservancy of Georgia and one under the direction of the U.S. Fish and Wildlife Service. Together these areas stretch across almost 3,000 acres along the upper Little Ohoopee River. Ohoopee Dunes is named for a central ridge of Kershaw sand dunes. Within Georgia, there are three types of sand dunes. The first occurs at the ocean shoreline marking the current coastal boundaries. The second type sits along the fall line where continental bedrock meets coastal plains and provides evidence as to where ancient coastlines used to sit. Unlike either of these formation types, riverine sandhills, like those found at Ohoopee Dunes, formed as a result of strong winds depositing river bottom sand along the shores of rivers—in this case, during the late Pleistocene era over 20,000 years ago. Ohoopee Dunes is the most extensive system of this type in Georgia.

Within the confines of the Ohoopee Dune Natural Area, there are a variety of natural communities. Dry dunes and longleaf pine forests sit adjacent to hardwood stands and river floodplains. Visually, though, the dune community is the most striking and the most characteristic of the preserve. Hosted within these communities are a variety of tree and plant species. Some of the flora residents are generalists that are adapted to a variety of drier, sandy soil environments. Some, though, are considered specialists and can only be found in communities with these specific kinds of sandhills. Specialist species found here that are considered by the state as threatened include sandhill rosemary and sandhill milk vetch, for example. One of the reasons why plants like the sandhill rosemary thrive so well in dune environments is that it depends on fire for successful reproduction. The nature of dune communities means that burns are patchy, often leaving islands of vegetation untouched in a unique pattern difficult to find in natural environments. Many sandhill and habitat transition zone species need fire for their survival but would not benefit from fires that burn long and hot, like the fires of a forest. The spotty nature of vegetation in dune environments is perfectly conducive to plants with selective fire needs.

One interesting characteristic of the plant environments found in these dune areas is the stunted nature of plant stature and growth. The trees are short and twisted, and shrubs populate many of the natural communities. Lichen and mosses cover the ground. The soil simply does not have the nutrient resources or water access to support larger plant varieties. Longleaf pine and turkey oak are found here along with dwarf oak and oak hammock. Despite the widespread support limitations, many species of both plant and animal call the dunes home. The desertlike environment hosts several types of threatened and endangered flora and fauna. The habitat supports unique evergreens, such as woody mints and rosemary, which provide protective wildlife areas along with erosion control for the dry, sandy soil. Animals found in the area include the threatened eastern indigo snake, the gopher tortoise, and the endemic Ohoopee Dunes moth. The unique natural character of the dunes encourages communities and residents found in few other places in North America.

The eastern indigo snake is one of these unique inhabitants. It is the longest breed of snake in the United States, with specimens reaching over 100 inches long, and it sports lustrous black scales with patches of red or cream on the face and neck. Its preferred habitats are the sandhills of northern Florida and southern Georgia. Originally, this species became threatened as a result of detrimental overcollecting of the animals as pets and deaths caused by the gassing of tortoise burrows in an effort to collect rattlesnakes.

Ohoopee Dunes. (Alan Cressler)

Human habitat expansion has played a significant role in the reduction of the snake's natural territory as well, multiplying the threat to a dwindling population. The eastern indigo snake requires a variety of habitats to successfully complete its annual cycle. One habitat necessity is the presence of tortoise burrows, like the ones made by the gopher tortoises residing at Ohoopee Dunes. During the winter, eastern indigo snakes use the burrows as protection from the cold and dehydration. In its Georgia habitats, these thermal refuges are necessary to the survival of this species. Small vertebrate animals provide the main source of nourishment for the eastern indigo, and the dunes at Ohoopee provide ideal habitats for small mammal support. Turtles, turtle eggs, young tortoises, lizards, and birds can all fall prey to this predator. Another reason these dunes provide such a perfect habitat for the eastern indigo is that the species prefers open, undeveloped areas for its home range. Large tracts of undeveloped land, like the preserve at Ohoopee, are essential for the maintenance of large population numbers. While burrow gassing and pet-trade collection are on the decline, the presence of humans and the effects of their habitation continue to threaten existing populations. Agricultural activity, construction, pesticides, and rodenticides all cause direct mortality, as well as contribute to the fragmentation of natural habitats, reducing the successful spread and growth of viable eastern indigo snake communities.

Natural management techniques aimed at protecting these important habitats include a variety of preservation measures. One of the most important maintenance goals involves protecting and preserving the wide-ranging diversity of plant and animal communities that call the dunes home. The decimation of any species that is part of this delicate balance threatens the survival of all. Dune plants and animals rely on each other for food, protection, and shelter, as in the example of the interconnected relationship between the eastern indigo snake and the gopher tortoise. The lands currently protected may not be sufficient to sustain all of the integral species found at Ohoopee Dunes. Through research and creation of educational materials, managing entities hope to educate the wider public, resulting in a more common respect for the delicate nature of the dune environments. While human presence and impact cannot be eliminated, recreational access to the dunes can be controlled, offering a balance between the needs of the natural communities and the people who value these areas of natural beauty.

Further Reading

Chafin, Linda G. *Field Guide to the Rare Plants of Georgia.* Athens: University of Georgia Press, 2007.

Mara, W. P. *Racers, Whipsnakes, and Indigos (Herpetology Series).* Neptune, NJ: TFH Publications, 1996.

Nourse, Hugh. *Favorite Wildflower Walks in Georgia.* Athens: University of Georgia Press, 2007.

LOUISIANA

Louisiana is a land of diversity and novelty. Both environmentally and culturally, this relatively small southern state presents a complex puzzle. Well known for its bayous, swamps, and the people who inhabit them, Louisiana possesses a wealth of less-celebrated inland natural resources. In addition to the Mississippi alluvial plain and the western gulf coastal plain, the central plains of Louisiana or "piney woods" cover a large area of the state. Once covered in oak, hickory, and pine forests, the northeastern and central portions of the state are now populated by loblolly and shortleaf pines. Two-thirds of this region is forested, supporting a robust lumber and pulpwood industry. Adjacent to this area is the Mississippi alluvial plain. Alluvial, by definition, suggests that soil, clay, gravel, and other material settled in the area because of flowing water, as in a riverbed or floodplain. The final large piece of the Louisiana puzzle is the western gulf coastal plain. While the effects of human habitation are a concern, the Mississippi alluvial plain and the western gulf coastal plain were most recently damaged by natural forces: Hurricane Katrina. Widespread wetlands and forested areas, already affected by long-standing human presence, took a beating in 2005 when Katrina made landfall, and the region still struggles with environmental and economic recovery. These natural forces, combined with a history of timbering and open range livestock have permanently altered the coastal plain ecosystem. While much of Louisiana's restoration effort and money is spent recuperating the losses of Katrina, ongoing preservation activities aim to stabilize and expand the foundations laid nearly a century ago.

Historically, Louisiana's major pressing environmental concerns have focused on the Mississippi River's potential for flooding and wildlife conservation. The first wildlife conservation law was passed in 1857, with a formal, fully formed wildlife protection agency emerging in the early 1900s. Some of the first general environmental actions taken were to construct flood control measures by building a system of floodways and spillways for the Mississippi River in the late 1920s. These actions, combined with dredging for oil and exploration for sources of natural gas, slowed the natural process of silt flowing into the wetlands. This allowed salt water to seep in, creating brackish environments not suited for many of Louisiana's native flora and fauna. Despite these issues, concerted, widespread state environmental action did not truly begin until the early 1980s. The Department of Environmental Quality formed to address questions of air and water quality, solid waste management, control of radioactive materials, and hazardous waste disposal. Unique to Louisiana's concern over its wetlands are the uses to which the wetlands are dedicated. Not only are these habitats important natural environments, they are also the foundation of major agriculture and fishing industries. Partially because of this heavy industrial character, in 1993, Louisiana became one of the first states in the country to exercise federally approved strict solid waste landfill regulations. The late 1980s and early 1990s also saw the emergence of the Nature Conservancy in Louisiana in response to critical environmental challenges. The advent of Hurricane Katrina in 2005 complicated and compounded restoration and preservation issues immensely. Projects such as the Cameron Creole Watershed—Marsh Terracing Project highlight the state's efforts to preserve natural habitats and protect human interests by terracing marshes to prevent erosion while building up stable hurricane evacuation routes along Louisiana Route 27. Out of necessity and ingenuity, Louisiana continues to offer unique solutions to unique environmental problems, setting precedents for wetland conservation around the globe.

One of the most active and effective environmental organizations in Louisiana is the Louisiana Environmental Action Network, or LEAN. As a citizen action league, LEAN emerged as a combination of more than 100 grassroots organizations focused on helping communities become safer, healthier places to live. It functions as an umbrella organization that provides member groups and individuals with information, support, and resources to enact significant environmental change. As a leader of conservation and restoration action and a groundbreaking association, LEAN works with citizen groups to develop, implement, and enforce legislative and regulatory safeguards; support grassroots groups across the state; hold yearly conferences; and keep the media informed about important issues while constantly encouraging governmental leaders to take action. Operating under the motto of "powered by people, fueled by knowledge," LEAN has encouraged and supported great change in Louisiana policy and action on the environmental front both before and after Hurricane Katrina. By empowering citizen action, LEAN leads the way in effective, permanent change in both environmental policy and accomplishment. Because of the unique challenges faced by Louisiana, innovative and effective solutions such as LEAN have emerged to set a standard for future preservation efforts.

Abita Creek Flatwoods Preserve

Abita Creek Flatwoods Preserve is a pine-dominated wetland community organized solely for environmental preservation and public appreciation purposes. The Nature Conservancy of Louisiana controls the area and focuses its efforts on the restoration of degraded lands to high-quality savanna conditions as well as monitoring and documenting the restoration process. Selective timber cutting and prescribed burns are two important tools used by the conservancy to rebuild the preserve's natural ability to self-sustain. Longleaf pine savanna, pond cypress woodland, longleaf flatwoods, and riparian forests characterize this small but important natural site. Although the area is open to the public during the daytime, there are no developed facilities except for a boardwalk that takes visitors along a prescribed path through the preserve. The rules concerning visitation to the preserve aim to strictly enforce maintaining a distance between visitor and nature. Pets are not permitted, and collection, removal, and damage of plants, animals, artifacts, and minerals are strongly prohibited. Camping, hunting, fishing, and trapping are all banned in the effort to preserve the gains made by restoration efforts. Abita Creek Flatwoods Preserve stands as an example of strict control and regulation entirely aimed at the reestablishment and stabilization of this unique habitat, which hosts many rare, threatened, and endangered plant species.

Generally speaking, wetlands are areas of standing water that support dense populations of aquatic plants. Pond lilies, cattails, and sedges dot the landscape, interspersed with stands of cypress and gum. Wetlands are important geographical components because they provide food and protection for a wide variety of plant and animal species and provide buffer zones for neighboring ecosystems, protecting them from flooding and other natural forces. Because wetlands sit at the divide between fully wet environments and drier ecosystems, they exhibit characteristics of both types of locations. Additionally, they tend to be very fragile systems that are particularly vulnerable to human infringement. People involved in development and agriculture often see no value to the maintenance of wetlands because their presence limits human construction and use drastically. As a result, wetlands are often drained to make them more accessible and more profitable. In addition to providing important natural habitats and buffer zones for surrounding areas, wetlands also function as filters for the water that flows through them, helping reduce the effects of pollution and cutting down on silting deposits in adjacent waterways. In many ways, wetlands perform important functions not only for their natural residents, but also for surrounding ecosystems that depend on them for protection and stability.

This preserve is part of a larger system called the Pleistocene Terraces, or what are more popularly known as the Florida Parishes. In this collection of southeastern parishes, which are Louisiana's equivalent to counties, the pressure to develop the land for human habitation and agricultural purposes is greater than any other area of the larger Lake Pontchartrain basin. St. Tammany Parish, the home of Abita Creek, has been the fastest growing parish in Louisiana for more than a decade. As a result, agricultural land use, which was largely the historical focus in this area, is quickly giving way to residential and commercial demands. Development interests, when faced with the challenge of wetland utilization, often choose to drain them to facilitate construction. The Nature Conservancy of Louisiana has acquired and currently manages more than 30,000 acres in St. Tammany Parish alone, much of which is wetlands. The major goal is to restore and preserve the wetlands of southeastern Louisiana to enhance the natural health of these important ecosystems and their neighbors. Because of the ever-expanding human presence, the water quality of rivers and streams on the Pleistocene Terraces suffers.

Controlled access, restoration efforts, and careful management of the Abita Creek Preserve is setting the standard for wetlands care and maintenance.

The Pitcher Plant Trail Boardwalk at Abita Creek Flatwoods Preserve provides access for the public to view communities of longleaf pine savanna and bayhead swamp. A walk along the almost-mile-long trail offers the opportunity to view several rare species of plant and animal, including the carnivorous yellow pitcher plant for which the boardwalk is named. Pitcher plants coexist with other species of carnivorous plants, as well as grasses, wildflowers, and sedges. Educational stations positioned along the boardwalk provide information concerning the area's natural habitats, its residents, and management strategies. Particular attention is paid to the use of prescribed burning, an important management tool that facilitates seed germination and resprouting and discourages the growth of competing vegetation. The reduction of intense-burning fuel sources and the control of pest problems are also important side effects of prescribed burning. Because burning is a controversial practice, educating visitors on the needs for and benefits of this practice is important. Built almost entirely by volunteers and through materials grants, the boardwalk represents intelligent, well-planned efforts at public education and access while simultaneously preserving natural environment integrity and viability.

Further Reading

Carle, David. *Burning Questions: America's Fight with Nature's Fire*. Santa Barbara, CA: Praeger Trade, 2002.

Streever, Bill. *Saving Louisiana? The Battle for Coastal Wetlands*. Jackson: University Press of Mississippi, 2001.

ATCHAFALAYA BASIN

Located in south-central Louisiana, Atchafalaya Basin, also known as Atchafalaya Swamp, is the largest swamp in the United States. It is created by a combination of wetlands and river delta at the point where the Atchafalaya River and the Gulf of Mexico meet. Within it are bayous, marshes, and cypress swamps that slowly give way to more brackish wetlands. Spartina, or cordgrass, marshes form the border between the basin and the Gulf of Mexico. Encompassing more than one million acres, there are significant expanses of bottomland hardwoods, swamplands, bayous, and backwater lakes. One thing that makes it unique among basins of this type is the fact that it has an expanding delta system along with very stable wetlands. The basin is consistently wet enough and the constant threat of flooding makes it difficult to develop and inhabit, so the area is sparsely populated. In the past, the Atchafalaya has functioned as the main channel for the Mississippi River, which is accomplished through the process of delta switching. Over the last 100 years, the Mississippi has been changing its main channel to the Atchafalaya because of the effects of manmade alterations on the river. The river is now in the process of forming a new delta in the Atchafalaya Bay, and, as a result, this one piece of the Louisiana shoreline is gaining ground rather than losing it.

The larger basin area can be divided into three distinct regions. The northern portion is composed of bottomland hardwood forest. In the middle are swamps containing cypress, willow, and tupelo tree communities. The lower portion is a mix of freshwater and brackish marsh. Ecologically speaking, the 800,000 acres of forested wetlands and 500,000 acres of marsh play the most significant role in this ecosystem. Endangered species such as the Florida panther, the peregrine falcon, and the ivory-billed woodpecker all find refuge in these fertile, protective lands. The nonprofit environmental preservation organization Atchafalaya Basinkeeper records 15 endangered species of animal and bird, 29 rookeries, more than 40 mammalian and reptile species, and at least 20 amphibian varieties. As the most productive swamp in the world, this is worthy of the active efforts underway to ensure the basin's preservation.

One controversial preservation issue involves the controlling of floods along the river. Through strategic channeling of the river's waters to control the periodic floods that inevitably occur, surrounding salt marsh wetlands have suffered greatly and threaten the environmental sustainability of the basin. One of the side effects of wetland degradation is the erosion of the buffer zone created by the wetlands. Inhabited and agricultural lands that were once protected from submersion by the wetlands' presence are now succumbing to the previously restrained sea waters. One serious role the salt marshes play along the coast is one of protection against the effects of hurricanes and the accompanying surges. The artificially altered flow of the river is now carrying marsh-dependent silt over the edge of the continental shelf, degrading the health and stability of the marshes even further. Between the 1950s and 1970s, the oil industry dealt an additional severe blow to the marsh environments by digging trenches into the marshlands in order to better position barges to serve as platforms. Over time, the trenches' edges have eroded away, leaving wide, shallow channels in their wake. The loss of delta lands is considered by many to be one of the most significant environmental threats the United States faces today because of the complex and important role these coastal areas play.

The unique habitats that form the coastline of the Gulf of Mexico, of which Atchafalaya Basin is an integral part, provide important support systems for both resident and migratory animal populations. These areas, for example, allow communities of migratory birds to utilize local food resources as a staging ground for their flight. More than half of all migratory bird species use the Atchafalaya Flyway every year. They also serve as important avian breeding grounds. Resident fish and wildlife population counts are staggering, with some numbers suggesting a natural populace of over three times that of the Everglades. The crawfish industry harvests 23 million pounds annually. The bay contains one of the largest fish crops in the United States. Hunting, fishing, and recreational boating are all part of the leisure life of the Atchafalaya. These resources are valuable pieces of the natural landscape and are important to the local, regional, and national economy. Unfortunately, a large majority of the basin does not enjoy state or national preserve status. Barely 15,000 acres are protected in the Atchafalaya National Wildlife Refuge, and the rest is vulnerable to human development and alteration.

Most of the basin land is privately owned and controlled. In the early 20th century, the main industry in the area was the logging of cypress trees. Landowners, though, also began leasing mineral rights to oil and gas companies, establishing a permanent presence for these interests. Without any level of protection, developmental use of basin land poses many threats. The detrimental effects of logging in cypress stands and bottomland hardwoods will continue to reduce forested areas. Private control of large expanses not only restricts public access, it also limits effective contribution action. Dredging has disrupted natural water flow and created aquatic dead zones. At least one lake in the area is heavy polluted with mercury. Levees have changed and cut off freshwater flow, contributing to saltwater infiltration, which is having damaging effects on delicate freshwater environments. In an effort to mediate these ongoing threats, the Louisiana Department of Natural Resources and the Corps of Engineers developed a master plan that involves, among other measures, land acquisition along with environmental easements aimed at addressing logging issues. One interest that is actively involved in reducing the impact of cypress logging is Atchafalaya Basinkeeper, and, recently, the combined efforts of this and other groups accomplished their goal: the cessation of cypress logging for mulch along the Louisiana coast.

Cypress wetland forests are one of the most productive types of wetland ecosystems in the world. Their presence in swamps is absolutely necessary to sustaining the natural balance and health of the area. Bald cypress trees live for many hundreds of years, producing cypress balls that many forms of wildlife eat. Because the bald cypress sheds its bark, insects tend to congregate under the peeling layers, providing feasts for woodpeckers and other birds. Older cypress trees develop cavities in their trunks that are used by a wide variety of wildlife as homes and nesting places. Even their branch placement plays a role in the natural community; because the branches are perpendicular to the trunk, they are nesting waders' trees of choice due to ease of access and use. Cypress swamps host migratory and neotropical songbirds, help maintain fishery health, filter the water that flows through of pollutants and excessive nutrients, and perform a vital function as natural carbon sinks. Not only do they filter the groundwater, they remove carbon dioxide from the atmosphere and store it, helping mitigate the effects of global warming. As the largest of its kind in North America, the cypress swamps of the Atchafalaya Basin are recognized as valuable, integral components of Louisiana's coastal landscape, and, as a result, protection and preservation efforts continue to increase.

Further Reading

Atchafalaya Basinkeeper. http://www.basinkeeper.org/index.htm.

Reuss, Martin. *Designing the Bayous: The Control of Water in the Atchafalaya Basin: 1800–1995*. Washington, DC: U.S. Government Printing Office, 1998.

Tidwell, Mike. *Bayou Farewell: The Rich Life and Tragic Death of Louisiana's Cajun Coast*. London: Vintage, 2004.

BAYOU COCODRIE NATIONAL WILDLIFE REFUGE

The Nature Conservancy purchased a tract of 11,000 acres from the Fisher Lumber Company in 1992. Over five years, the conservancy then sold the land to the U.S. Fish and Wildlife Service, which manages this important state scenic river and refuge encompassing more than 13,000 acres today. The bottomland hardwood forests that cover much of the area are some of the last and relatively least disturbed timber expanses in the Mississippi River Delta. One of the largest goals of the preserve is to protect these important bottomland hardwood environments. Migratory waterfowl, diverse wildlife species, and nongame migratory birds all find refuge in these woods, making the preservation of these environs important to a widespread natural community. Working in tandem with these conservation goals is an access plan that allows for hunting, fishing, hiking, and nature appreciation.

The company of resident wildlife includes recognizable forest dwellers such as white-tailed deer, squirrels, and raccoons. As a migratory stop during the winter months, mallards, shovelers, pintail, and teal can often be spotted. Many wood ducks make their home at the refuge year-round, nesting in trees and wood duck boxes provided by the U.S. Fish and Wildlife Service. Woodstorks, egrets, and herons also find the bayou's habitat suitable as permanent homes. Avian species on the decline find a haven in the refuge as well, with migratory songbirds such as prothonotary, hooded, and Kentucky Swainson's warblers utilizing these much-needed resources to ensure their survival. Additionally, there are three protected species that can be spotted on preserve land and in the skies above it. Bald eagles and peregrine falcons roost in the high trees during winter months. Louisiana black bears find the contiguous forestland an ideal corridor connecting the Tensas River National Wildlife Refuge and the Red River Wildlife Management Area. This wide variety of species suggests that Bayou Cocodrie offers diverse environmental hamlets suitable for many natural wildlife communities.

Cypress swamps and hardwood forests populated with gum, elm, ash, and oak trees cover more than 75 percent of the refuge. One thousand acres of this land has been designated as a natural resource area because of the old-growth characteristics of this dwindling hardwood stand environment. Until the 1960s, the Lower Mississippi River valley was largely made up of bottomland hardwood forests, much like the 1,000-acre natural resource area preserved and studied today. In the early 1970s, much of this forest land was clear-cut to make way for agricultural interests. Today, one of the focal efforts is on reforestation. The idea is to reintroduce species that dominated the landscape before intense human intervention. The U.S. Fish and Wildlife Service suggests it will take 30 years or more for the trees being planted today to fully restore these woodland remnants to conditions ideally suited for widespread wildlife habitation. Additional benefits to restoration include wind and rain erosion control, making the replanting of trees across the bayou a priority in creating a sustainable, valuable, natural environment.

Further Reading

Dickson, James. *Wildlife of Southern Forests: Habitat and Management*. Blaine, WA: Hancock House, 2001.

U.S. Fish and Wildlife Service. "Bayou Cocodrie National Wildlife Refuge." http://www.fws.gov/bayoucocodrie/.

CADDO BLACK BAYOU

Caddo Black Bayou is a spring-fed area that contains braided streams, bottomland hardwood forests, cypress and tupelo swamps, and a sandhill forest that is home to a variety of rare plants. The Nature Conservancy of Louisiana owns and directs this small site (just under 500 acres) and directs its efforts toward protecting the bottomland hardwood forest, the cypress swamp, and the sandhill forest. Bottomland hardwood forests are treed wetlands that sit beside large river systems. Although these types of forests can be found throughout Louisiana, the Mississippi alluvial floodplain is predominantly populated by this type of forest. Seasonal flooding that creates alternating wet and dry seasons is the principal maintenance cycle that supports bottomland hardwood areas. They play important roles in the larger ecosystems of which they are a part, including contributing to the safeguarding of water quality; providing healthy, protective environments for local wildlife and fish species; and regulating periodic flooding effects. Bottomland hardwoods are highly productive, largely due to the effects that floods have on the soil's particulate and organic matter as well as nutrient concentrations. The decimation of bottomland hardwoods directly affects the surrounding ecosystem as well as the wildlife populations that call these areas home.

What is left today of bottomland hardwood forest in Louisiana is estimated to be only 50 to 75 percent of the original coverage that would have been present prior to European settlement. The biggest historical threat to these forested areas was the clearing of land for agricultural purposes. Fragmentation of bottomland environments set the stage for widespread decline in the health and viability of any old-growth areas. Some larger tracts of bottomland hardwood have survived human presence and development, but none exhibits the characteristic traits of old-growth stands. Restoration efforts began in the early 1980s, and, to date, almost 400,000 acres of Louisiana land have been reforested. The biggest challenges to the recovery of these important systems are the fragmentation issues resulting from agricultural clearing and the restoration of wetland forest functions. In addition to land reclamation efforts, wildlife research and survey issues play a significant role in bottomland hardwood forest conservation efforts. Of specific concern is the maintenance of appropriately diverse tree populations to support the variety of natural residents at Caddo Black Bayou. Not only are different tree species homes for different forms of wildlife, leaf litter on the ground and woody debris provide shelter and food sources for ground-dwelling mammals and amphibians. The entire system depends on a delicate balance of species type and distribution to maintain the optimum conditions for bottomland hardwood forest health and survival.

The management techniques and conservation strategies that are most effective and immediate in forest and bayou management are the focus of preservation at Caddo Black Bayou. These strategies include the monitoring of nuisance species and measures to control the species, if necessary. Silvicultural, or forest management, techniques also play a significant role in maintaining species diversity within the preserve. Cooperation among neighboring parishes in Louisiana to address water management issues that affect the water table at Caddo Black Bayou is important as well. Oil and gas drilling is an important cooperative effort, because the use of directional drilling minimizes the environmental impacts of drilling activity on wetland habitats. Overall, it is important to pay attention to the variety of issues that are necessary for maintaining wetland forest health to ensure a sustainable future for Caddo Black Bayou.

Further Reading

Allen, Barbara. *Uneasy Alchemy: Citizens and Experts in Louisiana's Chemical Corridor Disputes*. Cambridge, MA: MIT Press, 2003.

United States Geological Survey. *A Guide to Bottomland Hardwood Restoration: General Technical Report SRS 40, 40*. Washington, DC: USGS, 2001.

Catahoula National Wildlife Refuge

Catahoula National Wildlife Refuge is located in central Louisiana, approximately 12 miles east of Jena. As one of the older refuges in the South, established in 1958, the area is dedicated as a wintering area for migratory waterfowl. The total acreage is just over 25,000 and is divided into two units. The smaller headquarters unit, at almost 7,000 acres, borders the northeast shore of Catahoula Lake. The second, larger unit is called Bushley Bayou and was acquired in 2001 through a partnership between American Electric Power, the Conservation Fund, and the U.S. Fish and Wildlife Service. Lowland hardwood forest dominates this preserve's landscape, and the wetland is maintained through seasonal flooding coming from the Black, the Red, and the Ouachita rivers. A variety of wildlife resides in the area, including white-tailed deer, songbirds, small mammals, raptors, reptiles, amphibians, and waterfowl. During the winter, waterfowl populations are especially high, with peak populations recorded at more than 75,000 ducks, for example. In 2001, Catahoula National Wildlife Refuge was designated a globally important bird area, and Catahoula Lake was recognized as a wetlands of international importance by the Ramsar Convention. Administered by the U.S. Fish and Wildlife Service, the headquarters for the refuge is located about 30 miles northeast of Alexandria, Louisiana.

Some of the important measures taken at Catahoula National Wildlife Refuge include strict rules governing wildlife observation and bird-watching activities. Education is an important focus of refuge activities. Restriction of public access does not accomplish the same positive results as do widespread education efforts. Monitoring human activities in the refuge ensures that wintering fowl experience as little disturbance as possible and that they have the proper energy reserves to deal with the stress of difficult weather conditions and their eventual migration. Additionally, visitors are educated on the dangers of manmade objects such as fishing lines and six-pack rings. The sharing of this information then benefits more than just the preserve. Visitors take their knowledge into their own environments, helping spread the positive effects of their newly acquired information, and ultimately making more environments safer for wildlife as a result. Part of the education process involves learning about the effects of human presence on the breeding process and how that presence can disrupt this important event. An important piece of this education is communicating the reasoning behind leaving alone a bird that appears to be in distress, or even dead. Often, people are not able to discern the true condition of wildlife that may seem to be in danger. For example, a baby bird that is floundering on the ground may simply be learning how to fly, with the parents waiting in the distance until there is no human presence to interfere. In another example, hummingbirds can go into a state of torpor and may appear to be dead, but they are simply conserving energy when they are not feeding. Actual dead birds might carry parasites or disease that is dangerous to humans. All of these situations require the nonintervention of bird-watchers to ensure a successful outcome both for the bird and the person. Without education programs, such as the comprehensive plan being executed by the Catahoula National Wildlife Refuge, vital nesting and habitation grounds would be in danger of damage and destruction from unknowing missteps made by uneducated human visitors.

Further Reading

Alderfer, Jonathan. *National Geographic Birding Essentials*. Washington, DC: National Geographic, 2007.

CHENIER PLAIN

The Chenier Plain is characterized by a muddy strip of coastline west of Atchafalaya Bay in southern Louisiana. It begins at the Southwest Pass and stretches westward to Sabine Pass at the Louisiana-Texas border. Moving inland from the waterline, the muddy swatch of land marks the boundary between the Gulf of Mexico and the fully formed marsh grasslands of the plain. Wave activity in the Gulf of Mexico moves fluid mud to the boundary zone, where it literally becomes part of the landform. The new land is then eventually colonized by the marsh grass and other associated vegetation, increasing the stability of the new land. Aerial photos taken of the Chenier Plain show manmade irrigation canals from the 1980s that end hundreds of feet away from the current shoreline. This evidence allows for accurate measurement of exactly how much land has been created by this process over the last three decades. As an active delta zone, however, the effects of human presence and intervention are easy to see. Levees, jetties, and dredging—all aimed at aiding in navigation and negotiating flood control—prevent the incursion of sediment necessary for land building and marsh expansion. Nature needs and human demands must be balanced to provide the optimal results for both local populations and environmental concerns. To understand the plain's role in both natural and human environments, Gay Gomez suggests that three themes stand out as the most important focal points of study: regional distinctiveness, continuity and change, and environmental perceptions of human groups that share an interest in the Chenier region.

The foundation of understanding this region then rests on the attitudes and actions of those involved most closely with the wetlands. Not only must the knowledge and opinions of specialists be taken into account, it is also important to consider the experiences and positions of those that live on these lands. In this modern age, land will never exist independently of human use and habitation. Understanding the viewpoints, however, is just the first step. According to Gomez, it is also necessary to look at the historical forces of change and continuity in a region over time. Whatever the present situation, it is the product of a long line of changes in the land and its inhabitants, which directly affect the value placed on the region by those that use and live on the land. The final question of understanding, then, is deceptively simple. What makes a place so special? It is just as important to *know* a place as it is to have knowledge about a place. By combining outside knowledge with internal experience of a region, a truer understanding emerges.

In the case of Chenier Plain, the importance placed on this environment has evolved largely around what is considered economically important. Alligators, ducks, and fur-bearing mammals have long fallen into this economically significant category. Recognition of the fact that these animals play an indispensible role in the natural environment along with the economic well-being of the region has been important to the stabilization of their habitats and the development of intelligent use of these animal resources. In examining *A Wetland Biography*, however, it is pointed out that there are elements and species involved in the cycle of life on Chenier Plain that do not have such a direct connection to the human habitation the plain supports. The suggestion is that the public's growing interest in nonconsuming outdoor recreation activities, such as wildlife viewing and bird-watching, will play a significant role in the local economy of Cameron Parish and other local areas that are home to accessible parts of the Chenier Plain. Economics and aesthetics need not be mutually exclusive. The efforts at Chenier Plain should focus on environmental conservation for the purposes of both public enjoyment and economic utilization sustainability. What is necessary, then, is to arrest the environmental degradation that is taking place across the region as a result of human interference and activity as well as natural forces. One of the biggest concerns is increasing salinity in areas dependant on brackish or freshwater conditions. Water control structures have been constructed with backward flow stops to reintroduce needed freshwater to more southern regions of the plain. While not completely correcting the problem, this construction measure has had a significant effect on average salinity over time, helping preserve this important balance. By endeavoring to understand the hydrologic balance of fresh water and salt water necessary to maintain the plain's health, specialists hope to enact conservation and restoration strategies that will help preserve this important economic, cultural, and natural resource for future generations.

Further Reading

Gomez, Gay M. *A Wetland Biography: Seasons on Louisiana's Chenier Plain*. Austin: University of Texas Press, 1998.

McBride, Randolph A., Matthew J. Taylor, and Mark R. Byrnes. "Coastal Morphodynamics and Chenier-Plain Evolution in Southwestern Louisiana, USA: A Geomorphic Model." *Geomorphology* 88, no. 3 (2007): 367–422.

Meselhe, Ehab. "Chapter C.6: Hydrodynamic Models of Subprovince 4." Department of Engineering, University of Louisiana at Lafayette. http://data.lca.gov/Ivan6/app/app_c_ch6.pdf.

Copenhagen Hills

Copenhagen Hills straddles Caldwell and Catahoula Parishes with four miles of shoreline sitting along the Ouachita River in northeastern Louisiana. Selected for its botanical importance as well as the many globally endangered habitats it supports, the Nature Conservancy of Louisiana restricts access to this important 1,500-acre natural treasure. Twenty-seven rare plant species, including nine that are found only in Louisiana, thrive in the habitats at Copenhagen Hills. The calcareous soil of the area is formed by the weathering of calcareous rock and fossil shell beds. Chalk, marl, limestone, and often a great deal of phosphates can be found in the ground, making for fertile growth conditions. The rich history contained within the preserve's soil cannot be underestimated. The ground contains fossil-rich marine sediments that are almost 40 million years old. As calcareous soil, with a high pH, these hills along the Ouachita River provide the perfect conditions for fossil preservation and presentation. As a result, the goal of the managing entity, Louisiana's Nature Conservancy, is twofold. Restoration of the prairie and woodlands is the primary goal, but running a close second is the preservation of the fossil-laden sediments that offer many clues to understanding the area's ancient past.

It is this unique soil composition, among other factors, that accounts for the unusual flora found at Copenhagen Hills. In the past, prairie covered this area, creating acidic conditions that pulled out much of the calcium and magnesium that would have otherwise remained in the soil; this, along with soil movement caused by the steep slopes and erosion resulting from the flow of the Ouachita River, set up the soils of this four-mile stretch of riverside land to support a unique combination of vegetation species. Some of the wildflowers rare to Louisiana flourish here, including Waiter's violet, coralroot, and whiteleaf leather flower. Little is left of what used to be expansive prairie; the environment has almost entirely disappeared from the state. The prairie habitat was and is one of the most diverse environment types in Louisiana. In hosting a wide variety of grasses, wildflowers, and insects, an equally wide variety of wildlife species are provided with the fare they need to survive. Restoration of these dwindling habitats, like the prairie reinstatement efforts underway at Copenhagen Hills, are slowly but steadily reestablishing prairie environs to Louisiana. Broadcast seeding of native prairie grasses and flowers is an important foundational step in this process. In addition, it is necessary to transplanting prairie sod from established prairie habitats to provide some initial stability for young, fledgling environments. In Louisiana, over 3,000 acres of prairie could be restored to self-sustaining status. The efforts at Copenhagen Hills are part of a grander effort to reestablish prairie presence where once it thrived.

Further Reading
Mohlenbrock, Robert H. "Uncommon Property: In Northern Louisiana, Soil with an Ancient Link to the Sea Invites a Unique Flora." *Natural History*, May 2007.

CYPRESS ISLAND

Located between Lafayette and Breaux Bridge, Louisiana, this 9,500-acre preserve protects an expansive bottomland hardwood forest and cypress-tupelo swamp, with its centerpiece being Lake Martin. As one of the more accessible wildlife areas in Louisiana, the island receives thousands of visitors every year. The site is open during daylight hours and boasts a two-and-a-half-mile walking trail along the site's levee plus a one-mile system of trails through the preserve. There are times during the year, for wildlife and habitat protection, that parts of Cypress Island are closed. The walking trail along the levee is not accessible during alligator nesting season, which runs from June through October, and the rookery is closed from February to July in order to assure prime breeding conditions for the resident avian populations. The overall goal of the Nature Conservancy of Louisiana is to restore approximately 20,000 acres of natural cypress-tupelo swamp while providing environmentally friendly public access for enjoyment and recreation purposes. At Cypress Island, a parking area, picnic areas, restrooms, and a boardwalk are in the works using eco-friendly and culturally appropriate development plans. Cypress Island offers the perfect opportunity for public access to and education concerning this rare and fragile swamp environment, furthering the understanding and acceptance of preservation and restoration practices in Louisiana's wetlands.

The preserve's main wildlife feature is an amazing rookery that supports thousands of nesting birds every spring. A walk along the levee trail offers the opportunity to observe white ibis, snowy egrets, green herons, and roseate spoonbills in their natural environment. The trail also crosses migratory songbird paths, providing a unique diversity of

Lake Martin, bald cypress covered with Spanish moss. (pointnshoot)

bird-watching opportunities for nature enthusiasts. The sustainability of this significant rookery depends on a successful compromise between the preserve, its oil and gas drilling neighbors, and local farmers looking to protect their crawfish ponds. Preservation of Cypress Island is integral to abating the decline of the Lower Mississippi Valley ecosystem, according to Keith Ouchley, who is closely associated with the controlling entity, the Nature Conservancy of Louisiana. Texaco donated almost 3,000 acres, which included Lake Martin, to the Conservancy in 1994 and then followed that up with over 6,000 more acres as the land proved it was running low in gas and oil deposits. Working with the conservancy, Texaco aims to "balance competing needs in an environmentally sensitive area." While Texaco retained the mineral rights to the area, it also donated $500,000 to the conservancy for community education. Although the conservancy has no legal rights or control over the mineral extraction activity that takes place at Cypress Island, EnerVest Management Partners, which leases the mineral rights, tries to cooperate with the conservancy by avoiding the more critical, sensitive areas of the preserve in the effort to "respect the beauty of the environment."

Local residents, though—especially the crawfish farmers of the area—suffer the negative consequences of the feast provided to these nesting birds by their farm ponds. Preventative measures have little impact; selective elimination of nuisance birding, noisemaker shells, and pyrotechnics have been ineffective at reducing the number of birds on these sustenance-rich ponds. Some evidence suggests that feeding the birds helps thin out the pond, ultimately resulting in larger crawfish, which have the potential to increase farmer income. Without more conclusive evidence, though, that this is the case, current efforts focus on educating farmers in different techniques to control the large rookery population's access to the ponds. By digging the ponds deeper and planting excess vegetation, avian access can be managed rather than eliminated. The birds need crawfish, and the lake, to survive as a tourist attraction, needs the birds, so a balance must be found. During this period of compromise and negotiation, an additional problem is of utmost concern to the conservancy: the death of the lake itself. It has no natural system of drainage, and, with the addition of tons of bird droppings every year, it has become necessary to drain the lake into surrounding wetlands and bring in fresh water to renew the lake through a canal system. Ultimately, the greatest need is to keep the environment as quiet as possible, limiting and controlling both public and industrial access. Through careful conservation measures, this unique avian haven will become a self-sustaining, self-renewing resource for the birds that depend on it for survival as well as a valuable educational experience for the visiting public.

Further Reading

Ault, Alicia. "Recipe for a Refuge in Louisiana: Wetlands, Wading Birds, Oil Wells." *New York Times*, July 24, 2001. http://www.nytimes.com/2001/07/24/science/recipe-for-a-refuge-in-louisiana-wetlands-wading-birds-oil-wells.html?pagewanted=2.

Hancock, J., J. A. Kushlan, R. Gillmor, and P. Hayman. *The Heron's Handbook*. New York: HarperCollins, 1987.

FREDERICK'S SWAMP

This is one of several preserves in Louisiana managed by the Nature Conservancy that is not open to the public. Many habitat remnants across the state are at a delicate stage of restoration and preservation, making public use and enjoyment a risk not worth taking at this point in the site's conservation program. Frederick's Swamp houses one of the few remaining tracks of mature woodland in the Bayou Teche area. The Nature Conservancy points out that, originally, two and a half million acres of coastal prairie existed in Louisiana, but today there are less than 500 acres that survive only as widely scattered patches. The conservancy chose this site because of its mature woodlands as well as its low lying lands that host bald cypress and tupelo gum trees, with ridges dominated by oaks. This preserve is one of the central efforts of the conservancy and interested partners to protect the cypress swamp of Bayou Teche.

Historically, cypress swamps have been the target of the logging industry because cypress wood is particularly resistant to rot and for a long time was a popular wood used for construction. As a result of this exploitation, widespread cypress populations dwindled over the first half of the 20th century. Swamp formation is a long, slow process of conversion. Swamps begin as lakes or ponds. Over time, shrubs and trees fill in the land, and, as the plants die and decay, the water level lowers and the swamp forms. The result is poorly drained soil with large amounts of organic matter. Restoration of cypress swamps is not an easy task, because fire plays a significant role in the establishment of cypress habitat. Cypress trees recover very quickly after a fire, taking hold in the environment before other trees have a chance to grow. Easily identifiable, mature cypress can grow as high as 100 feet, and their distinctive swelling at the base of the tree functions to stabilize the tree. Also contributing to their unique stature are knees, or roots that stick up out of the water, which add further stabilization as well as facilitate gas exchange with the surrounding air. These swamps provide important habitat for rare and endangered wildlife, such as the Louisiana black bear and ivory-billed woodpeckers. A critical part of the swamps' role along the gulf coastline, though, is their function as a buffer zone, helping protect more inland areas from flooding and storm surges, as well as helping reduce some of the damage inflicted by the area's frequent hurricanes. Continued logging demand threatens recovering cypress swamps and forests, but through aggressive conservation measures along with legislative and public education efforts, small remnants like Frederick's Swamp will have the chance to recover and contribute to the larger area's health and stability, helping increase the gulf coast's environmental and economic viability.

Further Reading

Dennis, John V. *The Great Cypress Swamps*. Baton Rouge: Louisiana State University Press, 1988.

Steinberg, Michael K. *Stalking the Ghost Bird: The Elusive Ivory-Billed Woodpecker in Louisiana*. Baton Rouge: Louisiana State University Press, 2008.

KISATCHIE NATIONAL FOREST

Kisatchie National Forest stretches across seven parishes and 600,000 acres, encompassing bald cypress groves and old-growth pine in the heart of the sportsman's paradise that is Louisiana. Divided into five distinct units called ranger districts, the forest system offers unparalleled opportunities for recreation and education in a uniquely pristine and highly accessible natural treasure. Established as a national forest in 1930, restoration was the overall initial goal, with preservation activities coming to the forefront as natural regrowth and stability became established. Today's Kisatchie Forest holds a wealth of information for the interested visitor and offers a wide range of experiences for those who venture onto its lands.

The aquatic habitats of Kisatchie National Forest reach across many miles of the preserve. With more than 5,000 miles of streams, the aquatic resources of the forest offer outstanding recreational opportunities, as well as valuable protective habitats for local fauna species. Small streams function as nursing grounds for a wide variety of native fish. Perennial flowing streams are home to the Louisiana pearlshell mussel, federally listed as a threatened species. With 80 percent of the mussel's range within the boundaries of the forest, the importance of protecting the habitat conditions for this rare mussel cannot be overestimated. The U.S. Forest Service focuses on monitoring and protecting the midsized stream habitats to facilitate the mussel's survival. Larger streams on the lands are utilized for canoeing, swimming, fishing, and nature enjoyment, rounding out the aquatic experience at Kisatchie. Lakes in the area offer recreational opportunities, with bass-, sunfish-, and catfish-stocked ponds; camping facilities; and duck hunting. Some of the forest's lakes, though, are regulated to provide a more quiet experience by outlawing the use of electric motors. Even more remote are the wildlife ponds scattered across the preserve that offer visitors a truly primitive chance to get away from it all. With so much to choose from in the realm of aquatic environments, Kisatchie National Forest provides important opportunities for habitat conservation in conjunction with diverse alternatives for recreation and relaxation.

One unique program underway at the forest is the restoration of a rare orchid breed to the area. The brainchild of a local high school student, who is still involved with the project, the goal is the reinstatement of 200 rare Kentucky lady's slipper seedlings. Now found at only two locations in the forest, the decline of this orchid species is a result of logging, herd grazing, invasive plant competition, wild hog introduction, and orchid collection. Unfortunately, orchid seedpods hold thousands of powderlike seeds that are extremely difficult to cultivate in a controlled environment. Kevin Allen, the high school student and an amateur botanist, monitored orchid populations in the forest, looking for the occurrence of fertile seedpods. Because these orchids have naturally infrequent flowering cycles, the wait was long and the search was tedious. After three years, Kevin found a flowering specimen and initiated self-pollination. A few weeks later, he was able to collect a seed pod and send it to a lab, which was able to produce seedlings using a tissue culture method. From there, the seedlings went to Central Louisiana Orchid Society growers, who succeeded in cultivating 95 percent of the seedlings. Because the seed was collected locally, the seedlings that will be planted in Kisatchie will be directly descended of the local variety, preserving the genus of the local population. The importance of this, as pointed out by the U.S. Forest Service, is that other plants from different range areas would not exhibit the characteristics that have evolved as a result of the forest's extreme southern location. Centuries of evolutionary adaptation would be lost in the transplanting process. Because of the dedication of an eclectic group of contributors, a unique and beautiful element of Louisiana's natural heritage is on its way to recovery.

Kisatchie National Forest boasts a comprehensive wildlife management plan as well. Rare, game, and nongame species all play a role in the maintenance plan the Forest Service has enacted to preserve the natural landscape of the forest. The main focus of rare species preservation revolves primarily around the red-cockaded woodpecker. Annual surveys, monitoring activities, habitat conservation, and community augmentation are all important parts of the efforts to improve and preserve the red-cockaded woodpecker and its environment. This unique woodpecker prefers mature pine forests with an abundance of living trees, which is unusual for woodpeckers in general. They typically prefer older trees infected with a fungus called red heart rot, which causes the inner wood of the tree to become soft. Instead of boring cavities out of dead trees, the red-cockaded woodpecker chooses living trees, taking up to three years to complete their cavity excavation. These cavities are an important piece of the natural mosaic of Kisatchie National Forest. Birds and small mammals often take over abandoned cavities to make their homes. Larger woodpeckers often take advantage of the work already completed to bore larger holes, which, in turn, then house larger birds and mammals. Reptiles, amphibians, and insects also appropriate these woodpecker-made resources, adding to the diversity of wildlife that depends on these crafty birds. Wildlife management plans in the forest include encouraging red-cockaded woodpecker nesting by predrilling cavities and placing nests in order to reduce the workload on the birds. As an integral part of the wildlife family at Kisatchie, these rare birds are fortunately making a comeback due to the increasing stable environment created by the Forest Service's aggressive restoration and preservation efforts.

As the only national forest in Louisiana, Kisatchie's 100 miles of hiking, biking, and horseback riding trails, more than 40 developed recreation sites, a designated national scenic river, and a 13-mile water trail coexist with important research, restoration, and preservation activities that make this large preserve one of the most important examples of successful compromise between recreational interests and environmental needs in the South. The paths blazed by this success story set the example and the bar of comparison high.

Further Reading

McFarlane, Robert W., and Ellen Mabry. *A Stillness in the Pines: The Ecology of the Red-Cockaded Woodpecker.* New York: W. W. Norton, 1994.

Mohlenbrock, Robert. *This Land: A Guide to Central National Forests.* Berkeley: University of California Press, 2006.

U.S. Forest Service. "Kisatchie National Forest." http://www.fs.fed.us/r8/kisatchie/index. html.

LAFITTE WOODS PRESERVE

As the controlling interest in Lafitte Woods, the Nature Conservancy of Louisiana facilitates access to and enjoyment of this preserve, which is one of the last remaining tracts of live oak and hackberry on Grand Isle. Sitting just west of the mouth of the Mississippi River, this island is perfectly positioned to be an important stopover for birds migrating across the Gulf of Mexico. Walking trails in the woods and an elevated boardwalk give bird-watchers and nature enthusiasts outstanding access to 20 acres of tidal salt marshes and their resident communities. In this small, 35-acre preserve, more than 300 avian species have been documented as either transitory or permanent inhabitants.

To support this heavy wildlife load, efforts focus on the restoration of woodlands to a state as close to their original condition as possible. Development pressure on the island is tremendous, and undeveloped land is hard to come by. These natural habitats are an important part of the barrier island environmental landscape, and every tract of land that can be restored and preserved adds to the natural beauty and health of the island's ecosystems.

Two elements make this particular barrier island important in terms of restoration and preservation: the tracts of live oak and hackberry forest and the birds that depend on those tracts. As mentioned, more than 300 bird species have a connection to the island, and that equals approximately one-half of the avian species in the United States. Without healthy stands of live oak and hackberry, the massive number of birds that utilize the islands as a stopover each year would have nowhere to live and feed. These trees grow easily in moist bottomland soil, but hackberry, in particular, is tolerant to a wide variety of soil conditions. Not only is it tolerant of high alkaline content, it also is hardy in more salty conditions, like those found at Grand Isle. Although these trees are versatile in their tolerance of soils, they are extremely vulnerable to injury. The slightest damage can set off an internal decay process that is often detrimental for the tree. Protective measures, restoration action, and condition monitoring are absolutely necessary to maintain these habitats that are so vital to the thousands of birds depending on this small island as a migratory haven each year.

Further Reading

Alden, Peter, Gil Nelson, Brian Cassie, Jonathan D. W. Kahl, Eric A. Oches, Harry Zirlin, and Wendy B. Zomlefer. *National Audubon Society Field Guide to the Southeastern States*. New York: Alfred A. Knopf, 1999.

MARY ANN BROWN PRESERVE

Although small, the 100-acre Mary Ann Brown Preserve, donated to the Nature Conservancy of Louisiana by Mr. and Mrs. L. Heidel Brown in memory of their daughter, offers a unique mature stand of beech and magnolia forest. Experts point to the combination of sweet loess soil and the microclimates created by the preserve's deep ravines as the main supporting mechanisms for an unusual collection of plant and animal species. Particularly interesting is the large diversity in woody species found in the area. Two miles of access trails offer visitors the opportunity to explore the centuries old trees. Despite its diminutive size, the Nature Conservancy maintains this site as one of its more accessible land tracts, partially because of its striking natural beauty but also because of its relative hardiness in the face of public use and access. Camping areas are available for school and scout groups with prior arrangement, and a pond and pavilion at the center of the preserve are offered for day events.

What visitors see when traversing this unique area is a collection of beech and magnolia trees, some of which are centuries old. The landscape is typical of the Tunica type, with the loess bluffs of the Tunica Hills displaying a well-balanced mix of northern and southern flora species. In addition to the remaining magnolia and beech trees, there are more fern varieties here than anywhere else in Louisiana. Ferns are an ancient family of plants, with evidence of their existence reaching back 360 million years. This means they predate flowering plants by 200 million years. Ferns are delicate plants that only grow in areas with a sufficiently moist climate, and they prefer low-lying areas close to creeks or streams with a heavy forest canopy to provide adequate shade. In fact, moisture is the key element to the survival of ferns, because it is necessary for reproduction. Reproduction for ferns is a more difficult and more situation-dependant process than it is for most other plant species. On the underside of fertile fern fronds are small patches that contain the fern's reproductive spores. These spots contain many sporangia, or the spore casings that hold the individual spores. Under the right conditions, these patches will release the spores, which look like a fine powder. If the conditions are right, these spores will grow into tiny gametophytes. Gametophytes are not full ferns from a genetic perspective; they contain only half of the required genetic material. In appropriately moist conditions, the male and female reproductive organs contained on a single gametophyte will self-fertilize and produce a sporophyte. This is the beginning of an adult fern. Ferns can sometimes reproduce without fertilization through the spreading root system of existing plants or by the sprouting of baby ferns at the tips of their fronds, which eventually fall to the ground and take root. It is important that the environment contains enough moisture in the soil and the air, along with an abundance of nutrients and suitable temperatures. The delicate nature of ferns also demands protection from wind, excessive sunlight, and freezing. Conditions that encourage survival and conditions that support reproduction are two different things. Mary Ann Brown Preserve facilitates both survival and reproduction for many species of ferns, adding to the unique character of this small but important preserve.

Further Reading

Kirkman, L. Katherine, Claud L. Brown, and Donald Joseph Leopold. *Native Trees of the Southeast*. Portland, OR: Timber Press, 2007.

Ranker, Tom A., and Christopher H. Haufler. *Biology and Evolution of Ferns and Lycophytes*. Cambridge, England: Cambridge University Press, 2008.

Pushepatapa Creek

As one of the smallest preserves under the care of Louisiana's Nature Conservancy, Pushepatapa Creek stands out in importance for its protection of the beautiful mountain laurel. In fact, this preserve is the only site in the state where this unique species can be found. Along the 21-mile stretch of creek, this spectacular species can be found in abundance. Mountain laurel prefers soils that are well drained and are somewhat acidic. In the areas where they grow, they form a thick, impenetrable understory layer that, when it is full bloom, displays unsurpassed natural beauty. In the environment at Pushepatapa Creek, the mountain laurel has adapted to the higher levels of water in the soil as well as the lower levels of sunlight caused by the presence of the oak, hickory, and pine forest cover. Despite its ability to survive in what are unusual conditions for this species, the growth rate of mountain laurel is relatively slow. This trait makes the laurel community at Pushepatapa particularly delicate. If not protected, the widespread growth of this species so rare to the Louisiana landscape would disappear from the land entirely.

As part of a natural habitat, mountain laurel does not contribute to the sustenance cycle of local wildlife. In fact, the leaves, flowers, and fruit of the mountain laurel are poisonous and may be lethal to both animals and humans. Despite this issue, several species of deer, the black bear, and the ruffed grouse have been known to utilize the mountain laurel as a source of winter forage in times of food shortages. The main benefit in restoring and preserving mountain laurel thickets is its beneficial protection against water runoff and soil erosion. The most common public consumption use is the placement of the species as ornamental accents and floral display enhancements. It is important in areas that support heavy growth of mountain laurel to maintain an equitable balance of ground cover to encourage the growth of an overstory. Mountain laurel is often abundant in areas where insect presence has had a detrimental effect on the health of larger tree species, and there is debate about the limiting effect mountain laurel has on the growth of overstory species. The assumption is that thick patches of mountain laurel tend to choke out larger species that create forest cover, but, in several different environments across the United States, this assumption does not hold true. Another common management tool that is under debate is the use of burning to limit species occurrence. It appears that periodic burning can increase the presence of mountain laurel because the process of burning encourages asexual reproduction in the species. Pushetapata Creek, as a pine hardwood region of the Louisiana coastal plain, is a small but important area of interest and conservation for this unique and beautiful species.

Further Reading

Jaynes, Richard A. *Kalmia: Mountain Laurel and Related Species*. Portland, OR: Timber Press, 1997.

TALISHEEK PINE WETLANDS PRESERVE

Talisheek Pine Wetlands Preserve in St. Tammany Parish is the largest intact pine wetland in southeast Louisiana. This important habitat supports many rare plant and animal species, with several noted occurrences of the federally threatened gopher tortoise and the rare mud salamander, for example. Currently at nearly 3,000 acres, this delicate site is not open for public visitation. The managing entity, the Nature Conservancy of Louisiana, is in the process of restoring the pine savannas in order to better support the wide variety of native animal species. At this preserve—which is the second largest conservation site under Nature Conservancy direction in Louisiana—long-leaf pine restoration is one of the utmost concerns, mainly because little remains of this habitat that used to cover more than 1.3 million acres of Louisiana land. The diversity of flora and fauna species this environment supports is important to maintaining the historic natural conditions of the area, which functioned for a long time as a vital system of water purification and flood control. The preserve's significance as the largest of its type in southeastern Louisiana makes it uniquely important in the concerns of the conservancy and their preservation partners, resulting in a strong focus of effort to support the natural health of valuable wetlands.

Adjacent to the Talisheek Pine Wetlands Preserve is a tract of land now owned by Ecosystem Investment Partners (EIP). This 2,500-acre tract was selected by EIP because of its potential for wetland pine savanna restoration as well as its capacity to help offset the impacts of human development north of New Orleans. The idea was that Louisiana's Nature Conservancy could work with EIP in a partnership that would utilize the strengths of both organizations. The conservancy's conservation and stewardship experience combined with EIP's financial and mitigation bank management resources promised to greatly further the efforts to reestablish and protect the dwindling pine savanna habitat. One of the foremost goals is using the restoration of this land to offset the environmental impact of the increasing rapid development taking place north of New Orleans. To balance the loss of more than 300 acres per year, 600 acres of mitigation is necessary. This partnership aims to greatly impact that mitigation effort. As a conservation bank, the restored land will function as a supportive habitat to native endangered species such as the gopher tortoise. Conservative estimates suggest that the EIP environment, once it is successfully renovated, could support 50 gopher tortoises or more. To ensure that these restoration efforts are permanent and sustainable, non-wetland forest easement will surround the valuable savanna lands, functioning as a buffer zone of environmental protection. It may be possible, through the intelligent and selective silviculture practices of thinning and harvesting, to revert the loblolly and slash pine lowlands to their natural longleaf pine state. The area suffered a severe blow in 2005 from Hurricane Katrina. Although many of the hardwood species in the preserve area fell, much of the pine remained standing, which is extremely beneficial for the area's restoration efforts. Additionally, the ground cover on the preserve was not severely impacted, and so, by the time Nelwyn McInnis of the Louisiana Nature Conservancy was consulted in late 2008, McInnis was able to say that the preserve is "well on the way to recovery." Rejuvenation of this important natural habitat promises to play a significant role in local and regional environmental health, recreational value, and economic contribution.

Further Reading

Jose, Shibu, Eric J. Jokela, and Deborah L. Miller, eds. *The Longleaf Pine Ecosystem: Ecology, Silviculture, and Restoration.* New York: Springer, 2007.

Kirkman, L. Katherine, Claud L. Brown, and Donald Joseph Leopold. *Native Trees of the Southeast.* Portland, OR: Timber Press, 2007.

Shearer Publishing. *The Roads of Louisiana.* Frisco, TX: Mapsco, 1997.

WHITE KITCHEN PRESERVE

White Kitchen Preserve is one of the last intact overflow swamp systems in the entire Southeast. Its animal habitants include a large water bird rookery as well as a bald eagle nest that has been used for more than eight decades. Access to the preserve is facilitated by a boardwalk constructed with the help and support of Chevron that allows visitors to walk out into the marsh and experience this unique environment firsthand. Additionally, swamp boat tours of the area are available, letting visitors get right in the middle of this outstandingly preserved natural site. The Pearl River basin, of which White Kitchen Preserve is a part, consists of cypress tupelo swamp intertwined with freshwater marsh and is surrounded by a rich ridge of loblolly pine that supports the native water bird rookery. This rare and valuable environment, like so many along the Gulf Coast, suffered tremendously in the wake of 2005's Hurricane Katrina. The resulting tidal surge destroyed more than 60 acres of marshland, leaving a large, unbroken water expanse instead of the grassy marsh habitat that used to thrive here. Unfortunately for the natural areas affected by the hurricane's devastation, the damage to human lives, property, and economy has overshadowed the environmental impact. It is estimated that more than 320 million trees were killed by the hurricane. The carbon emitted from these felled trees is roughly the same amount as is absorbed by all of the forests in the United States combined. Although hurricanes are natural forces and thus an integral part of the local environmental cycle, human alterations of the landscape—including building construction, dam additions, and habitat fragmentation—have drastically affected the ability of impacted coastal environments to recover on their own. Areas with intact, functioning ecosystems fared the best in the face of the hurricane's force, but only time and intelligent human direction and intervention can put these important sites permanently on the road to recovery.

Further Reading

Miller, James, Karl V. Miller, and Ted Bodner. *Forest Plants of the Southeast and Their Wildlife Uses.* Athens: University of Georgia Press, 2005.

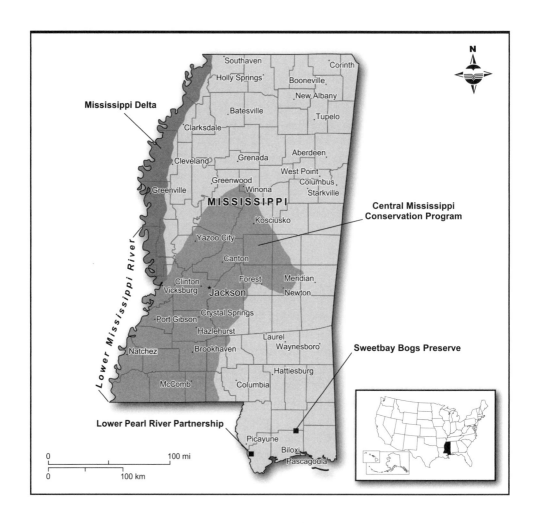

Mississippi

The state of Mississippi contains three major types of ecosystems: the Mississippi alluvial plain, which it shares with Louisiana and Arkansas; the Mississippi Valley loess plains that cuts the state in two; and the southeastern plains covering the entire eastern half of Mississippi. The loess plains region starts in western Kentucky near the Ohio River, then stretches all the way to Mississippi and into the tip of the Louisiana boot. Plains and rolling hills characterize the landscape, except near the Mississippi River, where bluffs are more common. Loess, wind-deposited finely grained silt or clay, stands out as a regional characteristic as well. The bluff hill soils are steep and tend to erode easily. Now covered in a patchwork of forests and agricultural land, the loess plains gives way to the southeastern plains, dominated by longleaf pine with patches of oak and hickory. The bluff regions are home to a large variety of plant and animal species found few other places in North America as well as bluff forest systems, which are found only in the eastern Mississippi black prairies. Some of the biggest state concerns include the preservation of hardwood groves and the control and removal of invasive species. Natural water flow has been affected by human habitation and crop cultivation, so restoration of natural flow paths is a priority. Mississippi's natural resources are a top priority for restoration and preservation, especially in light of the damage caused by Hurricane Katrina, and many agencies and individuals work together today toward common goals.

In addition to drinking water programs and the regulation of noncommercial oil field waste disposal, the Mississippi Department of Environmental Quality oversees the environmental regulatory programs across the state. In 1978, the Mississippi legislature formed the Mississippi Department of Natural Resources (DNR) by consolidating five state agencies. Another restructuring took place in 1989, and the DNR became the Mississippi Department of Environmental Quality (MDEQ). The following offices comprise the MDEQ: the Office of Geology, the Office of Land and Water Resources, the Office of Pollution Control History, and the Office of Administrative Services. As in other states across the country, efforts at restoration and preservation take place in Mississippi under the initiative of the Nature Conservancy. While the international conservancy has been active in Mississippi since the mid-1960s, it opened a permanent state office in 1989. Through the policymaking and enforcement of the MDEQ, the action of the Nature Conservancy and other organizations, both private and public, a great deal of work on Mississippi's natural environment has taken place. For more than a century, the Mississippi River has been a conduit of transportation, communication, and industry, and Mississippi has felt the side effects, both positive and negative, of the river's many roles. The effort to find a balance between human use and environmental sustainability is an ongoing project, and Mississippi has enacted some unique preservation measures in the effort to address all needs.

Using MDEQ and Nature Conservancy programs as representative examples shows a broad spectrum of preservation, protection, and restoration efforts across the state. Mississippi Delta projects, like the Black Bear Restoration plan led by the Nature Conservancy of Mississippi and the Bear Education and Restoration Group, focus on habitat restoration and protection for locally threatened animal species. As part of the State Acres for Wildlife Enhancement program, project participants can enact a restoration strategy that provides protected habitat for the threatened Louisiana black bear and the endangered American black bear on eligible agricultural lands. Rivers and creeks across central Mississippi are part of programs designed to preserve biological diversity in natural community environments. In another landmark effort, in 1976, the Nature Conservancy initiated the Pascagoula River Project, which was, at the time, the largest public land conservation purchase (35,000 acres) ever undertaken in the United States. Today, the conservancy, several conservation organizations, and government agencies combine efforts to protect and manage 75,000 acres along the Pascagoula River. Other major efforts focus on coastal wetland restoration, especially in the wake of Hurricane Katrina. By facing its unique challenges head on, Mississippi is well on the way to preserving its exceptional natural resources and treasures.

CENTRAL MISSISSIPPI CONSERVATION PROGRAM

In 2005, the Nature Conservancy of Mississippi established a program with the focused goal of preserving endemic biological diversity, protecting important conservation sites, and defending delicate natural communities. There are very specific areas of concern, and they are enumerated by the Mississippi chapter of the Nature Conservancy. The long list of high-priority conservation areas across 29 central Mississippi counties includes: Amite River, Bayou Pierre, Bayou Sara, Big Black River, Clark Creek, Durand Oak Prairie Easement, Homochitto National Forest, Lower Buffalo River, North Bienville National Forest, Noxapater Creek, Pearl River, St. Catherine Creek, Strong River, Tallahaga Creek, Tangipohoa River, Thompson Creek, and Upper Yockanookany River. This program is a key contributor to several partner-based initiatives across the state. In working with organizations such as the Mississippi Department of Environmental Quality, Central Mississippi's Planning and Development District, the Mississippi Forest Legacy Program, and the Best Management Practices Wetlands Task Force, the conservancy hopes that the combined efforts will result in successful restoration and, more importantly, successful maintenance and protection of central Mississippi's valuable, fragile natural communities and ecosystems.

Each of the listed sites included in the conservancy's Central Mississippi Conservation Program represent an area of special concern and action. The majority of partnership action is directed toward work involving watershed and hydrological restoration and sustainability. The main significance of areas such as the Amite River basin rests in their important role in flood damage reduction, along with the equally important status as a habitat for rare and endangered species. In the case of the Amite River, riparian sand and gravel mining severely altered the river's hydrological characteristics, contributing to advanced erosion and ultimately reducing its effectiveness in flood control and natural damage mediation. In the case of Bayou Pierre and Bayou Sara, the high priority is the restoration of aquatic life support capability. Excessive sediment and nutrients along with pesticides and pathogens all play a role in the degrading strength of Bayou Pierre to adequately support native aquatic species. Many of the bayou systems across the state of Mississippi suffer from some of the same impact and control issues, putting bayou understanding and protection at the top of many lists of environmental concern.

River systems across the state have been impacted by human presence as well, although, because many of these rivers' roles differ vastly from that of the bayous just discussed, management plans and outcome expectations are decidedly different. The Big Black River suffers from some of the same water quality and maintenance issues as Bayous Pierre and Sara, although the extent of human influence and impact is not nearly as great. It is arguably the least disturbed river in the western Mississippi Delta region, supporting not one single dam along its almost 300-mile length. Even navigation and flood control intervention have been minimal, leaving the flow of this major river system fairly intact. The Lower Buffalo River, however, has a history of significant industrial development, and, as a result, the lower six miles of the river is designated as an important area of concern by the International Joint Commission, whose overall charge is the preventing and resolving of disputes between the United States and Canada. Specifically, these issues involve boundary and transboundary waters and air quality, and the Buffalo River falls within the joint commission's interests. Many rivers in central Mississippi suffer from the same environmental impacts. The management strategies of Pearl River—along with the Yockanookany and the Strong rivers, two of its tributaries—largely utilize fire management for the surrounding forest lands in addition to controlled access measures aimed at restoring damage caused by Hurricane Katrina, correcting the negative impact of artificial flow changes, and preserving the rivers' integrity. Rivers such as the Tangipahoa suffer from fecal coliform contamination, making the river dangerous to its natural inhabitants as well as the humans who use the river for various recreation purposes. The state as a whole funnels more than 50 billion gallons of fresh water a day into the Gulf of Mexico. With this kind of aquatic impact taking place on a daily basis, it is of upmost importance that the health and sustainability of Mississippi's water resources and its associated natural communities stand in the forefront of environmental action and concern.

Several of the high-priority activities of the conservancy in central Mississippi involve the protection of creek environments. Thompson Creek and Clark Creek, for example, are two of the most scenically valuable outdoor recreation areas in the region. The mix of hardwood and pine forests complements the creeks' meandering courses through the hills and over beautiful waterfalls. As part of the Pearl River basin, Noxapater Creek preservation plays an integral part in the ongoing efforts to restore the vitality of the Pearl River. As a National Wildlife Refuge, St. Catherine Creek offers superior habitats for migratory waterfowl, a variety of endangered animal species, and a wide range of more common natural residents. From swimming holes to fishing hot spots to rejuvenating hot springs, the creeks of central Mississippi are at the heart of efforts to create and maintain the strongest natural environments possible in central Mississippi.

Further Reading

Benke, Arthur C., and Colbert E. Cushing. *Rivers of North America.* San Diego, CA: Academic Press, 2005.

Bradburn, Anne S. "Preservation of Species: An Alternative Method." http://www.bgci. org/congress/congress_rio_1992/bradburn.html.

Irvine, K.N., K.M. Frothingham, M.C. Rossi, S. Pickard, J. Atkinson, and T. Bajak. "Contaminated Sediment in the Buffalo River Area of Concern: Historical Trends and Current Conditions." http://www.buffalostate.edu/geography/documents/irvine %20et%20al%202003.pdf.

LOWER MISSISSIPPI RIVER

The Mississippi River holds the honor of being the fourth longest river on earth. It runs for 2,350 miles, starting far north at Lake Itasca, Minnesota, and stretching all the way to the Gulf of Mexico. Its watershed is over one million square miles, which means it includes more than 40 percent of the United States and even a bit of Canada. Its drainage basin is the third largest in the world, and, in addition to producing the seventh highest discharge of any river, is also one of the most complex riverine ecosystems in existence. These natural qualities testify to the important role the Mississippi River plays not only in North America but also in the Western Hemisphere and the world. These facts, though, do not address the river's significance to human mobility, economy, and culture. According to the Lower Mississippi River Fisheries Coordination Office, more than one billion tons of commodities are transported along the length of the Mississippi annually, and this tonnage includes over 50 percent of the nation's grain production. The economic and social impact of these numbers cannot be ignored, and they do not represent the totality of human dependence on this key riverine system. Conservation and protection of this valuable natural resource are at the forefront of several significant environmental programs. A major part of this focus centers on the Lower Mississippi Alluvial Valley and the mouth of the mighty Mississippi.

The Lower Mississippi Alluvial Valley runs from the meeting of the Ohio and the Mississippi rivers in Illinois all the way south to the Gulf of Mexico. At the mouth of the Mississippi is a rich expanse of four and a half million acres of characteristically coastal prairies and marshes. These areas are an extension of the forested alluvial valleys to the north, and together they form an important, virtually unrivaled, wetland ecosystem. The lower section of the mighty Mississippi bears little resemblance to the 1,400 miles of northern river. The entire length of the lower stretch is free flowing. Historically speaking, the Mississippi and its tributaries, by overflowing into a wide alluvial valley, represented the largest floodplain fishery in North America, as described by the Fisheries Coordination Office. As a result of the river's dynamic nature, it constantly both created and drained many channels, resulting in a wide variety of both permanent and seasonal wetlands. Human presence, though, affects the health and sustainability of the Lower Mississippi River basin's natural habitats, and the expansion of housing developments, agricultural pursuits, and industry interests have all taken their toll on its unique and irreplaceable habitats.

For many decades, active conservation efforts throughout the Lower Mississippi River basin have tried to mediate some of the damaging effects of human presence. The U.S. Fish and Wildlife Service, the Nature Conservancy, and other nonprofit organizations combine their efforts in the direction of wildlife refuges, management of plant and animal communities, and conservation of ecosystem integrity. Significantly increased participation in voluntary conservation programs such as the federal Wetlands Reserve Program helps organized preservation efforts greatly. As private landowners become more educated about the benefits of preservation and restoration, their conservation efforts increase in the hopes of improving water quality, contributing to effective flood control, and reducing the effects of erosion. One of the biggest focal points of these efforts involves finding and maintaining the delicate balance that will support human use of the Delta region while simultaneously preserving the environmental sustainability of its natural communities. As the most heavily utilized river system in the United States, the Lower Mississippi River poses unique challenges in the search for this compromise.

As mentioned, the Lower Mississippi River is the most heavily trafficked river system in North America. This fact puts the Lower Mississippi at the center of concerns that involve not only the environmental state of the river and its watershed but also its continued ability to contribute to the societal identity and economic well-being of its local residents. The river provides unique access to the interior of the continent and functions as a valuable transportation method. It has drawn people to the region since long before the arrival of Europeans in the New World. Twenty-six of the 48 continental states heavily depend on the Mississippi River and its connected riverine systems for economic stability as well as environmental health maintenance. The compromise between these varied functions is an extremely complex and often controversial issue. The lower river holds a unique environmental position. Not only does it depend on the treatment of the Lower Mississippi River basin, but there are also six river systems upstream that directly feed into the Mississippi, thus affecting environmental stability and quality. Heavy industry, manufacturing, and marine transportation all threaten the natural health of the area. An additional challenge rests on the fact that, despite the vital economic position of the Mississippi River Delta, local communities do not often benefit from the economic activity generated by the mighty power of the Mississippi. As a result, residents turn to the government for assistance in achieving balanced river use, environmental protection, economic stability, and cultural preservation because the resources simply do not exist in the Delta region to promote a self-sustaining reality for the area's natural or human communities.

Riverfront community and economic development is a focus of local efforts to utilize both the river's natural and economic potential. In a dramatic deviation, though, from industrial use of the riverfront in the past, the goal of these communities is to develop greener alternatives to waterfront land use. By promoting environmentally sound development and utilization of shoreline property, local communities aim to create an attractive environment for residents, investors, and business interests. For many, investment in community infrastructure and maintenance means investment in the river's restoration and conservation. The hope is that by creating a cycle of responsible economic growth and sound environmental policy, the two goals can work hand in hand to create a permanent base of fiscal success that couples with natural preservation. Utilizing government sponsorship in establishing a community-led initiative to simultaneously develop and protect this valuable resource, the American Heritage Rivers Initiative has inspired much positive work along the Lower Mississippi beginning in Memphis, Tennessee, stretching all the way to the mouth of the river in southern Louisiana. As a result of this initiative, the Lower Mississippi American Heritage River Alliance coordinates regional efforts and governmental sponsorship while, at the same time, allowing local populations to formulate and lead their own visions for this important national resource. The Lower Mississippi River stands as a successful example of what people can do when they direct their efforts toward coexisting with natural habitats in ways that benefit everyone and everything involved.

Further Reading

Charlie, Thomas. "Saving the Mighty Miss: Years of Tinkering by the Army Corps of Engineers Has Inexorably Harmed the Fragile Ecosystem of the Lower Mississippi River." *State Legislatures* 32, no. 4 (2006): 30–34.

Hessie, Larry W. *Restoration Planning for the Rivers of the Mississippi River*. Washington, DC: National Biological Survey, 1993.

LOWER PEARL RIVER PARTNERSHIP

The Pearl River was named by French explorers for the pearls found at the mouth of the river as they began a journey of discovery down the river in the late 1600s. What they found was a region rich in human history and biological diversity. From the pre-Contact days of the Choctaw and Acolapissas to the present use of the river and its tributaries for boating and fishing, this river has long played an important role in the natural personality of the Deep South. The combination of rivers, creeks, swamps, forests, and marshes offer diverse environments for natural communities to thrive in and for local populations to utilize. Not only is the Pearl River watershed important for its recreation and natural environment characteristics, it also is a major natural element of support for the fishery industry of the southern Gulf Coast. The Pearl River hosts more than 100 fish species and more than 40 types of freshwater mussel, making it one of the most diverse species habitat systems in North America. The water, though, is not the only important element of this valuable habitat. Swallow-tailed kites call this region home also. In 2005, according to Mississippi's Nature Conservancy, there were 27 nesting pairs observed around the Lower Pearl River. The significance of this number is that kites generally require a minimum of 100,000 acres of solid forest in order to adequately maintain a healthy population. Currently there are more than 120,000 acres of land protected around the Lower Pearl River region. In a joint effort that crosses the Mississippi-Louisiana state border, the states' Nature Conservancies along with both Departments of Environmental Quality formed the Lower Pearl Partnership to work with various stakeholders, including local agencies and landowners, to restore and protect the Lower Pearl River region for the benefit of all of its natural residents.

One of the area's more demanding natural residents is the swallow-tailed kite. With the same requirement of at least 100,000 acres of continuous forest for successful population breeding and support, this kite represents one of the most striking and one of the most identifiable raptors that sail the southeastern skies. The swallow-tailed kite is a medium-sized hawk that sports contrasting black and white coloring all along its body; thin, pointed wings; and a distinctive forked tail. Dining on flying insects as well as amphibians or reptiles perched at the top of trees, the kite spends a great deal of its time aloft. Like many raptors, the kite rarely flaps its wings while flying. Instead, it almost continuously rotates its tail to hold a heading, make sharp turns, or follow tight circles as it flies. Federally, this species is not considered endangered or threatened, but the reality for kite populations in the United States is that their range and habitat are shrinking. Because they are so acreage dependant, it is becoming increasingly difficult for kite populations to find forest expanses large enough to support significant populations. The preservation of the Lower Pearl River basin, then, plays an important role in the long-term survival of this unique species. While it is not currently threatened, the measures taken across the Lower Pearl region will help ensure that kites, along with their many neighbors, have a suitable, sustainable habitat for many years to come.

Pearl River in Mississippi. (Michelle Harrison)

Despite the relative health of the Pearl River, there are some significant threats to its well-being. Some of the primary issues include problems such as excessive sedimentation, altered hydrology, increased toxicity, substrate destabilization, habitat disturbance, and flow alterations. Private landowner participation in restoration and protection activities is a must. Forest industry development must be controlled and monitored to reduce impact. Residential and commercial development must respect best management practices in order to maintain a healthy watershed. Pollution runoff into the river system is a concern for all of these invested partners. By implementing and following established best practices, the Lower Pearl River watershed and basin will emerge as a healthier, better protected wildlife refuge and recreation haven. According to the Watershed Protection and Management Program, best management practices in this context are intended to be "effective, practical, structural, or nonstructural methods [that] prevent or reduce the movement of sediment, nutrients, pesticides, and other pollutants from the land to surface or ground water, or which otherwise protect water quality from potential adverse effects of silvicultural activities." Almost every human development or industrial activity has an associated collection of best practices to moderate the negative effects of construction, manufacturing, natural resource exploitation, and recreational use. Without standard guidelines, protection efforts across the country would vary greatly in quality and impact. By respecting the best practices recommendations for the use and development of the Lower Pearl River, the process of coordinating conservation techniques between widely varying stakeholders becomes a little bit easier.

Further Reading

"International Stormwater BMP Database." http://www.bmpdatabase.org.

Kemper, Karin E., Ariel Dinar, and William Blomquist. *Integrated River Basin Management through Decentralization.* New York: Springer, 2006.

Meyer, Kenneth D. "Swallow-tailed Kite (*Elanoides forficatus*). *The Birds of North America Online,* no. 138 (1995). http://bna.birds.cornell.edu/bna/species/138.

MISSISSIPPI DELTA

"Economic development of the Delta cannot be separated from its ethnic realities and cannot be planned apart from careful management of its resources and protection of its environment. This report envisions a coming time when ecological mindfulness and economic development are no longer seen as incompatible but as indivisible." This statement by the Lower Mississippi Delta Development Commission of 1990 embodies the direction many are taking today in the effort to find the compromise between human use of the environment and responsible protection of it as one of society's most valuable resources. By combining the goal of improving the well-being of ethnic and racial minority populations with the aim of achieving a sustainable level of environmental justice, the commission and those taking action based on their findings hope to demonstrate how partnerships can identify and reduce the impact of environmental degradation, resulting in benefit to human and natural communities alike. The entirety of the Mississippi Delta region encompasses 219 counties that occupy a wide strip of land that follows the Mississippi River from Illinois and Missouri down through Kentucky, Tennessee, and Arkansas, and then on into Mississippi and Louisiana. More than eight million people live on this strip of land, and the health of their local environment affects not only the conditions in which they live, but also the means with which they support their families. To address these varying and complex issues, federal and state agencies, academic institutions, and local organizations are working together to formulate a plan that addresses the needs of this important region of the United States. As a result, three concerns have become the focus of activism in the area: the need for economic development, the importance of improving health conditions for underserved populations, and the necessity of ensuring that both environmental justice and social justice concerns are met.

The commission's final report, entitled "Realizing the Dream . . . Fulfilling the Potential," addresses many issues, both social and environmental, that impact the overall health of the Delta region. Through the commission's exploration into the foundational issues concerning the Delta region, it identified a major area of connection in that problems found along the Delta are common to all seven states through which the Mississippi flows. From a societal perspective, health, education, housing, agriculture, tourism, and natural resource use along with the development of community infrastructure, business interests, and entrepreneurial opportunities are all concerns of towns and cities across the Delta region. If efforts focus on these collective needs in conjunction with the restoration and protection of natural habitats and environmental resources, the Lower Mississippi region will emerge stronger and more self-sufficient in the process. Three goals resulted from the commission's studies and research. First, by the year 2001, improvement in environmental quality should meet or surpass national environmental standards, and a particular focus to develop more comprehensive disaster protection and recovery plans should be emphasized. Also by 2001, environmental research and community environmental awareness should be at the center of ongoing educational efforts across the Delta region. Finally, all states along the Delta must have perfected methods of hazardous and solid waste disposal in the ongoing effort to protect water and air quality. While many continue to suggest that human development and environment conservation cannot work together toward the same ultimate goals, it is the position of the Lower Mississippi Development Commission that the two cannot happen separately. Environment preservation greatly enhances quality of life by producing local pride and sense of place and by enticing investment and development. Communities benefit directly from well-planned protection programs. On the other side of the coin, the local environment benefits from educated, invested residents who actively work toward the preservation of their natural surroundings, especially when their quality of life and economic stability are tied to the health of the environment. The overarching goal, then, of the Lower Mississippi Development Commission is that sustainable development involves all facets of society, from health and education to nature and its protection, and should address the concerns of all in order to be successful.

One interesting connection between Delta communities and their environmental surroundings is the growing body of evidence suggesting that environmental health risks are disproportionately shouldered by local poor populations. Environmentally induced illnesses seem to be related to both socioeconomic class and ethnicity, at least based on observational conclusions. One major connection infers that residential proximity to pollution sources plays a major role in environmentally caused health concerns. It is important to develop a better understanding of the demographic nature of populations living near pollution-threatened areas. In addition to residential location, the fact that many of these populations live in urban areas where pollution levels are elevated affects health concerns. Additionally, there seem to be higher instances of contaminated fish consumption and higher rates of employment in inherently dangerous jobs. The combination of these factors greatly increases the occurrence of pollution-based health issues and concerns. From these studies, plans can be developed to minimize the impact of health threats on disadvantaged local populations. Education efforts will play a major role in mediating these concerns, as will the encouragement of racial and ethnic minorities to enter fields focusing on environmental and health studies, helping create closer connections for threatened communities to the solutions they seek. Federal efforts have recently emerged that support these goals. The Department of Health and Human Services (DHHS) and the Environmental Protection Agency (EPA) responded to an executive order signed in 1994 that established a foundation suggesting that "each Federal agency shall make achieving environmental justice part of its mission by identifying and addressing, as appropriate, disproportionately high and adverse human health or environmental effects of its programs, policies, and activities on minority populations and low-income populations." The result is that efforts such as the Delta project focus on developing practices that involve the fair treatment and involvement of all people, regardless of ethnicity, income, or education level in the formulation of environmental policies and practices. Additionally, no population that suffers under political underrepresentation or economic disadvantage should bear disproportionate impacts of pollution and other environmental hazards. Both the DHHS and the EPA have recognized the Mississippi Delta Project's efforts as an outstanding model of interagency cooperation and environmental justice action, identifying this far-reaching effort as a leader in environmental and social interest balance and coordination.

In addition to the Delta Project's efforts at education, restoration, and protection of this region as an important natural resource, the National Park Service has undertaken a heritage study and environmental assessment geared toward gaining a better understanding of the interplay and interdependence of Delta heritage and environment. The foundation of this program rests on the concept that visitors and residents need to understand the magnitude, importance, and diversity of the environmental systems that comprise the Delta region. Severe poverty issues exist across the Delta region, complicating efforts directed at public education and action. Additionally, concerns exist regarding the adequacy and quality of local food supplies. Ultimately, most of the social issues in the lower Delta region revolve around the persistent and widespread poverty of local communities. Because environmental health and societal stability are so closely tied, many of the efforts underway in the Lower Mississippi Delta involve the dual goals of shoring up the resident population's economic sustainability in conjunction with preservation plans that involve education and regional investment in the health of Delta ecosystems. Without addressing the needs of both the environment and its human communities, the future of the Delta region would be on shaky ground.

Further Reading

Bell, James. *The Evolution of the Mississippi Delta: From Exploited Labor and Mules to Mechanization and Agribusiness.* Bloomington, IN: iUniverse, 2008.

Connell, C.L., M.K. Yadrick, P. Simpson, J. Gossett, B. McGee, and M.L. Bogle. "Food Supply Adequacy in the Lower Mississippi Delta." *Journal of Nutrition Education and Behavior* 39, no. 2 (2007): 77–83.

Helferich, Gerard. *High Cotton: Four Seasons in the Mississippi Delta.* Berkeley, CA: Counterpoint, 2008.

SWEETBAY BOGS PRESERVE

The Sweetbay Bogs Preserve was the first land purchase made by the Mississippi chapter of the Nature Conservancy. This acquisition in December 1989 marked the beginning of Nature Conservancy action in the state of Mississippi. Located in Stone County near Red Creek in the Pascagoula River watershed, this relatively small preserve at just under 200 acres is home to several rare flora species and a variety of unique types of fauna. Grass of Parnassus, the flame flower, pineland bog button, and bog spicebush grow alongside various species of carnivorous plants such as sundews and butterworts. The site was named, though, for its characteristic sweetbay trees that are spread out across the tract of land. The area has been the focus of scientific study for quite some time. Biologists have recognized this small patch of land for decades as one of the most important natural communities in the state. It is a classic example of a hillside seepage bog, which are rarely found as far south as this one. Bogs are an integral part of longleaf pine ecosystems, which once covered the coastal plains, but now, due to human expansion and exploitation, this important natural community is vanishing.

The bogs are generally open, rather treeless wetlands that are associated with longleaf pine ecosystems. Fine, sandy soil that is highly acidic and low in nutrient concentration characterizes the substrate. Under this sandy layer is clay or sandstone, which facilitates constant seepage of groundwater to the surface. One important element to the maintenance of these ecosystems is periodic burning. Fire is necessary to restrict the growth of shrubs and competing tree species, while simultaneously encouraging flowering and seed production by native species. The delicate nature of bogs and their constituent species means that they are extremely sensitive to human presence and land use. Any activity that affects the watershed of which they are a part is often detrimental to the health of the bog. Water flow patterns and water storage capacity must be preserved and protected in order to support the survival of this habitat type. Additionally, fire suppression is a serious threat, because periodic burning is important for limiting invasive species and supporting the growth of native bog plants. The most recent threat involves the use of adjacent land for recreational purposes. In 2008, developers looked at land just above the bog as a site for a stock car racing track. The physical development of the area combined with the damaging effects of heavy motorized vehicle use would condemn the bog to extinction. Debates continue between developers and individuals interested in protecting the integrity of the bog as to the ultimate impact of racing activity on the surrounding wetlands. In this case, compromise between the needs of the environment and the desire for development may not be possible. Here, as in many areas across Mississippi and the South as a whole, competing interests vie for control, while a solution for successful cohabitation continues to prove elusive.

Further Reading

Bridges, E. L., and S. L. Orzell. "Longleaf Pine Communities of the West Gulf Coastal Plain." *Natural Areas Journal* 9, no. 4 (1989): 247–63.

Eastman, John. *The Book of Swamp and Bog: Trees, Shrubs, and Wildflowers of the Eastern Freshwater Wetlands*. Mechanicsburg, PA: Stackpole Books, 1995.

NatureServe. "NatureServe Explorer: An Online Encyclopedia of Life." Version 6.1. http://www.natureserve.org/explorer.

Bat Cave Preserve, 102

Gorges State Park, 104

Grandfather Mountain Preserve, 106

Great Dismal Swamp National Wildlife Refuge, 108

Great Smoky Mountains National Park, 110

South Mountains Game Land, 112

NORTH CAROLINA

The environmental landscape of North Carolina includes four major ecosystem types: Blue Ridge, piedmont, southeastern plains, and middle Atlantic coastal plains. North Carolina shares the southeastern plains with South Carolina, Georgia, and Mississippi and the middle Atlantic coastal plains with South Carolina. The majority of state lands, though, are either piedmont regions or Blue Ridge. In fact, most of the Blue Ridge land in the United States falls within North Carolina's borders. This landscape varies from narrow ridges to hilly plateaus and into higher-elevation mountainous terrain. The Environmental Protection Agency designates the southern Blue Ridge region as one of the richest areas of biodiversity in the eastern United States, including, for example, oak forests, northern hardwoods, and, in higher elevations, spruce and fir stands. Hemlock, oak-pine communities, and shrub, grass, and heath balds are common as well. There is even quite a variety of wetlands, including southern Appalachian and swamp forest bogs, bottomland forests, and high-elevation seeps. The piedmont areas are the nonmountainous portions of the old Appalachian Highlands and sit adjacent to the Blue Ridge region in North Carolina, functioning as a transition area between the mountains to the northwest and the coastal plains in the southeast. In earlier decades, this area experienced widespread agricultural cultivation, but in more recent years there has been some reversion to pine and hardwood forest and an ever-increasing presence of urban and suburban habitation.

The history of preservation and protection in North Carolina includes a variety of efforts by public and private organizations and individuals. One major active organization is the Conservation Trust for North Carolina. Its stated mission is to "protect [the] state's land and water through statewide conservation and cooperative work with land trusts to preserve . . . natural resources as a legacy for future generations." In North Carolina there are more than two dozen land trusts engaged in protecting natural areas of ecological, scenic, recreational, agricultural, cultural, or historic value. By combining grassroots efforts with community organization and professional business practices, land trusts permanently protect lands of significance through either purchase or donation of the land and the enacting of preservation and restoration measures specific to each site's individual needs. Just as many other states in the country focus on finding a balance between development and protection, the Ecosystem Enhancement Program focuses on supporting a growing population while managing the needs of ecosystems across the state. Recently, the Nature Conservancy of North Carolina celebrated its 30th birthday. It has grown from two staff in 1977 to 40 staff members today, and the organization constantly strives to learn from its past, adjusting what does not work to find what does. Four of the preserves under the protection of the conservancy—the Green Swamp, Bluff Mountain, Nags Head Woods, and Bat Cave—have been recognized for their unique characteristics and inhabitants. The conservancy attributes a great deal to its experiences with these sites, specifically acknowledging the benefit of hindsight, showing how important an initial foothold can be to long-term goals.

Today, groups like the Nature Conservancy and the Conservation Trust work with private and state agencies to continue working toward a balance between the needs of development and the necessities of preservation. As the Conservation Trust points out, for example, there are more than 1,000 species on the federal endangered and threatened list, and 18 percent of all the animal and plant species in North Carolina are on that list, giving the state a vested interest in developing manageable, sustainable plans for habitat preservation. Land trusts, among other groups, work with the North Carolina State Wildlife Action Plan to integrate the plan into conservation efforts already in the works and funding strategies for current and future projects. North Carolina also created a groundbreaking program with the Ecosystem Enhancement Program, which is a model for wetlands mitigation. The program's main strength is that it focuses on facilitating economic growth while supporting ecosystem enhancement to counterbalance the side effects of development through proactive rather than reactive actions. Public and private partnerships are the foundation of the program, and it has been designated as one of the top 50 innovative government programs of its kind. Unique challenges encourage unique answers, and North Carolina makes every effort to assist both human development and environmental preservation in unique ways.

BAT CAVE PRESERVE

A small but extremely significant natural site, Bat Cave Preserve covers just under 200 acres in western North Carolina. It is owned and operated as a joint venture between the state's Nature Conservancy chapter and a private landowner in the area. Because of the delicate nature of the bats' habitat, the preserve is only accessible through a controlled field trip program that runs from June through early August. Although trips to the area are possible during the summer, the cave is never open to the public in order to protect the bats and their fragile environment. A strategically timed trip to Bat Cave, though, is definitely worth the effort and planning. There is a steep trail that travels a mile into a mature hardwood forest. At the end of the hike is Bat Cave. Standing in the vicinity of the cave provides visitors with some relief as a cool mist constantly flows out of vents that line the cave's sides. According to the Nature Conservancy of North Carolina, Bat Cave is the largest known granite fissure cave in North America. Instead of being formed by water flow and grinding rock movement, fissure caves take shape as a result of rock splits and boulder movements, making the cave a unique underground environment. The conservancy also points out that, while this impressive cave structure is the draw for most visitors, the surrounding slopes offer an amazing opportunity to explore and observe an outstanding variety of native flora and fauna. Rare and endangered species cover the ridges and peaks of the mountain geography. The main preservation goal, though, is to firmly establish and maintain the critically endangered Indiana bat in its natural habitat. By supporting education concerning the site's importance through limited visitation access, the conservancy aims to expand understanding related to the needs of the bats and other cave residents while protecting the Indiana bat and other local species from the dangers posed by human presence.

One natural environment preservation effort involved a coordinated effort between the Nature Conservancy, the Coalition to Control Kudzu without Herbicides, and AmeriCorps volunteers to remove invasive outbreaks of kudzu, a nonnative, aggressive vine common across the South and Southeast. Local populations call kudzu porch vine, miracle vine, and foot-a-night vine, and, although its introduction 100 years ago was intended to beautify landscaping, by the end of the century, the plant came to alter and dominate many natural environments. Although it is visually attractive, its fast-growing nature means that it can strangle native vegetation and clog water passageways quickly, threatening local ecosystems. While the efforts in 2007 removed relatively little kudzu, the plant's presence, if unaddressed, would have led to a significant spread of its local range and ultimately could have negatively affected the sustainability of natural community habitats. Efforts such as this preventative kudzu removal project help ensure a proactive protection plan that addresses problems early rather than being a reactive battle that can only struggle to keep up with already-established threats. This is one successful example of total site management aimed at preserving a collective environment rather than focusing on specific species. The product is a better managed, more comprehensive approach that ultimately produces more victorious results.

Arguably, though, the main resident of focus is the Indiana bat. This species is a dark- or chestnut-colored medium-sized bat that is listed as endangered by the U.S. Fish and Wildlife Service. While the bats live rather spread out during the summer months, they cluster together to hibernate, which is the main reason why there is no access to the Bat Cave area during the winter. Disturbance of the bat community during their hibernation period would cause them to become agitated and fly around, using up the valuable energy stores necessary for them to survive through the winter. The lack of protected environments and the effects of human development have significantly contributed to a 50 percent decline in Indiana bat population numbers since 1975. An important part of the bats' hibernation habits is the type of cave they hibernate in, which tend to be rare. Stable, low temperatures are necessary for the bats to achieve the lowered metabolic rates necessary to effectively conserve fat stores to get them through the winter. In addition, a feeding colony of bats—which can contain thousands of individuals—needs thousands of insects, so the cave environment has to specifically address the colony's needs or the group will not survive.

In an effort to help the species recover some community stability, in 2007, the U.S. Fish and Wildlife Service drafted an Indiana Bat Recovery Plan. The goal of any species recovery plan, according to the document is to "describe actions considered necessary for the conservation of the species, establish criteria for delisting species, and provide estimates of the time and cost for implementing the measures needed for recovery." Depending on the time year, threats to Indiana bat populations vary. Modifications to caves, mines, and the surrounding areas are a danger to hibernation habitats. The loss and degradation of forest habitats that house populations during their breeding period severely affect the survival and multiplication of the species. In addition to threats such as these, gaps in knowledge and understanding of the Indiana bat's ecology restrict scientific ability to plan and implement the most effective conservation strategies. Based on the quantity and quality of hibernation areas, the stability of census numbers, and evidence of expanding breeding populations, the U.S. Fish and Wildlife Service suggests that the species could be delisted within a decade. Through protection of both summer and winter habitats combined with public outreach and education programs, the service hopes to achieve community stability and ultimately federal delisting, and, although small, Bat Cave in North Carolina is part of this larger effort to better protect and understand this unique, endangered species.

Further Reading

Culver, David. *The Biology of Caves and Other Subterranean Habitats*. New York: Oxford University Press, 2009.

Gillieson, David. *Caves: Processes, Development and Management*. Hoboken, NJ: Wiley-Blackwell, 1996.

U.S. Fish and Wildlife Service. "Indiana Bat (*Myotis sodalis*)." http://ecos.fws.gov/species Profile/SpeciesReport.do?spcode=A000.

Gorges State Park

Plunging waterfalls, rugged river gorges, sheer rock walls, and one of the greatest concentrations of rare and unique species in the eastern United States are found within Gorges State Park. The park rises to a 2,000-foot elevation, and that, combined with an average rainfall of 80 inches per year, creates a temperate rain forest unique to the Southeast. Covering more than 7,000 acres, this relatively new park is in the early phases of planning and development, offering a unique opportunity to watch the growth of restoration and protection programs in action. Dedicated in 1999, the park is bordered by lands managed by the North Carolina Wildlife Resources Commission and the U.S. Forest Service, as well as South Carolina's Lake Jocassee. To facilitate immediate public access, an interim development plan was put into place that constructed visitor parking, restroom facilities, picnic areas, and hiking trails. These temporary facilities allowed the public to utilize the new state park while the managing organizations grappled with a variety of development challenges. The terrain and quickly rising elevation of Gorges State Park pose particular challenges to access development. According to land surveys, more than half of the slopes in the park are at a grade of more than 25 percent. In light of this reality, combined with the goal of protecting the area's natural communities, a master plan emerged with an overriding concept that focuses on developing a wilderness experience in the park utilizing low-impact facilities while limiting developmental access to the more easily reached outer areas of the park. The planning of Gorges State Park as a public resource represents a model of modern environmental development and preservation by focusing on maximum protection for the local ecosystem that balances favorably with public use, access, and education.

Despite the developmental focus on preserving the wilderness experience that characterizes Gorges State Park, there is evidence throughout the area that humans have been there and altered the natural landscape to a certain extent. One of the most damaging events occurred in 1916, when the dam that contained Lake Toxaway broke. Despite the almost 100-year respite, debris piles from the torrential flood still remain as evidence of the destruction. Singer Sewing Machine Company bought large tracts of land after the

Gorges State Park on the border of North and South Carolina. (Victor Nunnally)

flood and commenced logging, which lasted for decades. In the late 1940s, Singer sold its lands to Duke Energy Corporation, which had an interest in utilizing the steep slopes and high rainfall amounts to develop hydropower projects. It was at this point that early efforts at environmental protection began. The Crescent Land and Timber Corporation, a subsidiary of Duke Energy, took over management of the land and began closing roads and limiting public access to protect the natural state of the area. Later, in the 1970s, conservation studies began, and, by 1982, almost 300 acres of what eventually became Gorges State Park was placed on the North Carolina Registry of Natural Heritage Areas because of its natural preponderance of rare and threatened species. By the late 1990s, Duke decided it no longer needed the land for its hydropower projects and put the area up for sale. This is where the North Carolina Division of Parks and Recreation stepped in and purchased the land with the goal of creating the newest state park in North Carolina. In a unique partnership comprised of industry, the environmental community, and the state of North Carolina, more than 10,000 acres ended up under the protection of the North Carolina Wildlife Resources Commission and the North Carolina Department of Parks and Recreation, establishing a large and important preserve for many future generations.

Further Reading

Adams, Kevin. *North Carolina Waterfalls: A Hiking and Photography Guide*. Winston-Salem, NC: John F. Blair, 2005.

Frankenberg, Dirk, ed. *Exploring North Carolina's Natural Areas: Parks, Nature Preserves, and Hiking Trails*. Chapel Hill: University of North Carolina Press, 2000.

Grandfather Mountain Preserve

Rocky summits, cliffs, and breathtaking views of the Blue Ridge Mountains and piedmont landscape characterize the beauty of nature at Grandfather Mountain Preserve. The Nature Conservancy states that rock outcrops, spruce-fir forests, heath balds, and hardwood forests are the foundation for habitats that support more than 60 rare plant and animal species, making Grandfather Mountain one of the most biologically diverse mountain areas in the region. Its backcountry areas are accessible by a network of hiking trails that range in difficulty from easy forest treks to rugged climbing experiences that reach all the way to the 5,694-foot Calloway Peak. Late spring and early summer treat visitors to a dazzling array of colorful wildflowers as well as outstanding opportunities for bird-watching, especially during traditional migratory periods. The Nature Conservancy of North Carolina currently works with Grandfather Mountain, Inc., a private corporation, to manage the nearly 2,000 preserve acres, pieces of which have been added to the site over the last decade, helping to expand the reach and effectiveness of concerted preservation efforts.

Grandfather Mountain Preserve. (Mike Kight)

Grandfather Mountain stands as the highest peak in the Blue Ridge range and is renowned throughout the southern Appalachian region. Unfortunately, the spruce-fir forests that grow in the higher altitudes have lately been suffering from a triple threat. First, growing levels of air pollution are making it harder for these stands to thrive. Additionally, exotic insect infestations have taken their toll on the health and welfare of these and many other tree species. Finally, northern hardwoods growing at altitudes above 5,400 feet are dying off at alarmingly high rates. In response to these and other threats, Grandfather Mountain is currently the only privately owned park in the world that is designated by the United Nations as an International Biosphere Reserve. When conservationist and founder of the Sierra Club, John Muir, visited Grandfather Mountain, he is quoted as saying it was truly "the face of all Heaven come to earth," which testifies to the strength and beauty of this place. In deciding to award Grandfather Mountain the status of International Biosphere Reserve, the United Nations had to take several issues into consideration. First, it should be a resource that is representative of the larger region of which it is a part. Second, it must have a legally protected core area as well as a history of scientific study and research. It must also be active in the education and training of resource management professionals as well as the general public. And, finally, it should function as a focal point of regional dialogue concerning current environmental and economic growth issues. By meeting all of these criteria, this designation encourages developing ways for local communities to enjoy economic prosperity without destroying valuable environmental resources. A biosphere reserve is not, however, land controlled by the United Nations. The designation simply functions as a method of value recognition and an encouragement system that focuses on finding the balance between development and conservation activities. Grandfather Mountain stands, both figuratively and literally, as a premium example of the gains made in defining, finding, and maintaining the balance between human and environmental interests.

Further Reading

Little, Charles. *The Dying of the Trees: The Pandemic in America's Forests.* New York: Penguin, 1997.
Tager, Miles. *Grandfather Mountain: A Profile.* Boone, NC: Parkway, 1999.
Williams, John Alexander. *Appalachia: A History.* Chapel Hill: University of North Carolina Press, 2001.

GREAT DISMAL SWAMP NATIONAL WILDLIFE REFUGE

The area of this large, unique national refuge covers more than 100,000 acres of forested wetlands and spans the border between southeastern Virginia and northeastern North Carolina. While protection of the land as a refuge is relatively recent, occurring in 1973, human habitation of the area has a history stretching back more than 13,000 years. Following European settlement, though, interest in the swamp was low. It was not until George Washington visited the area in the 1760s when he organized the Dismal Swamp Land Company to begin draining and logging the wetlands. This profitable venture took hold and continued all the way through the 1970s. The result is that Dismal Swamp has been greatly altered by human intervention over the centuries. What remains today represents barely half of the original swamp coverage. Additionally, there were 140 miles of roads constructed to facilitate access to the timbered areas. The building of these roads severely damaged the swamp's natural water flow because ditches were dug to provide soil for the road bed. This resulted in dramatic drainage of the swamp's naturally contained water. This redistribution also created pools of stagnant water that greatly affected the quality of the swamp's ecosystem. The logging removed natural species such as cypress and Atlantic white-cedar stands that were eventually replaced with other nonnative trees, affecting the natural interdependence cycle as well as the diversity of species. Initial acts of preservation and restoration began in 1973, when the Union Camp Corporation donated almost 50,000 acres of land to the state chapter of the Nature Conservancy. By 1974, the conservancy had transferred the land to the Department of the Interior, resulting in the official establishment of the Great Dismal Swamp National Wildlife Refuge in 1974.

Since then, the main goal of resource management programs involving the swamp has been to restore and maintain the natural character of swamp as it existed before human intervention began changing its native landscape and distinctiveness. Water resources, native vegetation, and varied wildlife are the mainstays of restoration programs, because all three categories are important in defining the natural personality of the swamp. Eight plant community types make up the swamp's natural vegetation collection. Pine, Atlantic white cedar, maple blackgum, tupelo bald cypress, and sweetgum oak poplar stands were all native tree species to the area. There are three types of nonforested environments to consider also: remnant marsh, sphagnum bog, and an evergreen shrub habitat. The plants considered native to the preserve depend heavily on periodic burning, a process that has been suppressed for centuries. Red maple is now the most predominant tree type, because it thrives in the drier, unburned conditions created by human presence. The main goal of restoration is to reestablish native species and to provide conditions that support successful community maintenance.

In addition to these vegetation communities, a great variety of bird, mammal, reptile, and amphibian species also call the refuge home. More than 200 types of birds have been identified at the refuge, and almost half of these use the refuge as nesting grounds. A variety of mammals can be found throughout the wetlands as well. Otters, bats, raccoons, minks, foxes, and squirrels dominate the animal communities. White-tailed deer can be found throughout the area, also, and, although not as common, it is possible to see black bears and bobcats occasionally. Several poisonous snakes, such as the cottonmouth and the copperhead, along with 18 types of nonpoisonous snakes roam the preserve. More than 50 varieties of amphibians have been observed during study of the refuge's animal communities. To restore and preserve habitats that are conducive for the survival of native flora and fauna, the U.S. Fish and Wildlife Service adopted a comprehensive conservation plan in 2006. Under this plan, land acquisition would occur only in approved areas, and resource management operations and visitor services would expand as finances became available. Based on an extensive examination of the refuge and its natural resources, along with a wilderness assessment, it was possible to develop a comprehensive conservation plan aimed at restoring the land to the highest prehuman impact quality possible and then subsequently maintaining the site's ecological health and viability. Studies did not simply look at the physical environment and biological resources, however. Cultural resources and socioeconomic realities were also addressed to produce the most comprehensive information possible. The end result included a management blueprint that addresses habitats, species, land protection, and public use issues along with a refuge administration plan capable of overseeing this massive restoration and preservation effort. Without the time, money, and energy spent studying and developing an all-encompassing strategy, this complicated effort would not stand a chance in the face of the amount of work that needs to be done to restore and maintain this valuable preserve.

Further Reading

Simpson, Bland. *The Great Dismal: A Carolinian's Swamp Memoir.* Chapel Hill: University of North Carolina Press, 1998.

U.S. Fish and Wildlife Service and National Wildlife Refuge System. "Great Dismal Swamp National Wildlife Refuge." http://www.fws.gov/northeast/greatdismalswamp/.

GREAT SMOKY MOUNTAINS NATIONAL PARK

The Great Smoky Mountains National Park recognizes no state borders. It straddles North Carolina and Tennessee with its majestic, overpowering peaks. The National Park Service ranks this awe-inspiring mountain range as the most visited national park in the United States. It helps that 800 miles of maintained trails crisscross the park, ranging from short but beautiful excursions to truly strenuous hikes that could require more than a day to complete. In addition to the wide variety of trekking opportunities, camping, fishing, picnicking, wildlife viewing, and auto touring are popular as well, functioning as the mainstays of national park attractions across the country. In fact, the Great Smoky Mountains offer the most of many different natural elements. For example, more than 1,500 bears live in the park, providing a draw for nature-loving, wildlife-observing tourists. The Smoky Mountains house more biological diversity than any other area in the world's temperate zones. About 100 native tree species inhabit the park's land, which is more than all of the varieties found across the entirety of Northern Europe. When visiting during the blooming season, visitors can be treated to more than 1,600 kinds of flowering plants. With this wealth of natural riches, it is no wonder that the park attracts so many visitors each year.

Another valuable element of the Smoky Mountain experience, though, is the rich history of Appalachian culture that has been coexisting and interacting with the area's amazing natural bounty for generations. Pre-Contact Native American societies were followed by early European settlement in the 1800s. By the 20th century, the area hosted the logging industry and then later the Civilian Conservation Corps. It was the activities of the 20th century that drastically altered the face of the land from its natural condition. Settlers of the late 1800s lived off the land by hunting wildlife, cutting trees for constructing buildings and fences, and clearing land for agricultural use and for pasturing livestock. Although the Cherokee, who originally inhabited the land, were very advanced societies, their land use practices did not rival the dramatic changes caused by European use. Change occurred again in the early 1900s as the lumber industry entered the area. Within a couple of decades, local communities that had been entirely self-sufficient changed to societies dependent on manufactured goods and store-bought food. Logging activities threatened to permanently change the forested mountain lands, and, as a result, the National Park Service stepped in and established the Great Smoky Mountains National Park in 1934 to protect the quickly disappearing natural communities.

While only 20 percent of the original forested area remained untouched at that point, the forest was saved by the quick declaration of federal protected status. One difficult logistical result was the forced relocation of more than 1,000 landowners. They left behind churches, mills, school, and homes. In an effort to recognize the human history of the park alongside the environmental significance, more than 70 of these structures have been preserved. Great Smoky Mountains National Park contains the largest collection of historically significant log buildings in the eastern United States.

The historical and environmental significance of this magnificent park draws 10 million visitors a year. This kind of human presence must be continually monitored and mediated to minimize the impact of so much continuous human interaction. Air and water pollution are a constant threat, and, when combined with the preponderance of invasive species, this means park staff and administration must constantly address and assess the continually changing environment in order to better implement preservation techniques. Nonnative species made their way into the park both through intentional and accidental human introduction. The main problem with new species introduction is that nonnative varieties tend to compete heavily with indigenous plants and animals, often proving to be extremely competitive. The result is the takeover of fragile, specialized ecosystems that are necessary for resident rare plants and animals to survive. To complicate matters, nonnative species, because they did not evolve in their new environment, have no

Great Smoky Mountains National Park. (Ron Miguel [Kamoteus])

natural predators, so the invaders can often increase their numbers at alarming rates. The nature of many flora and fauna species that came to North America from Europe is one of competitive dominance. Many species naturally evolved in Europe to be more competitive, largely because of the lack of available natural resources. In order for a plant or animal species to be successful, it had to develop a competitive edge. When transplanted to North America, that competitive nature often quickly overtook the delicately balanced communities of the New World. These issues are still relevant, posing a constant challenge to the protection of local natural ecosystems. If a park resource is threatened, eradication of the threatening nonnative species may be necessary in order to preserve the indigenous environmental character of the Great Smoky Mountains. Through the efforts of staff and dedicated volunteers, the unique personality of the park will survive for the enjoyment of future generation and the guarantee of stable, sustainable native ecosystems.

Further Reading

Frome, Michael. *Strangers in High Places: The Story of the Great Smoky Mountains.* Knoxville: University of Tennessee Press, 1994.

Linzey, Donald W. *A Natural History Guide: Great Smoky Mountains National Park.* Knoxville: University of Tennessee Press, 2008.

South Mountains Game Land

South Mountains Game Land is one of the largest tracts of undisturbed forestland in North Carolina. Its almost 18,000 acres sit directly adjacent to South Mountains State Park, the combination of which offers unparallel restoration and preservation opportunities. The North Carolina Natural Heritage Program suggests that the South Mountains have national biological significance. Rare ecosystems are home to a wide variety of plant and animal species that are found in few other locations in North America. Botanist Bill Moye conducted the only ecological survey of the area and, in the process, identified more than 20 rare plant species that are thriving in the South Mountains environment. Established in 1998, the game land is the culminating product of a massive four-year coordinated effort to safeguard this rare large stretch of dense forested land. The Nature Conservancy, the Foothills Conservancy of North Carolina, and the North Carolina Wildlife Resources Commission purchased what was formally known as the Rollins Tract in order to formally establish the South Mountains Game Land. At the center of this effort was a committed group of private citizens determined to preserve this prime piedmont environment for future generations. It started with just four people: Steve and Judy Padgett, Susie Hamrick Jones, and Bill Moye. Within months of their first meeting, the North Carolina Wildlife Resources Commission and the North Carolina Division of Parks and Recreation were on board, and the foundation of a coalition was formed.

Next to join was the North Carolina chapter of the Nature Conservancy, but shortly after, an out-of-state industry interest bought the land and began selling timber access rights. Within a few years, the coalition was able to negotiate a manageable price, which resulted in the purchase of the Rollins Tract. The rest is now history as preservation action continues in this delicately balanced ecosystem. Although the large coalition partners were largely responsible for compiling the almost $14 million necessary to purchase the site, the Nature Conservancy specifically recognizes the efforts of Susie Hamrick Jones. "Without people like Susie, who are willing to risk failure in order to achieve great things, the Nature Conservancy could not reach its goals." The importance of individual contributions could not be any clearer.

Further Reading

Howell, Benita, J. *Culture, Environment, and Conservation in the Appalachian South*. Urbana-Champaign: University of Illinois Press, 2002.
North Carolina Birding Trail. *The North Carolina Birding Trail: Mountain Trail Guide*. Chapel Hill: University of North Carolina Press, 2009.

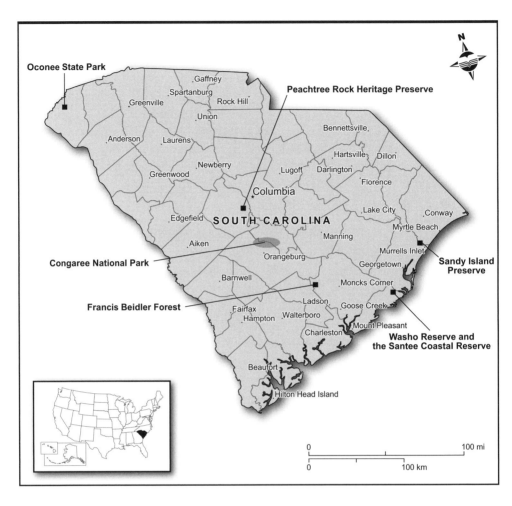

Oconee State Park

Peachtree Rock Heritage Preserve

Gaffney

Spartanburg

Greenville

Rock Hill

Union

Bennettsville

Anderson

Laurens

Hartsville

Dillon

Newberry

Lugoff

Darlington

Greenwood

Florence

Columbia

SOUTH CAROLINA

Edgefield

Lake City

Conway

Manning

Myrtle Beach

Aiken

Murrells Inlet

Orangeburg

Georgetown

Sandy Island Preserve

Congaree National Park

Barnwell

Moncks Corner

Francis Beidler Forest

Ladson

Goose Creek

Fairfax

Walterboro

Hampton

Mount Pleasant

Charleston

Washo Reserve and the Santee Coastal Reserve

Beaufort

Hilton Head Island

0   100 mi

0   100 km

South Carolina

South Carolina shares with North Carolina its three major ecosystem regions—southeastern plains, the middle Atlantic coastal plains, and the piedmont—and, when combined, the southeastern plains and the middle Atlantic coastal plains comprise over half the state's lands. Much like the southeastern plains in Mississippi and Georgia, the South Carolina expression of this ecoregion is characterized by a patchwork of croplands, pastures, woodlands, and forests. Two general types of trees are found in the forests and woodlands of South Carolina: conifers, such as pine and cedar trees, and broadleaf trees, such as maple, oak, and elm. Longleaf pine is the predominant natural tree, but smaller stands of oak, hickory, and pine, along with mixed forest areas dot the landscape. The middle Atlantic coastal plains that South Carolina shares with other coastal states consists of lower-elevation plains scattered with marshes, swamps, and waterways. Many of the wetlands are classified as salt marshes or transitional areas occurring where the water can range from near ocean levels of salinity to almost freshwater quality in upriver marshes. Despite these general characterizations, salt marshes in South Carolina are at the mercy of high and low tides, which causes rapid changes in water temperature, salinity, and depth. Animal and plant populations, then, must be able to withstand the sometimes rapid changes in the salt marshes. Like many natural communities across South Carolina, salt marshes depend on a delicate balance of conditions to thrive, and the state constantly strives to maintain and protect that balance. It is important to note that salt marshes have not always been considered important natural resources. Today fewer than half of the original salt marshes are left in the United States, with many of them being damaged and destroyed during the 1950s, 1960s, and 1970s. Because of the lack of value recognition, many of these marshes were filled in to create land for habitation, industry, and agriculture. Ditching for mosquito control and diking have also had a large impact on the marshes. The loss of marshes is a serious problem, affecting not only natural habitats for important flora and fauna but also the filter function that marshes naturally serve. With more than half of the nation's population living and working in coastal communities, the importance of marsh preservation cannot be underestimated.

Major protection efforts involving salt marshes and other critical natural communities headed by the state happen under the guidance and direction of the South Carolina Department of Health and Environmental Control (DHEC). In 1973, the state legislature combined the State Board of Health and the Pollution Control Authority. The mission statement—"promoting and protecting the health of the public and the environment"—testifies to the agency's dual purpose: to find the balance between the impact of development and the protection of environmental communities. The Office of Environmental Quality Control, as the regulatory division of the DHEC, consists of four major program plans: the Bureau of Air quality, the Bureau of Land and Waste Management, the Bureau of Water, and Ocean and Coastal Resource Management. Over 30 years of focus on both human and environment health and sustainability has given South Carolina an impressive portfolio of environmental action plans. In response to an ever-increasing population, South Carolina continues to rise to the challenges of environmental preservation and protection, continuing the fight for the longevity of its natural environment resources.

CONGAREE NATIONAL PARK

As home of the largest remaining old-growth floodplain forest on the continent, Congaree National Park functions as an outstanding example of vital and ongoing preservation efforts in an area of rare environmental significance. Congaree is also a designated wilderness area, an international biosphere reserve, and a globally important bird area, all of which emphasize this site's role in the larger ecosystem. Before it was a national park, it was first established as a natural national landmark and area of interest in 1974. The Congaree Swamp National Monument gained international biosphere reserve status in 1983. In 1988, it added wilderness area to its designations. In 1989, Hurricane Hugo swept through the area, snapping treetops and changing the natural landscape. Overall, though, the effects of the hurricane were beneficial. The removal of dense overgrowth allowed for expansion of undergrowth species, ultimately creating a healthier ecosystem. Fallen trees proved to be excellent sources of shelter for many plant and animal species, resulting in a more varied collection of microenvironments. By 2001, the monument had become a globally important bird area, and in 2003, it was added to the domain of the National Park Service as the nation's 57th park.

In support of this collection of official designations, the area's species diversity is outstanding. With more than 90 tree species, many of which hold state and national records for size, this level of diversity is unmatched by most areas of similar environmental character. The number of different tree types in this one national park equals half the number found in Europe as a whole. In addition to this dazzling array of species, the forest's health is exceptional. One sign of a healthy forest environment is the occurrence of downed trees. Naturally felled logs signify a normal cycle of growth, death, and decay.

The standing trees of the forest function as homes and feeding sites for many avian varieties, including all eight woodpecker species found in the Southeast. To support this unique collection of flora and fauna, periodic flooding of the swamp is necessary. The extent of cyclical flooding is dependent on the amount of rainfall that occurs upstream in the Saluda and the Broad rivers' watersheds. If the swamp floods 10 or more times a year, then the flooding cycle is functioning as it should to maintain the health of the forest. These recurring floodwaters deposit rich soil that holds many nutrients necessary to support the giant trees found throughout the forest. Although the park can be accessed on foot, the most dramatic paths through this fantastic landscape are traversed by canoe. The 18 miles of hiking trails and the park's marked canoe paths offer visitors to Congaree National Park unparalleled access to this rare and valuable old-growth forest treasure.

Further Reading

Franzreb, K.E. "Implications of Home-Range Estimation in the Management of Red-Cockaded Woodpeckers in South Carolina." *Forest Ecology and Management* 228 (2006): 274–84.

Friends of Congaree Swamp. *Images of Congaree National Park, Hopkins, South Carolina.* Manning, SC: Totally Outdoors Publishing, 2005.

FRANCIS BEIDLER FOREST

Located between Columbia and Charleston, Four Holes Swamp encompasses 45,000 acres of black water sloughs and lakes, bald cypress, tupelo gum flats, and bottomland hardwood expanses. Fifteen thousand acres of this land are owned by the National Audubon Society; that is the Francis Beidler Forest. The initial preservation goal was the protection of one of two remaining old-growth forest stands in the state (the other is in Congaree National Park). While its total old-growth acreage does not match that of Congaree, the forest does boast the largest virgin stands of bald cypress and tupelo gum in the world. Many of the bald cypress trees in the forest are close to 1,000 years old, with the oldest tree's age being estimated at 1,500 years. Public access to the site has been facilitated by the construction of a boardwalk, the maintenance of miles of hiking trails, and the marking of a canoe path. In addition to these common usage methods, Beidler Forest's staff offers a wide range of activities throughout the year to facilitate visitor access and education opportunities. For individuals and small groups, the self-guided tour is the way to go, but larger groups can take advantage of a guided tour that offers the expertise of a staff member to complement the natural experience. In spring, events include off-boardwalk treks into the swamp, bird walks, "wine and warbler" tours, and night ventures. Workshops and other education efforts often take center stage, offering a well-rounded complement of activities for visitors no matter where their interests, abilities, and experiences lie.

One unique outreach and education program at Francis Beidler Forest is the Great Backyard Bird Count (GBBC). This annual four-day event recruits bird enthusiasts of all ages to participate in creating a yearly image of the bird population of the North American continent as a whole. The 12th annual GBBC in 2009 showed a record completion of checklists totaling almost 10,000 submitted by volunteers. Led by the Cornell Lab of Ornithology and the National Audubon Society, "the GBBC provides the most detailed real-time snapshot of bird distribution across North America," according to Rob Fergus, a senior scientist with the National Audubon Society. The affects of changing migration patterns, feeding habits, and weather patterns can all be analyzed by creating a census count of the migrating bird populations each year. During this count, for example, the big story was the emergence of a massive invasion of pine siskins and white-winged crossbills throughout the eastern United States. Historically, these birds have wintered in Canada, but, as a result of seed crop failures there, the birds were forced to find a more resource-rich place to winter. The GBBC counts also show declines in species across the continent and has documented the emergence of new species over the years. Francis Beidler Forest, along with hundreds of other sites and thousands of other participants, plays an important role in recording and understanding the natural world of North America and the changes taking place in it.

This barred owl was wide awake and looking for crayfish along the boardwalk in Francis Beidler Forest. (Will Stuart)

The man for whom the forest is named demonstrates environmental dedication at its best, much like the programs the forest hosts today. In 1875, Francis Beidler was awarded a grant to explore western territory in the United States. One of his earliest natural experiences was witnessing the eruption of the geyser now known as Old Faithful. It forever affected Beidler and his views of the environment. From then on, Francis worked diligently as a champion of environmental preservation long before these ideas were commonplace, much less popular. Not only did he embrace the cause of natural conservation, he traveled to Europe in 1907 to become educated in forestry practices. He took what he learned there and applied the techniques to his own lands in South Carolina. Without his education and dedication, what South Carolina has today in the rich lands of Francis Beidler forest may not exist. There is no doubt that 100 years of conscious effort directed at protection of the old-growth forest as a valuable natural resource is predominantly, if not entirely, responsible for the forest's current health and outstanding level of natural sustainability.

Further Reading

Davis, Mary Byrd, ed. *Eastern Old-Growth Forests: Prospect for Rediscovery and Recovery.* Washington, DC: Island Press, 1996.

Mitsch, William J., and James G. Gosselink. *Wetlands*. Hoboken, NJ: Wiley, 2007.

OCONEE STATE PARK

Oconee State Park sits in the Blue Ridge foothills of South Carolina. The park's facilities were constructed during the Great Depression by the Civilian Conservation Corps, so for more than 70 years, the park's easy hiking trails, cabins, and campgrounds have been attracting visitors of all ages. Although the site is only about 1,100 acres, its pristine lands and diverse wildlife offer a wealth of natural experiences in a small but beautiful package. Oconee State Park is the southern trailhead for the Foothills Trail, an 80-mile trek along the Blue Ridge escarpment all the way up to Table Rock. Additionally, the park is next to both the Chattooga and the Chauga rivers, along which many enjoy white-water rafting and fishing. Activity choices at Oconee and Table Rock offer something for everyone. Mountain birding is a popular pastime and is capstoned each year with the celebration of International Migratory Birding Day, when participants are educated on the 300 migratory bird species that cross North America each year. For early risers, a sunrise hike to Table Rock offers an unmatched opportunity to see the Blue Ridge Mountains at their finest. A unique historical-based offering includes a frontier encampment experience in which the staff offer educational experiences based on the area's history as a frontier outpost following the American Revolution. Period reenactments include rope making, cooking presentations, and black powder demonstrations. Local culture plays a role in the area's personality and experiences as music aficionados can immerse themselves in traditional bluegrass music at the Table Rock Lodge.

One of the most attractive natural highlights of the park is its position as the southern trailhead for the Foothills Trail. It begins at Oconee State Park and runs to Table Rock State Park. A spur trail then connects Caesars Head to Jones Gap State Park, completing over 80 miles of breathtaking hiking. The most striking feature of the trail is that it takes trekkers along the Blue Ridge Escarpment, the geological location where the southern Appalachian Mountains end and the Piedmont begins. In just a few miles, the elevation drops by more than 2,000 feet. There is more to the trail than the vast scenery, though. A wide variety of plant and animal species inhabit the lands surrounding the trail. Six major rivers drain into the area, as well. The trail crosses the highest point in South Carolina and passes one of the tallest waterfalls in the southeastern United States. One of the largest black bear populations in the country roams the surrounding forests of Jocassee Gorge. Rare plant species abound, and the history of the trail is riveting. Maintained by the Foothills Trail Conference, the organization publishes a guidebook to help adventurers plan excursions along its massive length. Few other outdoor retreats in North America can match the magic offered by this rich recreation opportunity.

Further Reading
De Hart, Allen. *Hiking South Carolina Trails*. San Ramon, CA: Falcon, 2001.
South Carolina Department of Parks, Recreation and Tourism. "South Carolina State Parks: Oconee State Park." http://www.southcarolinaparks.com/park-finder/state-park/750.aspx.

PEACHTREE ROCK HERITAGE PRESERVE

A unique preservation site in South Carolina is Peachtree Rock Heritage Preserve. It is an interesting area for its natural environments and its geological history and significance. The preserve's name comes from an unusual sandstone formation immediately visible as visitors enter the park. It is an upside down triangle of rock that stands about 20 feet tall and is the result of erosion wearing away the softer rock and sand in the lower levels and leaving the harder sandstone toward the top. Weathering, erosion, and ancient shore deposits have all added to the geological character of the area. Now sitting 15 miles outside the town of Lexington, Peachtree Rock once was part of the ancient shoreline during the Eocene Epoch 60 million years ago. The abundance of marine fossil evidence at the site was deposited by ocean wave action washing over the area, leaving behind the fossilized material, beachlike sand, and intertidal deposits. The surrounding lands are comprised of Eocene sands, Miocene river deposits, and Pleistocene sand dunes. The ancient character of the geography is unavoidable. Evidence of ancient marine life survives in the form of marine fossils and burrows in the rock created by the myriad life forms that swam this region million of years ago. The vandalism that has taken place on the rock and other formations throughout the site detract from the beauty as well as the scientific study viability, but much still remains to inspire those who venture into this ancient landscape.

The preserve encompasses almost 500 acres of land and contains not only the ancient rock formations described above but also a swamp tupelo-evergreen shrub bog, a longleaf pine ecosystem, and the only waterfall in the coastal plains area. In this relatively small area, more than 250 plant species have been documented. There a wide diversity in the plants appearing here, and the nature of these species varies greatly. In the valley near the waterfall, the wet soils host mountain laurel, tulips, and yellow poplar, while the drier soils on the ridge are populated by pines and turkey oak. There are occurrences of the federally endangered Rayner's blueberry growing on the seepage slopes within the longleaf pine forest. Species of salamander, skink, and beetle thrive in the undergrowth, while avian varieties of chickadee, titmouse, cardinal, and woodpecker roam the upper reaches of the forested areas. In partnership with the South Carolina Department of Natural Resources, this area is comanaged by the Nature Conservancy of South Carolina to protect what remains of the site's geological history while preserving the vast amount of natural diversity found here. Some efforts involve restoration activities. In 2007, 70 acres of exotic slash pine were removed, and the naturally occurring longleaf pine was planted as the replacement species. Prescribed burning was introduced in 2008 to encourage the growth of diverse flora species. While several hiking trails provide access to the preserve's interesting scenery and natural environments, the site itself is relatively undeveloped. There are no paved roads, no picnic tables, no restrooms, no trash cans, and camping is not permitted. Visitors must be prepared to take responsibility for maintaining Peachtree Rock Preserve's natural beauty and state of existence. As an area protected in its true natural state, it depends on the diligence of visitors and volunteers alike to remain that way.

Further Reading

Colquhoun, J. Donald, Paul F. Huddlestun, Paul G. Nystrom, and Jean Burn. "Stratigraphy of Peachtree Rock Preserve." *South Carolina Geology* 29, no. 1 (1985): 1–7.

SANDY ISLAND PRESERVE

This island is located between the Waccamaw and the Great Pee Dee rivers, and it is the largest undeveloped area left in the Waccamaw Neck. At more than 9,000 acres, the island is a true natural treasure of South Carolina and a treat to visit. No bridge, however, exists to facilitate visiting the island. Instead, there are four public boat landings near the island on both the Pee Dee and the Waccamaw rivers. With its diverse collection of natural environments, the island offers visitors the opportunity to explore a complex of wetland and upland communities. Combined with this natural trove are the remnants of rice plantation conversion from the 1800s. A few impoundments and water control structures remain in testimony to the human presence that once inhabited the area. Although the island is open for daylight visitation, there are many restrictions on public activities, including the prohibition against picking or collecting any piece of the natural landscape, from flowers and berries to rocks and shells. Camping, fires, and cookouts are also on the restrictedlist. Motorized vehicles, bicycles, and horses are not allowed, and the feeding of wild animals is strictly controlled. Additionally, there are no trash disposal areas, so it is important that visitors be prepared to take their own garbage. Limited hunting is allowed, but it is controlled by the Wildlife Management Area Agreement, and the specific rules and regulations regarding these activities are available through the South Carolina Department of Natural Resources. Visitors must also be careful to respect the rights of private landowners whose tracts are adjacent to the preserve. To the southeast of the park are privately owned parcels; to the north, the lands are federally controlled; and to the southeast is the Exchange Plantation, a conservation easement. The rest of the surrounding areas are urban developments, making the island a small natural haven in the midst of human habitation and land utilization.

As far as the natural community types are concerned, the island hosts a variety of environments. The uplands, which cover about half of the island, host plant collections common to sandhills regions as well as outer coastal plains. Mature longleaf pine dominates the uplands, and, consequently, fire is an important part of the northern area's natural management. The periodic burns on the island protect and encourage health, quality, and diversity in the longleaf pine forests. On the south end of the island, fire is repressed, and, as a result, turkey oak dominates that part of the landscape. Several rare species such as the continentally rare red-cockaded woodpecker call these forests home. A visitor in the right place at the right time might even observe a black bear utilizing the island as a travel corridor. With total island preservation in mind, the Nature Conservancy of South Carolina, which now owns the island, works to manage the longleaf pine forests using the periodic prescribed burn method. The invasion of feral hogs is a concern, and many efforts focus on relocating and controlling this disruptive force of nature. Amphibian and reptile populations are also closely monitored in the overall effort to preserve the island in as close to a natural state as possible.

There is a cultural tie-in to the preservation of this area, as well. As mentioned, there are no bridges connecting the island to the mainland, so trips into town, school attendance, and other daily activities are facilitated by boat travel. This reality has been fought for by the residents of the islands for years. The Gullah communities of the South Carolina coast have a long and often sad history with the area. After Emancipation, freed slave communities developed all along this area and existed self-sustainingly for almost 100 years. Once development began in the mid-1900s, these traditional villages and ways of life began to disappear. But there is one exception where the native Gullah community teamed up with environmental experts to save their piece of land and way of life, and that was at Sandy Island in South Carolina. The first major push to develop Sandy Island came in 1996, when the proposal to build an access bridge—largely to transport cut timber—emerged. Sandy Island residents, after observing the effects of development on other local African American communities, teamed up with environmental experts to block development efforts. The people needed to make informed decisions about their community and the surrounding natural environment, and, over the next few years, that is exactly what they did. Creative thinking and adventurous solutions helped preserve this valuable piece of cultural and natural history for generations to come.

Further Reading

Pyatt, Thomas. *The Gullah People of Sandy Island: A Tribute to the Gullah People of Sandy Island, SC*. Sandy Island, SC: Pyatt, 2005.

Saving Sandy Island. Videorecording, Written and produced by Betsy Newman. Columbia: South Carolina ETV, 2008.

WASHO RESERVE AND THE SANTEE COASTAL RESERVE

The adjacent Washo Reserve and the Santee Coastal Reserve work in tandem to protect their natural communities. The main focus of Washo Reserve is a 200-year-old cypress lake and cypress gum swamp that is home to the oldest continually used wading bird rookery on the continent. Of special importance are the many nesting ospreys that utilize the area. Their sheer numbers make this rookery one of the largest concentrations of ospreys in the eastern United States. By far the most unique attraction of the reserve is the vast array of majestic birds that live in the rookery, but there are other natural characteristics worth observing and experiencing. The maritime live oak and slash pine forest is the dominant environmental system for the coastal plain. Swamp tupelo, bald cypress, and black gum stands dot the landscape, but the live oak–slash pine mix is the most outstanding forest type. Within these stands live a variety of plant and animal species. Wood storks, bald eagles, and swallow-tailed kites make their homes among the branches. The longleaf pine habitats also attract red-cockaded woodpeckers, Bachman's sparrows, and brown-headed nuthatches to their sustenance-rich environments. Over-whelmingly, though, this site's importance rests on its function as a major wading bird rookery, which is what prompted the Nature Conservancy of South Carolina to acquire the land. In 1974, the Santee Gun Club donated 24,000 acres that would become the Santee Coastal Reserve, completing the area necessary for effective preservation efforts. Most of the property now falls under the jurisdiction of the South Carolina Department of Natural Resources, but the Washo Reserve remains under the direction of the South Carolina chapter of the Nature Conservancy. The cooperation between the two organi-zations allows for effective prescribed burns, managed aquatic vegetation, and monitored rare bird populations.

As part of this matrix of natural preservation, the Santee Coastal Reserve is a great birding spot, as well, although the focus is not so much on wading birds as it is in Washo Reserve. It boasts three main habitats that support avian life: old-growth longleaf pine forest, freshwater swamp, and freshwater and brackish marshland. The longleaf forests host many red-cockaded woodpeckers and Bachman's sparrows, while a trek into the swamp leads to a large heron rookery. Venturing out into the marshes offers the opportu-nity to observe ducks, shorebirds, rails, and other wetland species. The variety in this one accessible area will please any nature and birding enthusiast. To ensure the quality and survival of these varied and important environments, several restoration projects are un-derway at the Santee Coastal Reserve. First is the Cape Unit Restoration Project, which involves the restoration of 500 acres of tidal marsh in the reserve through the renovation of an existing dike. High tides, storm surges, and boat wakes have caused intermittent flooding from the Atlantic Intracoastal Waterway, and, by raising the level of the dike, it is hoped that Santee can be protected from some of these threatening forces. The tidal brackish marshes can only absorb so much extra water before their habitats become imperiled, and the marsh vegetation, along with the many duck varieties that live in the marsh, depend on its delicate brackish balance for survival. Another 150 acres of brack-ish marsh are threatened, and efforts to shore up resources northeast of McClellanville, South Carolina, along the South Santee River aim to protect this valuable habitat in much the same way. This tidal impoundment requires the construction of internal cross-dikes, spillway structures, and rice field trunks to facilitate flood control and drainage activity. The cross-dikes will contain the overflow of lowlands while restricting threaten-ing floodwaters. The exterior dikes have degraded and are no longer sufficient protection against the flooding that happens every year. When water channeling is needed, the spillways will provide paths for water drainage. Long, narrow wooden boxes with doors at each end—the rice trunks—can be utilized to selectively direct excess water away from areas it could harm. By dividing the area into five cells and addressing each land parcel as a separate management issue, the hope is that valuable wetland areas will be restored and preserved for species that depend on this region to survive.

Further Reading

Reynolds, Julius M. J., and M. Reynolds. *Sunrise on the Santee: A Memoir of Waterfowling in South Carolina.* Columbia: University of South Carolina Press, 2002.

Sanders, Albert E., and William D. Anderson. *Natural History Investigations in South Carolina from Colonial Times to the Present.* Columbia: University of South Carolina Press, 1999.

Zepke, Terrance. *Coastal South Carolina: Welcome to the Lowcountry.* Sarasota, FL: Pineapple Press, 2006.

TENNESSEE

Because it sits along a mountain ridge line, Tennessee's eastern half very much resembles its neighboring states to the south, Georgia and Alabama. The western half, however, resembles northern Mississippi and a large part of Kentucky more than it does the border states to the east or south. Tennessee shares the southeastern plains and Mississippi Valley loess plains with Mississippi, containing the northern reaches of these ecoregions. The areas shared with the states to the north, however, make up the heart of Tennessee: the ridge and valley lands, the southwestern and central Appalachians, and the interior plateau region. The ridge and valley ecoregion sits sandwiched between higher, rugged mountains to either side. Historically, the area experienced extreme faulting and folding activities, leaving parallel ridges and valleys of varying widths, heights, and materials in their wake. Springs and caves dot the region, which today holds a 50 percent forest cover. The southwestern and central Appalachians that sit to the east played a large role in defining the ridges and valleys. The southwestern area consists of relatively low-lying, open mountains with scattered forests, croplands, and pastures. The southern tip of the central Appalachians is higher in altitude and more rugged, with a cooler climate and infertile soils. Although this results in less agricultural activity, there has been more coal mining in this area, which often negatively affects the natural aquatic environments of mountain streams and lakes. Adjacent to this rugged region is Tennessee's interior plateau of open hills, plains, and tablelands. Both flora and fauna populations show immense diversity across this area that covers much of the state, with environments ranging from oak and hickory forests to bluestem prairies and cedar glades.

The Tennessee Department of Environment and Conservation oversees many conservation and restoration efforts across the state. According to the first Annual Summit for a Sustainable Tennessee, the state's "economy and population are growing, and although there are a myriad of benefits that come with this growth, there are also many costs to [Tennessee's] natural heritage, public health, and shared sense of civic life." The average land loss in Tennessee is more than 80,000 acres per year, ranking the state seventh in the United States when considering commercial and residential development. The organizers of the first summit in 2007 brought together environmental and community partners to find commonalities and create partnerships that could lead to a sustainable future. The Tennessee Environmental Council (TEC) and Tennessee Conservation Voters joined forces to assemble a gathering that would best represent a cross-section of Tennessee's communities, both human and environmental. In 1973, the TEC hosted what would become known as the Tennessee Environmental Congress. Because the congress would take place on a yearly basis, it provided a platform for issue-specific workshops and a foundation for a statewide environmental agenda involving governmental and legislative action. Building on the TEC's 30-year history of environmental activism and protection, the congress hoped to create a far-reaching collaborative partnership of environmentally interested parties. The TEC accomplished much, such as protecting the Great Smoky Mountains, cleaning up the Pigeon River, preventing degradation of the Rumbling Falls Cave system, and reducing pollution from the Tennessee Valley Authority's coal-fired power plants. By creating statewide partnerships, such environmental gains would be easier to perpetuate, resulting in a more sustainable Tennessee.

One current effort of the TEC focuses on trees as an important component of community environments. The Urban Community Forest Initiative (UCFI) aims to repopulate deforested areas that threaten ecosystems as well as public health. Trees anchor and fertilize the soil and provide important habitats for flora and fauna. Especially important is the direct benefit to human communities. The Urban Tree Initiative argues that, in addition to their important economic role, trees are emotionally beneficial to humans as well. Environmentally, as much as 60 percent of air particulate matter can be filtered by tree growth. Socially, it is even suggested that in areas with more trees, there is less crime. The initiative's plan is to work with homeowners associations across the state to begin the restoration of urban forests. Once the reforestation takes hold, the UCFI will help communities develop protection plans to ensure the permanency of restored natural areas. This is only one of many programs instigated by the TEC in the long-term effort to restore and maintain Tennessee's natural health and value. By addressing issues of air and water quality, land use, toxic substance handling, reforestation, and questions concerning green construction, the Tennessee Environmental Council has provided the foundation for a sustainable future for many of Tennessee's natural habitats.

CLINCH RIVER

The Clinch River begins its journey in southwestern Virginia and then winds its way through the Great Appalachian Valley, combining with several tributaries along the way to end up in eastern Tennessee. Along its 135 miles, the Clinch River hosts the largest variety of freshwater mussels of any river in the world. Unfortunately, this variety has been greatly reduced by human presence and interaction of the years. Before being dammed, the river was one of the largest harvesting grounds for freshwater mussels and pearls. This industry was dealt a death blow by the Tennessee Valley Authority's construction of dams during the Great Depression, which drastically changed the natural aquatic environment, which subsequently reduced mussel numbers and pearl output. More recently, coal-fired power plants and mining activity have introduced harmful pollution into the waters, endangering the fragile habitat of the river. Today the river still has more than 50 mussel species and at least 100 nongame fish, which support the varied aquatic life collection. This includes the many sport fish varieties that attract fishing enthusiasts from across the country.

The portion of the Clinch River that functions as part of the headwaters of the Tennessee River is the only ecologically intact section. This valuable preserve area boasts over 30 federally endangered or threatened species between the valley lands and the river itself. Concerns over preservation must, however, address the fact that human communities of the area have important concerns and considerations of their own. High unemployment and economic instability characterize many of the local populations. Preserving and protecting the environment must include plans that balance the needs of the towns scattered throughout the area. Sustainable economic utilization of the Clinch River and valley must be at the top of the goal list. In 1990, the Nature Conservancy included the Clinch and the Powell rivers' watersheds in their Last Great Places program.

Clinch River. (Alan Cressler)

This conservation effort is a joint venture of the Virginia and Tennessee chapters of the Nature Conservancy. With a current ownership of seven tracts of land across the valley region, additional acquisitions are planned over the next five years to complete preservation efforts. Some of the plan's actions include the creation of citizens' initiatives that focus on sustainable growth and the purchase and renovation of a 100-year-old church that serves as a community center, historical archive, and environmental information center. An important element of the program is creating officially protected areas where they are most needed. There are additional issues that must be addressed, though, in order to assure the achievement of long-term protection goals. Funding for restoration and preservation activities must be secure. Local and visiting populations must support and understand the reasoning behind the many plans and actions taken. Management strategies must constantly be evaluated and strengthened. Overall, without these coordinated efforts, preservation of important watersheds such as the Clinch River and its surrounding valley not only falters but often fails.

Further Reading

Fulgham, Richard Lee. *Appalachian Genesis: The Clinch River Valley from Prehistoric Times to the End of the Frontier Era.* Johnson City, TN: Overmountain Press, 2000.

Kilgore, Frank, and Stacy Fowler Horton. *The Clinch River: A World-Class Treasure.* St. Marys, WV: Mountain Heritage Books, 2007.

CUMBERLAND TRAIL STATE PARK

"Experience Tennessee hiking and backpacking at its best! The Cumberland Trail (CT) . . . became Tennessee's 53rd state park in 1998. The Justin P. Wilson Cumberland Trail State Park will contain a core corridor of three hundred-plus miles of trail . . . [and] this protected greenway will act as a buffer to protect water quality and provide natural habitat." This opening statement by the Cumberland Trail Conference's guide to the Cumberland Trail could not be more clear. Combining the goals of recreation access and natural conservation is a common theme across the country. In this case, the planning and execution of the Cumberland Trail route has targeted hikers and outdoor enthusiasts. The winning combination that has resulted in the Cumberland Trail is so successful because it was *designed* by hikers and nature enthusiasts, as well. The CT was and continues to be constructed and maintained mostly by volunteers whose efforts are managed by the nonprofit Cumberland Trail Conference (CTC), among other individuals and organizations. Along its 300 miles, hikers can access wildlife management areas, a national ark wild and scenic area, two state parks, two state natural areas, and two national parks. It is rare that one concerted effort can successfully connect so many geographically diverse areas. While being functional and inviting, specific care has been taken to ensure that the impact of human access is minimized to protect delicate habitats, unique environments, and threatened species. The very act of facilitating controlled recreational access brings watershed protection, wildlife conservation, and biosphere preservation to these remotely accessible, innately valuable natural areas.

It all began in the 1960s with the idea of constructing a hiking trail that would trace the eastern escarpment of the Cumberland Plateau, and, by 1968, the formation of the first organization that would play an instrumental role in the trail's development was complete. The Tennessee Trails Association was formed. The seeds of the trail then emerged in the early 1970s with the establishment of the Cumberland Trail State Scenic Trail. Work continued and more organizations joined the effort, with one of the most recent additions to the consortium being the Cumberland Trail Conference. The CTC, to this point, has documented more than 85,000 hours of volunteer time dedicated to trail development over the last six years. The very tangible result of this massive work effort is the construction of over 150 miles of trail. The Cumberland Trail is halfway there. The CTC continues to focus on trail building and maintenance with the Friends of the Cumberland Trail organization supporting park needs, historical research, resource management, equipment demands, and visitor facilities. A site of this scope and size requires a variety of efforts coming from many directions in order to not only continue expansion of the trail but also adequately maintain what has already been constructed.

The state park borders sections of what will become the 300-mile trail when completed, functioning as a buffer zone between human presence and trail sustainability. The establishment of these public lands is supposed to protect the environmental integrity and recreational appeal of this vast natural resource. These preservation goals are noble; however, when the state acquired these lands, most of the area was acquired without mineral rights. In 2007, the company that still owned the mineral rights in a section of the park called Deep Creek Gorge decided to employ bulldozers and front-end loaders in the removal of sandstone rock for the purpose of selling it to builders and landscapers. Acres of natural habitat were destroyed, and almost 100 yards of the Cumberland Trail were buried under debris in the process. At this point, the Southern Environmental Law Center (SELC) stepped in and combined forces with more than one dozen local, state, and national groups in an effort to contain the destruction and prevent further alteration of naturally valuable lands surrounding the Cumberland Trail. These limited lands, though, are not the only protection goal. Four hundred and fifty thousand acres in Tennessee, 28,000 of which are state parks and natural areas, suffer of the same kind of split in ownership of surface ground rights and mineral rights. After fighting negative rulings for more than a year, the Tennessee Court of Appeals agreed with the position of the SELC and its partner organizations. The contention was that rock should not be included in mineral rights access because the remove of the rock destroys the viability of the surface rights owners' property, meaning the land itself. The court stated that "basic common sense and equity" rightfully led to the conclusion that mineral rights owners cannot deny surface rights owners the use of surface property. The fight, however, is not over, and, as organizations continue to join the suit against mineral rights owners, there is more action that must be taken to prevent the detrimental removal of rock from state parks, wilderness areas, and wildlife preserves. Although the struggle may seem to never end, significant gains have been made, and precedent continues to be established, which strengthens the position of conservation efforts in Tennessee and around the country.

Further Reading

Andrews, Richard N.L. *Managing the Environment, Managing Ourselves: A History of American Environmental Policy.* New Haven, CT: Yale University Press, 2006.

Markham, Doug. *Boxes, Rockets, and Pens: A History of Wildlife Recovery in Tennessee.* Knoxville: University of Tennessee Press, 1997.

HUBBARD'S CAVE

As one of several sites in Tennessee that is owned by the state's Nature Conservancy chapter, Hubbard's Cave is rather unique in character and supports a rare, distinctive natural habitat that houses two of the country's rarest bat species. The gray bat and the Indiana bat find the conditions of this cave's environment perfectly conducive to hibernation. As the largest gray bat hibernaculum in Tennessee, there have been more than 100,000 bats documented in the cave complex, for example, which testifies to the cave's perfect suitability as a bat refuge. These two species, however, are not the only bat varieties that call the cave home. Many different bat types find the conditions ideally appropriate for their needs. Because of the accessibility of the cave, it has been necessary to install gates to keep visitors out during the hibernation period. All bats are extremely sensitive to disturbance during their hibernation period because they need every bit of fat reserve to get them through the winter. Any flying, any activity at all, risks their survival through the season. This makes the addition of gates to these delicate environments extremely important to ensure the survival of the hibernating colonies.

Even though the site is only 50 acres, its biological significance, combined with the role it has played in local area human history as well as prehistory, vastly outweighs its relatively small size. Human intervention has left its mark on the environment. During the Civil War, for example, it was mined heavily for saltpeter nitrate used to produce gunpowder. The mound used to grind the gunpowder still exists. The men who worked this mine left signatures as a historical testimony to their presence, with many dating back to the early 1800s. Unfortunately, modern graffiti has covered many of these signatures, obscuring a unique historical record. Evidence of human use, though, reaches much further back; torches have been found in the cave that that are 2,000 years old. Hubbard Cave is very much a part of the long human history of the area as much as it is a part of the natural character of the land.

The cave's major role in helping define that local natural character is as a hibernation haven for hundreds of thousands of migrating bats. At one point, over four million bats were recorded as wintering in the cave. The Nature Conservancy suggests that there may be no other cave in North America that supports this level of bat species diversity and that the wintering population numbers at Hubbard are some of the highest in the world. Out of the seven regularly reappearing species, the gray bat and the Indiana bat hold the most significance. In just over 20 years of ownership, the threatened gray bat's local wintering census has grown from 50,000 individuals to more than 500,000 today. The gates placed at the three openings to the cave have gone a long way in protecting wintering bat populations, as these dramatic population increases prove. At many bat sites, improper gating has caused some significant damage to the resident individuals. If gates are improperly constructed or installed, they can prevent the bats' access to the cave. More subtly, they can alter the air flow, temperature, humidity, and amount of light, all of which can drive hibernating colonies away because of their dependence on a delicate balance of environmental factors to make it through the winter. Another challenge is flooding that has resulted from both reservoir construction and natural forces, which forces these large bat colonies to seek other shelter. It is difficult for them to find caves that can support their large population numbers in their relatively limited southeastern range. Gray bats were placed on the federally endangered wildlife list in 1976, beginning the long chain of events that would raise awareness and ultimately action responses to the dangers facing these unique creatures. The measures are working, and, although there is still a long way to go, Hubbard Cave has definitely played a central role in reestablishing stable gray bat communities, much to the benefit of the ecosystem of which they are such an integral part.

Further Reading
DiSilvestro, Roger P. *The Endangered Kingdom: The Struggle to Save America's Wildlife*. Hoboken, NJ: Wiley, 1991.
Graham, Gary L. *Bats of the World*. New York: Golden Guides from St. Martin's Press, 2001.

OBED WILD AND SCENIC RIVER

The Obed Wild and Scenic River has changed little since the early days of European exploration. The area did not attract white settlement like some other areas of the country, largely due to its nutrient-poor soil. Fishing and hunting, however, were popular along the river because of its rich aquatic and land animal species populations. As an outstanding representation of what the Cumberland Plateau environment has looked like for hundreds of years, the Obed River and its surrounding lands offer valuable, unique opportunities for people to interact with a relatively untouched natural environment. Visitors can take advantage of the wildlife and environment experiences through the traditional methods of hiking and camping, and, seasonally, white-water paddling is available to those who wish to experience the park from a different perspective. There are no commercial guides, however, that operate on the Obed. Instead, boaters need to be experienced in class V white-water rafting as well as have a solid knowledge of white-water rescue. The natural state of the river provides outstanding environmental experiences for the educated and the careful but also harbors dangers for those treading in unknown territory. Primitive camping is available, but experience and preparation are necessary. Rock climbing offers further exciting opportunities, but, like the many other available adventures, those choosing to partake must do so with caution, making intelligent plans and activity choices along the way.

As mentioned, the history of the river reaches back over many hundreds of years, and, due to inhospitable settlement conditions of the area's geography, humans have maintained little long-term presence in and use of the region. This means that human interference and impact are low in comparison to many rivers across the country. Being designated a national park in 1976 solidified protection of the park as a natural national treasure, and it is possible to see what the land would have look and felt like centuries ago. Native American tribes lived in the region from about 1400 to the 1800s, but European incursion, fighting, and disease greatly reduced their numbers and eventually eliminated their presence. As a rule, despite their hundreds' of years of residence, the Native American impact on the lands in which they resided was often minimal and rarely permanent. Early white presence left little mark, as well. After European explorers and eventually hunters and trappers traversed the Obed area, however, came more settlement-oriented groups of people. It was as this point that more change to the environment begin to occur. Log cabins and land clearing became more common. By the time of the Civil War, though, homesteaders were more spread out. This paved the way for industry to move in, bringing gristmills to the Obed watershed. Flooding was a constant threat, however, eventually driving even this human presence away. The result is some of the most natural lands in the Southeast, an area that has been historically heavily settled and utilized by a constant influx of people.

Obed Wild and Scenic River. (J. Stephen Conn)

In addition to the vast protection resources offered by the National Park Service, the Obed Watershed Community Association (OWCA) lends its efforts to help protect the natural and cultural heritage of the Obed River watershed. Community education, research projects, conservation activity, and best management practices all play a role in the overall plan of execution for the area's preservation. Part of this plan includes a stream recovery project. Four streams in the area have been identified as impaired by the United States Environmental Protection Agency. This means that there are situations that are directly affecting the health of the stream and its natural inhabitants. The list may not remain limited to these four, because several other waterways are under consideration because of their declining health. The OWCA's Stream Monitoring and Restoration Project identifies the sources of the problems and works with private landowners, city officials, county agencies, and nonprofit organizations to restore and maintain the natural health of these endangered waterways. Grants will help pay for desperately needed repairs to the streams and surrounding lands. Intervention now is of the utmost importance, because the city of Crossville and the county of Cumberland are growing rapidly. Agricultural and forest lands are being converted for commercial and residential use. Developed lands do not allow for necessary rainwater absorption that replenishes the watershed. Well and stream content levels then suffer. The overarching goal is primarily an educational one, but before adequate instructive materials can be developed, a better understanding of threats and consequences must be attained. By combining previously completed research with recent observations and testing, a more complete picture of where the streams have been ecologically speaking, as well as where they are headed when it comes to sustainable health, will emerge.

Further Reading

Cushing, Colbert E., and Arthur C. Benke. *Rivers of North America*. New York: Academic Press, 2005.

Manning, Russ. *The Historic Cumberland Plateau: An Explorer's Guide*. Knoxville: University of Tennessee Press, 1999.

SHADY VALLEY PROGRAM

The broad bowl of lush, green fields ringed by the Blue Ridge Mountains is the expanse called Shady Valley. Sitting at almost 3,000 feet, this valley functioned as something of a safe haven for many plant and animal species during the last ice age. Its geographical position and elevation make it suited as a natural preserve for unique biosphere compositions. When the ice eventually retreated, left behind were wetland bogs fed by local streams and creeks. In 1978, the Tennessee chapter of the Nature Conservancy came into the picture and began actions directed at protecting the land and water resources of Shady Valley. Within Shady Valley are four preserves controlled by the conservancy: two wetlands called Orchard Bog and Quarry Bog, Schoolyard Springs, and the

John R. Dickey Birch Branch Sanctuary. Because of this diversity of preserve character, several types of projects are underway within the Shady Valley Program. One involves stream and wetland restoration. In the program, over 200 acres of restored wetlands and streams are constantly monitored and managed by the state's Nature Conservancy chapter. Another plan in action is the tracking of the local bog turtle population. This is the only place in Tennessee where North America's smallest turtle species still lives in its natural, wild environment. The monitoring shows that wetland restoration has not only expanded the turtles' range, it seems to have contributed to the promulgation of the species. One plant-focused initiative is the effort to bring back the red spruce to the valley. Historic land clearing took its toll on the massive numbers of red spruce in Shady Valley, and, by 2005, there was only *one* mature tree with seedling cones left standing. Staff members collected the seeds, and today young red spruce are growing across the preserve. The forth major program focuses on another unique plant inhabitant, the native cranberry. High elevation and cool temperatures create the perfect conditions for wild cranberry growth, and Shady Valley has that in abundance. The Shady Valley Ruritan Club created a nursery to shelter cuttings from a dwindling native plant population. Once the plants reach a mature stage of growth, club volunteers will transplant the sprouts into Orchard Bog Preserve so that they can benefit from the conservancy's restoration and preservation efforts already underway. In conjunction with these programs, each preserve offers unique characteristics and challenges to ensuring the survival of species and inhabitants.

Each of the preserves deserves a look at its individual needs and personality. Orchard Bog and Quarry Bog are rare examples of peat wetlands that once thrived across the planet. The end of the last ice age left the valley with rare bog environments that are more commonly found further to the north. While Orchard Bog is currently open for visitation, access to Quarry Bog is restricted to allow staff to focus on intensive restoration activities. Over the last 100 years, peat systems have been drained in order to use them for agricultural and livestock purposes. As a result, few examples of these important wetlands remain. The Orchard and Quarry Bogs are not only considered rare environments in Tennessee, but also when compared to the worldwide occurrence of these important wetland systems. The third system of the four is Schoolyard Springs. This small, 22-acre preserve harbors many rare plants that have thrived in this environment left by the wake of ice age recession. The sandy springs support an apparently endless flow of fresh water coming out of the springs. When the was even smaller, at only nine acres, the conservancy constructed a boardwalk to allow access and appreciation of this unique southeast habitat sphere. The John R. Dickey Birch Branch Sanctuary is open year-round from dawn to dusk and is the most easily accessible of the conservation sites that make up the Shady Valley Program. By far the largest of the four, at over 450 acres, the sanctuary works toward preserving the natural beauty and diversity of the area and aims to restore native warm-season grasses that provide nutritional resources and appropriate habitats for a variety of game birds, songbirds, and butterflies. Visitors to Shady Valley will not be disappointed, no matter what their environmental interests are; the program truly offers something for everyone interested in venturing out into the wild.

Further Reading

Pielou, E. C. *After the Ice Age: The Return of Life to Glaciated North America.* Chicago: University of Chicago Press, 1992.

Rydin, Hakan, and John K. Jeglum. *The Biology of Peatlands.* New York: Oxford University Press, 2006.

TAPOCO PROJECT

One of the larger areas of preservation activity in Tennessee is the Tapoco Project, which is next to the Great Smoky Mountains along with the Citico and Joyce Kilmer Wilderness Areas. Twenty-one rare or endangered species inhabit the land, along with a wide range of amphibians, birds, mammals, fish, reptiles, and plants, creating an amazing, extensive local biosphere. The management goal of the Nature Conservancy, the entity behind the establishment of the Tapoco Project, includes the acquisitions of many surrounding lands and ultimate transfer of those areas to other organizations. In 2008, the conservancy purchased almost 6,000 acres that had been under a conservation easement for four years and almost immediately gave control of the region to the U.S. Forest Service, the National Park Service, and the Tennessee Wildlife Resources Agency. The other 4,000 acres are currently protected under conservation easements, but the ultimate plans involve transfer of these acres to the Smoky Mountains National Park and the Cherokee National Forest. Although restoration and preservation are the overriding goals of all Nature Conservancy chapters, the final step of land management often includes transferring major tracts to the control of public organizations, ensuring that public access will be protected and maintained for generations to come.

Conservation and land acquisition involves the complicated efforts of many entities, both public and private. In May 2004, a group of over 150 stakeholders assembled for the signing of an agreement for the continued operation of four dams owned by ALCOA Power, a subsidiary of ALCOA Aluminum, the world's largest producer of many aluminum products. Five years of negotiation and compromise had led the company and many interested parties to this point. Among other issues and concerns, the protection of nearly 10,000 acres of undeveloped forest land were at the center of the agreement's concerns. Ultimately, this cooperation produced what has been called a "win-win-win" for everyone involved. Industry, environmental groups, and government agencies all came out ahead. This 10,000-acre bridge between the Great Smoky Mountains National Park and the Cherokee National Forest is now forever managed and protected under the Tapoco Program with the goal of eventual full administration by the National Park Service and others who specialize in maintaining the balance between human access and natural preservation. This rare and beautiful tract of land will be around for many years to come because those with the interest and the power were willing to work together to achieve an equitable solution for everyone involved.

Further Reading
Homan, Tim, and Vicky Holifield. *Hiking Trails of Joyce Kilmer-Slickrock and Citico Creek Wildernesses*. Atlanta, GA: Peachtree, 2007.
Manning, Russ. *40 Hikes in Tennessee's South Cumberland*. Seattle: Mountaineers Books, 2000.

TAYLOR HOLLOW

Taylor Hollow is classified as a class II natural-scientific state natural area. The Tennessee Department of Environment and Conservation (TDEC) has a vested interest in the almost 200-acre preserve owned by the Tennessee chapter of the Nature Conservancy. Located in Sumner County on the western Highland Rim, the site is described by the TDEC as "a botanically rich and a biologically diverse area that is one of only a very few areas remaining like this in Middle Tennessee that has been minimally impacted by human activity." Taylor Hollow's forest environment is considered old growth, although, in the past, there may have been some selective commercial cutting that took place. This mixed mesophytic forest—meaning the forest and its natural inhabitants are particularly adapted to moderate moisture levels—exhibits all the typical signs of old-growth establishment despite the possibility of previous logging exploitation. Snags and large standing trees are mixed with decomposing fallen logs and decaying organic forest matter, and this mixture of living and dead is one of the central identification points associated with old-growth forests. One unique flora species is the thriving occurrence of blue-eyed Mary. This variety is particularly sensitive to environmental disturbance and its widespread presence testifies to the relatively long-lived stability of Taylor Hollow. As one of the most diverse and one of the most unique forest environments in central Tennessee, Taylor Hollow demands and deserves extensive protection efforts.

Further Reading
Davis, Mary Byrd, ed. *Eastern Old-Growth Forest: Prospects for Rediscovery and Recovery*. Washington, DC: Island Press, 1996.
Yahner, Richard. *Eastern Deciduous Forest: Ecology and Wildlife Conservation*. Chicago: University of Chicago Press, 2000.

WALLS OF JERICHO

Another important class II natural-scientific state natural area, the Walls of Jericho encompass 750 acres of the larger 9,000-acre Bear Hollow Mountain Wildlife Management Area. Adjacent to the Skyline Wildlife Management Area of Alabama, the total combined acreage is over 21,000 acres. The effort to acquire this land was a complex and lengthy undertaking coordinated by the Alabama and Tennessee chapters of the Nature Conservancy. Situated in southern Franklin County in south-central Tennessee, the southern boundary of the site follows the Alabama-Tennessee state line where the Walls of Jericho are located. The walls are a naturally occurring geological feature that forms an amphitheater shape. Within the limestone that forms the walls are large holes about the size of soccer balls or basketballs. Water spouts from these holes during times of high water flow, creating a unique water-formed feature within the amphitheater. This formation is surrounded by bluffs, outcroppings, sinkholes, and caves, which add to the site's exceptional geological character. Of course, the special hydrological character of the walls is not the only thing that makes the site significant. There is a great deal of biological richness and natural diversity in the area that is difficult to match. Several rare and endangered plant species dominate the landscape and depend on the careful management and responsible protection of the walls as well as the surrounding ecosystems.

Scott Davis, the director of the Nature Conservancy of Tennessee, states that "this is truly a unique place, spiritual almost. It's like walking into a giant cathedral—you just want to be quiet." The Walls of Jericho and its environs were once the hunting grounds of Davey Crockett, and this is only a small part of the human history intertwined with the natural character of this rich region. Within this long history, the decision was made to close the area to public access in 1977, partially in an attempt to protect the headwaters of the Paint Rock River of northern Alabama, but also to preserve a link between large intact forests. Home to more than 100 fish varieties and 45 mussel species, the Paint Rock River headwaters are important as local natural habitats and as the beginning of an entire river system's worth of environmental health sustainability. In fact, two of the mussel species that live in the headwaters are found nowhere else in the world, and one fish variety is found in the Paint Rock River and one Kentucky river. The rare Tennessee cave salamander and migratory songbirds also find the area perfectly suited to their needs, adding to the natural diversity that is inherently native to this small but important watershed. The Nature Conservancy will reopen this amazing site to new generations of conservationists, scientists, and enthusiasts. The hope is that Forest Legacy funding will facilitate a transfer of the conservancy's almost 9,000-acre portion to the charge of the Tennessee Wildlife Resources Agency. As a core purchase in a comprehensive plan that involves more than one million acres across Alabama, Tennessee, and Kentucky, the Walls of Jericho add one small but centrally important piece to a larger protection puzzle.

Further Reading
Nash, Steve. *Blue Ridge 2020: An Owner's Manual.* Chapel Hill: University of North Carolina Press, 1999.

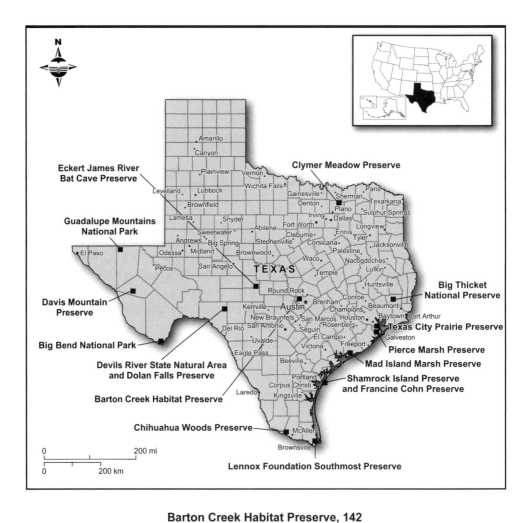

Texas

Although Texas shares the south central plains and western Gulf coastal plains with Louisiana to the east, most of its environmental character is unique among the south and southeast states. A combination of plains, prairies, plateaus, tablelands, and deserts comprise most of Texas. Arid grasses and shrubs dominate the Chihuahuan Desert, and the tablelands open up to range and grass rather than cropland. The Texas prairies are distinct in that the soil is finer and more suited to crop cultivation. As a result, much of this land has been converted to human use. The Edwards Plateau is particularly useful for grazing herds, and the abundant wildlife makes hunting a common land use. The many plains of Texas exhibit a large percentage of cropland, with areas of range and pasture interspersed. The central Oklahoma/Texas plains have proven to be a significant location for oil extraction, raising the value of this area of Texas greatly. In southern Texas, the brush country plains host a wider diversity of wildlife than anywhere else in the state. Combined, Texas offers many opportunities to see restoration and preservation in action in diverse environments and teaches valuable lessons about balancing the needs of ecosystems and the human community that call them home.

Texas's natural history demonstrates six major trends: growing extinctions, declining population numbers and geographical distribution, range expansion, species documentation, expanding threatened species lists, and the introduction of nonnative species. The history of environmental action in response to these changes is long and interesting. There is a gradual evolution from the protection of the right to access to the wider goal of protecting public health and preserving important natural resources. Water resources and access rights stood out as important at the turn of the 20th century, and the state's first efforts toward preservation addressed those concerns. By the mid-1900s, Texas began to address issues of air and water quality as well and eventually added waste disposal, both hazardous and nonhazardous, to its list of concerns. In 1993, Texas consolidated its environmental programs in the Texas Natural Resource Conservation Commission, which became the Texas Commission on Environmental Quality in 2002.

Present efforts focus on a variety of environmental concerns across the state. One of the biggest challenges Texas faces is meeting the disparate needs of the many environs within its borders. One area of recent discussion is the Christmas Mountains, which are adjacent to Big Bend National Park. In late 2007, debate raged over the fate of the area. One proposal suggested that the Christmas Mountains would be best served by private ownership, preserving the lands from public access and use. During the same period, the National Park Service put forth a proposal to assume responsibility for the mountains as part of Big Bend National Park. Ultimately, the question came down to one of public versus private ownership and under whose watch would the interests of both Texas and the Christmas Mountains best be served. This discussion demonstrates the vastly conflicting interests often at stake when it comes to environmental preservation. On one hand, private resources could restore and preserve the area better than the state is capable of doing, but it is also possible that the National Park Service, with its long history of resource management and established presence in Big Bend National Park, is best suited to be the steward of the Christmas Mountains. The 10,000-acre preserve donated to Texas in the early 1990s was sold, and only time will tell of the benefit or detriment private ownership will mean for this tract of land. Ideas about conservation and preservation vary across this vast state, complicating environmental issues and concerns. As the state with the second largest area and the second highest population, Texas struggles to address the concerns that come with simply being large. Areas of preservation across the state blaze paths of action for future Texas efforts to follow in its continuing fight to address its unique environmental challenges and concerns.

Barton Creek Habitat Preserve

Endangered bird habitat and watershed water quality depend on the cooperation between the Texas chapter of the Nature Conservancy and local landowners who have combined their efforts to protect the valuable, scenic landscape of Barton Creek Habitat Preserve. This 4,000-acre preserve is limited in its visitation opportunities, but the time and effort to arrange a visit are necessary for the reward of seeing this important ecosystem nestled up next to Austin in all its metropolis glory. Mature oak and juniper populate much of the land, while grassland areas dot the uplands, hosting several grass varieties, including little bluestem and Indian grass. Heading down the canyon walls toward the creek shore, the tree population exhibits more sycamore, pecan, and black willow. Many species of water-loving botanicals occupy the area as well, creating a uniquely diverse creek canyon community that is unrivaled in the area for its beauty and distinctiveness.

Many animals recognize the natural value of this ecosystem and choose to call it home. A significant number of golden-cheeked warblers, which are listed as endangered, nest in and around the Austin area. Mature oak forests are the draw for this tiny songbird, making Barton Creek a preference for these populations. The Barton Creek Habitat Preserve includes 1,800 acres currently suited for warbler nesting and hundreds more that will mature over the next 30 years to provide additional habitat refuge. The golden-cheeked warbler, though, is not the only endangered resident. The Nature Conservancy has set aside over 100 acres for the black-capped vireo as well. This small songbird (about five inches long) prefers areas of scattered trees and brushy growth. Oaks, again, are very important in their habitat choices. They seem to particularly care for steep slopes where trees would naturally have to be a bit scattered. This way, the vireo can choose clumped areas of trees that will hide their nests from view. Barton Creek has the potential to support specialized habitats such as those described here, but it is important that the Nature Conservancy continue its restoration activities to improve the natural environment so these delicate birds feel safe in building their homes on the preserve. Additionally, the conservancy's water protection measures not only strengthen Barton Creek, but, because the larger system of Barton Springs feeds into the Edwards Aquifer, the health of the creek plays a significant role in connected systems. As if part of a big jigsaw puzzle, Barton Creek fills its place and plays its role in the larger picture of Texas's natural health and sustainability.

Further Reading

Chu, Miyoko. *Songbird Journeys: Four Seasons in the Lives of Migratory Birds*. Orange, VA: Walker, 2006.

Loflin, Brian, and Shirley Loflin. *Grasses of the Texas Hill Country: A Field Guide*. College Station: Texas A&M University Press, 2006.

Proctor, Noble. *The Songbirds Bible: A Visual Directory of 100 of the Most Popular Songbirds in North America*. South Portland, ME: Sellers, 2006.

BIG BEND NATIONAL PARK

The home page of the National Park Service's Web site for Big Bend National Park says it is "a land of strong beauty—often savage and always imposing." The expanse of Big Bend encompasses three very different types of ecosystems. Within its borders visitors find stark mountains, vast deserts, and rushing rivers. The total size of the park is more than 800,000 acres. Big Bend National Park sits on the border of the United States and Mexico and manages more than 300 miles of that boundary that is the Rio Grande, include the spot where the Rio Grande turns sharply northeast, creating the big bend for which the park is named. This unique position means that the park functions under some distinct guidelines in its stewardship of the park and the river. Because the river forms a border between two countries, the park holds jurisdiction over the river only to the center of the deepest channel. The other side is the charge of the Republic of Mexico. Although the National Park Service and the government of Mexico do not work directly together, there are newly established protected areas on the south side of the border that go a long way toward cooperative protection of these valuable lands and waterways.

The U.S. side of the river holds important natural significance as the largest protected area of Chihuahuan Desert in the country. Its geological and paleontological history and evidence have drawn scientists to the area for decades. Geographically speaking, though, this is only one piece of the puzzle. It is truly a land of extremes. At the river, the elevation is just below 2,000 feet above sea level, but, in the mountains, the peaks reach upward of 8,000 feet. These extreme features breed an extreme character that hosts a dazzling array of habitats as well as the plant and animal life that populate them. It helps that the park is positioned in one of the least populated areas of the country. The largest towns are 70 and 100 miles away and sit to the north and northwest of the park headquarters, creating an effective buffer zone between the area's human population and the park. Towns to the west are a bit closer, but do not show population growth or numbers high enough to threaten the park. These lands, too, are sparsely populated for a reason. This is, in every sense, a terrain of extremes, and visitors must take extra caution when camping and hiking in the park. Getting lost in a vast preserve is always a possibility, and rescue in that large of a preserve obviously poses difficulties. The desert holds its own risks, including the threat of dangerous wildlife, exhausting heat, and inadequate water supplies. Visitors must follow all rules and suggestions for safety in order to enjoy the majesty and beauty of this one-of-a-kind national park.

Another interesting yet very different aspect of the park involves its position at the United States–Mexico border. Throughout the Rio Grande's long history, this border has been rather fluid, and people from both sides have crossed the line many times. It is ultimately, though, an artificial line. Political and social pressures have always played and will continue to play a large role in how this boundary functions in relation to the two countries it defines and the natural terrain it traverses. Events of September 11, 2001, affected Big Bend from an international boundary perspective. Increased border patrols mean increased presence in the park. But the 118 miles of border within the park that the United States and Mexico share run through a remote portion of the area. Border control is only one of several major issues visitors need to be aware of. Drug trafficking routes run through this section of the park, and any suspicious movement, transportation, or behavior should be avoided at all costs. Once visitors have left the area, park rangers should be notified of any concerns. Additionally, many Mexican immigrants look to cross into the United States using the park lands as their walking route. It is possible to see individuals or small groups of people walking through the desert lands with little or no provisions. Again, park management asks that visitors do not stop, but instead get to an area where rangers and staff can be notified of the issue. Big Bend is a naturally wild, strikingly beautiful national park, but visiting the park presents unique geographical, climatic, legal, political, and social challenges unlike any other national park experience in the country.

Further Reading
Morey, Roy. *Little Big Bend: Common, Uncommon, and Rare Plants of Big Bend National Park*. Lubbock: Texas Tech University Press, 2008.

Wauer, Roland H., and C. M. Fleming. *Naturalist's Big Bend: An Introduction to the Trees and Shrubs, Wildflowers, Cacti, Mammals, Birds, Reptiles and Amphibians, Fish, and Insects.* College Station: Texas A&M University Press, 2002.

BIG THICKET NATIONAL PRESERVE

The Big Thicket region of southeastern Texas exhibits a unique collection of plants and animals that are descendants of flora and fauna that ice age glaciers pushed into this biological crossroads centuries ago. It is not the number of rare species or amount of wildlife abundance that makes the preserve so special; it is the sheer quantity of biologically diverse varieties that coexist across the preserve that make it stand out as a unique natural site of intense scientific interest. Many major North American systems sit side by side at Big Thicket. The list of bordering regions includes southeastern swamps, eastern forests, central plains, and southwestern deserts. Once this thicket covered much more land, but today what remains of the mix of pine, cypress, and hardwood forest, interspersed with meadow and black water swamp, is just a sampling of the diversity that has historically been represented here. The natural inhabitant count includes 85 tree varieties, more than 60 shrub types, and over 1,000 flowering plants. Almost 200 avian species either live in the preserve or migrate through every year. Fifty reptile species roam the area along with many amphibians. For a long time, this area was left relatively undisturbed by human presence, allowing this wide diversity to thrive. Native Americans used this region for hunting but rarely penetrated into the deepest reaches of the forest. European settlers showed up relatively late to this area, leaving it more protected and less disturbed than many areas of the South. By the 1850s, though, the logging of pine and cypress began, which inaugurated the inevitable march toward dwindling natural environments. Sawmills showed up shortly after, and industry constructed railroads to haul out the wood. As ancient forests began to disappear, nonnative slash pine was planted in their place, furthering the changes already underway. Oil strikes in the early 1900s introduced even more industrial development. Rice farming, housing development, and other human activities combined to take their toll.

Today, however, the park enjoys the designations of national preserve (1974), international biosphere reserve (1981), and globally important bird area (2001)—all of which help set the land up for monitoring, restoration, and preservation activity. Its 83,000 acres are perfectly situated for aggressive protection measures aimed at preserving the unique site for generations to come. Access is facilitated by boardwalks, footpaths, and canoe trails, and the best seasons to visit are fall and spring to avoid the heat and insects of summer. Some of the best hiking in the preserve is along the 15-mile Turkey Creek Trail. Hikers begin in pine hardwood forests that host spots of sandy knolls. The trail continues through short-leaf pine and loblollies into mixed stands that are part of a beech, oak, sweetgum floodplain forest. The walk then leads to the creek, where hikers can see huge bald cypress trees with their knees sticking out of the water. Turkey Creek Trail is one of the best ways to reach the inner forests and experience the diversity Big Thicket has to offer. Visitors are not limited to land excursions. Two canoe trails—the Cook's Lake Canoe Trail and the Franklin Lake Canoe Trail—give adventurous access to the preserve's backwaters. The 37-mile canoe float trail of Village Creek is another option. While there are no rapids along this long, languid stretch, it is not fully developed, so access to the water must be accomplished at road crossing. Knowledge of rivers and swamps is essential to a safe, fun trip through this amazing preserve. Texas harbors in its backwaters and deep reaches one of the most fascinatingly diverse wild environments in the country: Big Thicket National Preserve.

Further Reading

Cozine, James. *Saving the Big Thicket: From Exploration to Preservation, 1685–2003*. Denton: University of North Texas Press, 2004.

Gunter, Pete A. Y. *The Big Thicket: An Ecological Reevaluation*. Denton: University of North Texas Press, 1993.

Watson, Geraldine Ellis. *Big Thicket Plant Ecology: An Introduction*. Denton: University of North Texas Press, 2006.

Chihuahua Woods Preserve

Some wild, unadulterated remnants of the Rio Grande Valley still exist as they once did. One of those remnants is the Chihuahua Woods Preserve. A variety of trees, thickets, and shrubs still characterize the plant life of the area, but according to the Nature Conservancy of Texas, less than five percent of the original thornscrub environment remains. What does remain provides both food and shelter for native wildlife, and an impressive collection of cacti thrive in this natural community as well. It is a small preserve, measuring almost 350 acres, and there are no developed visitation facilities at the site. Walk-in access is available during the daytime, but if individuals are not familiar with some of the natural threats of the area, visitation is not advised. Some of the dangers include the threat of Africanized bees, native rattlesnakes, and rabid animals. Serious precautions are necessary to protect from these dangers, with which many residents of south Texas are intimately familiar. Because of the limited visitation development and the natural character of the preserve, the staff requests that only small groups visit and do not bring children or pets. Camping, hunting, and fires are not allowed at the preserve, and, additionally, because the preserve sits near the United States–Mexico border, people are strongly encouraged to leave before nightfall, as poachers and trespassers could be on the property after dark. While the threats are varied, the beauty of the landscape along with the unique flora and fauna of the area warrant the time it takes to learn about the potential risks and plan a visit.

The short, mild winters that characterize the Rio Grande Valley region mean that Chihuahua Woods has a longer fall and spring season for enjoying the preserve. This preserve is small but indicative of the natural state of the valley before heavy human usage occurred. Some of the historic damage to the area included the clearing of shrublands for agricultural purposes. From a regional perspective, both banks of the Rio Grande are now covered with businesses, homes, and farms. The expansion of agricultural industry combined with clearing for building development continue to pose the most immediate threats to this environment, and pollution plays a role in local environmental degradation as well. Commercial harvesting of native cacti, which occurs throughout the region, inflicts significant damage to the environment because of the invasive digging and extraction methods used to gather viable specimens. While this preserve is arguably less accessible than most, in light of continuing environmental threats, its protection is an important part of preserving what remains of natural southern Texas.

Further Reading

Lockwood, Mark, Brad McKinney, Jim Paton, and Barry Zimmer, eds. *A Birder's Guide to the Rio Grande Valley*. Colorado Springs, CO: American Birding Association, 1999.
Longoria, Arturo. *Adios to the Brushlands*. College Station: Texas A&M University Press, 1997.

CLYMER MEADOW PRESERVE

North central Texas was once covered by blackland Prairie. Oak and savanna characterized the landscape, with scattered tall-grass prairie lands present throughout the area. Because of the rich soil and the temperate climate, these prairies lent themselves to agricultural pursuits. As a result, much of what was expansive prairie is now reduced to isolated sites of prairie remnants. Over 99 percent of these ecosystems have been cultivated, making the tall-grass lands the most endangered type of ecosystem as a whole in the United States. Clymer Meadow Preserve is one of the largest remaining prairie preserves of this type in North America. The 1,000-acre preserve is owned by the Nature Conservancy and private landowners. Because of its large size and relatively intact environs, Clymer Meadow is a subject of scientific study aimed at gaining a better understanding of prairies in their natural state. Plant and animal inventories, noxious weed control experiments, and soil content examinations have all contributed to a more in-depth appreciation for the delicate balance necessary to sustain prairie grassland health. The Nature Conservancy offers universities, primary and secondary schools, and research organizations special access for educational purposes. A successful reintroduction of bison to Clymer Meadow occurred for the first time in 150 years. Bison have long been a part of prairie maintenance, and their reintroduction is expected to encourage the restoration of this valuable habitat. The conservancy is borrowing bison to graze at the preserve in order to observe and examine the effect of bison presence on the sustainability of the site. The research and efforts made at the preserve have the potential to benefit struggling prairie lands across the continent.

One unique role Clymer Meadow has played in the human community is as a site for Native American education on the natural environments that once hosted their ancestors. A program called "Native American Seed: Helping People Restore the Earth," contains a recollection recorded by a participant in early prairie restoration efforts. Blogged at Native American Seed in 2007, the reminiscence reads as follows.

as for the Clymer Meadow, we have conducted conservancy harvests there a few times over the years, the first time back in the late 1980s. I lived in the old farmhouse on the hill with the harvest crew for three weeks. This was my first comprehensive gathering of all the ingredients for a real prairie restoration . . . of which we turned around and replanted all the sacred seeds to expand the Parkhill Prairie, which is maybe 20 miles away. Ol' pipe smokin' Arnold Davis was my mentor on this project . . . back in the day. He is no longer on this earth with us. In later harvests, the native seeds were used to expand the Clymer Meadow Preserve . . . and/ or offered for sale to others in the Blackland bioregion for ecological restoration purposes. The Clymer Meadow was the first prairie that Westy and Emily stepped foot on when they were but young chillin's. Having been born and raised in the blacklands, I find it is one of those rare magic places . . . anytime of the year.

This man's memories express what it means when people meet the land looking to restore something of the land's health and something of the people's legacy. Clymer Meadow, through its scientific research, natural education, and cultural edification activities, will continue to play a central role in discovering the past of the Texas prairielands, as well as preserving their future.

Further Reading

Hatch, Stephan L., Joseph L. Schuster, and Dale Lynn Drawe. *Grasses of the Texas Gulf Prairies and Marshes*. College Station: Texas A&M University Press, 1999.

Samson, Fred B., and Fritz L. Knopf, eds. *Prairie Conservation: Preserving North America's Most Endangered Ecosystem*. Washington, DC: Island Press, 1996.

Davis Mountains Preserve

Davis Mountains stand in stark contrast to their surrounding geography in formations called sky islands. The Nature Conservancy defines the phrase as "True ecological islands, isolated from similar mountain ranges by vast distances, preserving living remnants that occur nowhere else." The mountain preserve encompasses 32,000 acres and is buffered by an additional 70,000 acres of protected ranchland. Historical artifacts in the area testify to the important position the mountains have held in the human psyche for hundreds of years. Physical remnants of human habitation, like arrowheads and pottery, along with artistic and religious expressions, such as the fantastic pictograph collection at Madera Canyon and Wolf's Den Canyon, suggest that these lands have not only long been important, to many they were considered sacred natural areas. Given the unique character of the landscape and the variety of plant and animal life, it is no wonder that ancient societies were drawn to the mountains, much like we are today. Now, however, educational field trips and volunteer work days have replaced hunting expeditions and religious ceremonies. The Davis Mountains Preserve, because of its character and significance, offers visitors a chance to see widely diverse nature in action and learn about attentive preservation and active stewardship of important natural resources.

Because of their elevation and isolation, the flora and fauna that live above 5,000 feet are geographically isolated from other mountain communities because of the vast distances between these mountains and any other range. This makes these ecosystems unlike any other environments in Texas. Additionally, this collection of environments is delicate and adapted to specific cycles of fire and drought. Human intervention holds the potential to quickly and irrevocably damage these fragile areas. The complex nature of the interdependent relationships in the Davis Mountains environments also means that what recovery can be accomplished is a slow and laborious process. Overgrazing and land development, along with water resource redirection and depletion, are all threats the Nature Conservancy and cooperative individuals and organizations are trying to minimize. Additional goals include helping preserve the ranching legacy of west Texas by protecting the surrounding buffer zone of ranching lands. Also, the University of Texas McDonald Observatory's nighttime sky viewing could be severely affected if these areas were open to development. One final benefit of Davis Mountains' sustained health is the safeguarding of the hydrological system that begins at Mount Livermore. Streams, springs, and groundwater sources are the lifeblood of the region because of the overriding arid climate characteristics. With these important water sources contained largely within the preserve's 90,000 acres, healthy hydrological assets can be assured for years to come. Because the preserve is surrounded by the Chihuahuan Desert, there are few other places to turn for abundant, clean water supplies. The natural cycle of water exchange with the igneous aquifer is important for both the natural communities in the area and the human populations surrounding the preserve. Responsible stewardship of this one-of-a-kind Texas landscape will benefit all who visit and all who live in these beautiful, rugged lands.

Further Reading

MacLeod, William. *Davis Mountains Vistas: A Geological Exploration of the Davis Mountains.* Alpine: Texas Geological Press, 2006.

Tweit, Susan J. *Barren, Wild, and Worthless: Living in the Chihuahuan Desert.* Tucson: University of Arizona Press, 2003.

Devils River State Natural Area and Dolan Falls Preserve

On the western border of the Texas Hill Country, where the climate is dry most of the time, sits a rare ecosystem: the Texas Nature Conservancy's Dolan Falls Preserve. Dolan Springs, Dolan Creek, and the Devils River all contribute to this unique environment, which is located at the intersection of three distinct Texas natural regions: the Edwards Plateau, the Chihuahuan Desert, and Rio Grande plain brushland. The site contains almost 5,000 acres, but conjoining conservation easements increase the acreage to almost 20,000. The central water feature is the Devils River, which flows through canyons bounded by oak and sycamore stands accentuated by steep cliffs containing juniper and mesquite. Rare and endangered plant species abound, along with animal varieties found few other places in Texas. Many migrating species are drawn to the area as well, because the water source provides a path of migration through the surrounding dry lands. The environmental significance of these water flows is what attracted the attention of the Nature Conservancy in the first place. Conservation efforts focus on the riverfront, because it plays such a central role in the life of local flora and fauna. Inventories and research aimed at better understanding the natural interplay of resources and climate take place across the site. Additionally, the conservancy acquired 88,000 acres in 2003 to help protect the headwaters region of the Devils River. Water is such a precious resource in this arid Texas region that aggressive steps must be taken to protect its health and accessibility for generations to come.

One of the most significant pieces of the preserve's water resource collection is the Devils River. As part of the Edwards Plateau ecoregion and a buffer to the Chihuahuan Desert, the river is perfectly positioned to deliver valuable and necessary hydration to the almost constantly parched lands. Groundwater removal, damaged rangelands, water quality, housing development, and nonnative species incursion all pose severe threats to this uniquely irreplaceable landscape. Sixty miles of river flow through canyons, mesa hills, and deserts to meet with the Rio Grande at the United States–Mexico border. Keeping this massive stretch of vital water and its headwater region safe from the dangers of human use, abuse, and expansion is crucial for maintaining this rare remnant of a truly wild Texas. The landscape hosts more than regionally characteristic flora and the expected assortment of land and aquatic fauna. Fern Cave, an exceptional geological feature of Devils River, has functioned in the past as a maternity roost for more than 10 million Mexican free-tailed bats each year. Today, barely a quarter of a million return each year to give birth, and, although this is a significant population number, it does not compare to the counts of the past. Conservation can help restore some of this roosting activity. Fern Cave also represents the northernmost point of wintering sites for this species, making the area important year-round. While much of the environmental importance of this area is easy to discern, some natural gems, such as this expansive bat population, hide just below the surface, contributing unseen yet valuable elements of biological diversity. Sealing the river's significance is its historical legacy of human habitation reaching back over 5,000 years. The detailed and well-preserved pictographs found throughout the site draw anthropologists and archaeologists to the Texas Hill Country for a rare look into the region's fascinating native past. When added together, the protection effort that encompasses 25 of the river's 60 miles and almost 150,000 acres. Twenty thousand acres of this expanse includes the largest-volume waterfall in Texas: Dolan Falls. Another 20,000 acres constitute the Devils River State Natural Area, and an additional 22,000 acres comprise the Devils River Ranch, which is at the southern end of the river and boasts 13 miles of riverfront land. To quote an article titled "Devils River: Texas" in *Southern Living* magazine, "The Devils River is the stuff of Lone Star legend. A rugged survivor, it wends its way . . . through a mostly unpopulated, unforgiving corner of South Texas. . . . Its true character . . . is a sheer oasis, a magnet for life, a source of stark and extravagant beauty." Its preservation for future generations of humans, plants, and animals alike is now ensured, as long as visitors and stakeholders alike continue to recognize the legend that is the river.

Further Reading

Aulbach, Louis F. *The Devils River.* Washington, DC: Wilderness Area Map Service, 2005.

Clark, Gary. *Backroads of the Texas Hill Country: Your Guide to the Most Scenic Adventures.* McGregor, MN: Voyager Press, 2008.

Young,. "Devils River: Texas." *Southern Living* (2002).

ECKERT JAMES RIVER BAT CAVE PRESERVE

This amazing preserve is home to one of the largest continual collections of warm-blooded animals on the planet. Mexican free-tailed bats find this cave to be particularly conducive to their environmental needs. Unfortunately, because bats congregate in large number in relatively small, confined areas, even small acts of human intervention—or worse, intentional damage—can devastate an entire population. For a long time, bats were considered either nuisances or outright threats, and, as a result, many were run off or destroyed. Due to education efforts by organizations such as the Nature Conservancy and Bat Conservation International, the negative reputation of bats is slowly being reversed. Bats participate in seed scattering, helping facilitate the growth and regrowth of local plant species. They also play a tremendous role in regulating insect populations. Mosquitoes and crop pests are among their favorite prey, making them extremely beneficial to community health and economy. The habitat disruption that has taken place across the continent means that this valuable animal population is on the decline. It does not help that mothers only give birth to one pup per year, making recovery a slow process. With four million female bats in the cave from May through September and upward of six million after they give birth, the population census of Bat Cave is nothing to discount. Visitors are treated to an amazing site every night during the roosting season. Every evening in the hours before sunset, hundreds of bats fly around the cave opening. The mass of animals eventually merges into a spiral flying upward, forming a tornado of hundreds of individuals. As they reach higher into the sky, they break off into streams of hunting parties and fly out over the countryside in search of the body's weight worth of insects they need to consume to get them to their next feeding on the following night.

Mexican free-tailed bat emergence at TNC Eckert James River Bat Preserve in Mason County, Texas. (Jayson May)

Fortunately, Mexican free-tailed bats seem to be immune to an emerging mysterious bat disease called white-nosed syndrome. Bat communities across the northeastern United States are being devastated by this deadly disease. The cause of the affliction eludes scientists. The characteristics signs include the appearance of a white fungus around the ears, nose, and wings, and, while there is a massive research effort underway, there is still no treatment for this little-understood bat illness. The site of the Eckert James River Bat Cave Preserve is small—barely eight acres—but the population is so large, specialists can use this apparently resistant breed of bat to better understand the white-nosed syndrome threat. The larger effort concerning Bat Cave, though, is providing accurate educational information concerning the most popular myths that have followed this species for centuries. Only a few varieties of bats drink animal blood. Their use of echolocation means they never get caught in people's hair. The occurrence of rabies in bats is extremely low. All of these things have caused misunderstanding and irreparable harm to bat groups across the planet. This one education effort at the Eckert James River Bat Cave Preserve combines with many activities across North America to further understanding and acceptance of this integral, important native resident.

Further Reading

Kunz, Thomas H., and M. Brock Fenton, eds. *Bat Ecology*. Chicago: University of Chicago Press, 2006.
Tuttle, Merlin D. *Texas Bats*. Austin, TX: Bat Conservation International, 2002.

GUADALUPE MOUNTAINS NATIONAL PARK

Guadalupe Mountains in west Texas is a unique assemblage of natural and historical treasures. It holds the world's finest remnant of fossilized reef. A wide variety of flora and fauna call the park home. It is west Texas's only designated wilderness. Every trail, every sight, every step offers unparalleled solitude and beauty in this hiker's heaven. There are more than 80 miles that traverse the park, giving visitors access to natural wonders and fossilized graveyards alike. As the National Park Service states, it is easy for visitors to view the park as stark and forbidding; nothing but a "sea of harsh, barren desert." There is so much more to this outstanding national park than meets the eye. For those interested in the creatures that used to swim the waters that covered much of North America, Guadalupe Mountains' ancient fossilized reef holds a treasure of evidence. Approximately 250 million years ago, a vast ocean completely covered what is now this Texas desert land. The reef that remains today ran the length of the shoreline for over 400 miles. The ocean, though, slowly and eventually evaporated, leaving in its wake the massive reef buried under sediment and mineral salts, preserving it for millions of years. Today this vast collection of fossils offers geologists and scientists a rare opportunity to explore the remnants of an ancient shoreline.

After its time as an ancient reef, the area was covered with an ice age forest. Today it is a combination of lowlands, woodlands, and high mountain reaches. These changes are natural and expected parts of landscape development and evolution. Human presence, though, presents challenges of a different nature. Air quality and pollution levels are of particular concern in the area, because poor air conditions can have devastating effects on the widely varying natural communities across the mountains. In the local area, human habitation continues to expand, adding air regulation problems. Interestingly, pollution from as far away as Los Angeles finds its way to the park, compounding the problems and concerns. Another natural element that has been affected by humans is fire in the mountains' ecosystems. Understandably, humans tend to limit the occurrence and spread of fires in areas where housing, business, and industry have developed, but many types of natural communities depend on regular fires for their survival. The fire history of the park is not very well understood. It is difficult, due to the lack of scientific information, for park management and staff to make educated decisions about where and when to allow fires to burn. Currently, there is so much burning fuel in some areas that it would be impossible to conduct a prescribed burn to enhance the natural health of the forests. The search for the balance between necessary natural burning and the risk of

El Capitan's southeastern face at sunrise. Taken in the Guadalupe Mountains National Park. (David Lampert)

out-of-control ravaging fires continues in the hopes of addressing the needs of both the natural and human communities that inhabit the area.

One particularly interesting group of park residents are the mountain mammals that roam the lands. Most visitors will see few, if any, mammal species during a visit, however. Most animals seek shelter during the day, either from the weather or from predators. The most common sighting is of mule deer, which can be found throughout the park because they are very active during the day. Elk live in the park also, but in much fewer numbers. They are not as comfortable around human visitors, so there are few sightings of this majestic animal. Mountain lions and black bears roam the lands, as well, but seeing one of these elusive animals would be a rare experience. Smaller mammals abound throughout the forests and their understory growth. Coyotes, jack rabbits, and gray foxes are some of the smaller but no less integral animals that are part of this vast landscape. Amphibians and reptiles populate the environment, with desert rattlesnakes being among the most well known and most feared of all the animals in the park. Despite being poisonous, the risk of being bitten by one of these snakes is relatively small. And less than one percent of rattlesnake bite victims dies. The keys to survival are to remain calm, not treat the wound without medical help, and head immediately to the nearest hospital or medical treatment center. There are many risks when visiting wild areas such as the Guadalupe Mountains, but, with proper knowledge and preparation, a venture into the wildness can be both rewarding and safe.

Further Reading
Tennant, Alan. *The Guadalupe Mountains of Texas.* Denton: University of Texas Press, 1997.

LENNOX FOUNDATION SOUTHMOST PRESERVE

Southmost Preserve has been called the jewel of the Rio Grande Valley. As part of the Boscaje de la Palma region of the Lower Rio Grande Valley Wildlife Corridor, the site holds one of the last remaining stands of native sabal palms in the country. The Nature Conservancy of Texas suggests that the preserve may be one of the "most important pieces of land remaining in the country." The plant diversity is astounding, and the number of animal varieties is just as impressive. Rare flowering and green species along with the many palm and riparian stands create perfect havens for the many migratory avian species that use the major flyways crossing the preserve area. For example, the wooded fringes of the *resacas*—old and now dry channels of the Rio Grande—offer rare and valuable nesting grounds for at least two rare bird subspecies: the Brownsville common yellowthroat and the Lomita Carolina wren. The natural environments of the preserve house other endangered animals as well, including rare bat, tortoise, and rat species. The aquatic habitats host rarely seen amphibians, such as the Mexican white-lipped frog, the sheep frog, and the Rio Grande lesser siren. Because of this rich diversity, biologists have been drawn to the area for years, working toward a better understanding of this outstanding but dwindling remnant of Rio Grande Valley ecology. Despite a long history of agricultural use in the area, the sabal palm forest, resacas, and Tamau thornscrub environments are some of the largest and best examples of these natural communities in the southern United States. This is largely due to the fact that the preserve's private owner sought to find a sustainable balance between cultivation pursuits and conservation concerns, setting the stage for future activities.

In 1999, the Nature Conservancy purchased the site but continues to balance agriculture and protection efforts, while undertaking restoration activities in some of the more degraded and delicate areas. The restoration of brush habitats and resaca channels are the priorities of the conservancy when it comes to reestablishing native conditions. Exotic, invasive species pose a significant threat to the preserve's delicate balance, and so the Nature Conservancy has enacted programs aimed at minimizing and ultimately eliminating the damage foreign plants can cause. There is a native plant nursery on the 1,000-acre expanse that supplies reforestation projects across all of southern Texas. Some of the habitat it supports is perfectly suited for the ocelot and the jaguarondi, two of Texas's severely threatened wildcat species. The biggest potential benefit, though, for this particular preserve is the opportunity it presents to observe and study the coordinated compatibility of agricultural activities and conservation programs. Preserves such as Southmost are helping pave the way for future cohabitation understanding.

There is an unusual threat that looms over the future sustainability of this valuable coordinated effort. The recently proposed Mexico border fence, as it was planned in late 2008, would place the structure more than one mile north of the United States–Mexico border in many places. One of those places runs through the Lennox Foundation Southmost Preserve. Three-quarters of the site, including some of the most critical wildlife habitat, would be situated in a no-man's-land between the fence and the national boundary. The result is that much of the preserve would literally be stranded. Staff safety and stewardship success are at the top of the Nature Conservancy's list of concerns should the fence ever be erected. In December 2008, the Department of Homeland Security filed suit against the Texas chapter of the Nature Conservancy in an effort to condemn portions of the land within the preserve. The suit offered just over $100,000 for the approximately eight acres the fence would occupy. The problem, however, is the remainder of the land that would be cut off between the fence and the border. Seven hundred acres of valuable habitat would suffer as it sat inaccessible to preserve staff, biologists, and volunteers. Additionally, all of the preserve's facilities, including the home of the preserve manager would be caught between the fence and the river. As of January 2009, over 90 percent of the fence was complete, with the stretch that would occupy Southmost's land part of the incomplete portion. A local rancher and environmentalist pointed out in a report for National Public Radio that there are "some estimates that there's one percent of native natural land left along the river, and the wall is fragmenting that." Until the question of construction is answered, the fate of Lennox Foundation Southmost Preserve hangs in the balance.

Further Reading

Brush, Timothy. *Nesting Birds of a Tropical Frontier: The Lower Rio Grande Valley of Texas*. College Station: Texas A&M University Press, 2005.

Burnett, John. "Nature Conservancy Fights Planned Border Fence." National Public Radio, January 26, 2009.

Seale, Jan E., and Land Fund Valley. *Creatures on the Edge: Wildlife along the Lower Rio Grande*. McAllen, TX: Chachalaca Press, 1997.

MAD ISLAND MARSH PRESERVE

Sixty years ago, a large unbroken coastal wetlands system stretched along the Texas Gulf Coast at the very end of the Central Flyway, which is one of the four major avian migratory paths of North America. What remains of the upland prairies that are part of the Mad Island Marsh Preserve represents barely two percent of what was originally a much larger Texas prairie landscape. Today these 7,000 acres are an integral part of preserving what is left of the natural history of southern prairielands. The parts of the preserve that are marshy wetlands host a wide variety of aquatic plant species, including glassworts, cordgrasses, cattails, and rushes. The prairies that are adjacent to the marshes are better suited for different kinds of grasses like bluestem, wintergrass, and bristlegrass species. This botanical diversity provides both transient and permanent homes to almost 250 types of birds. Songbirds (both migrating and resident varieties), shorebirds, wading birds, and nesting birds find their feeding, roosting, and nesting needs fully filled by this coastal treasure. Ducks and geese find the lands and waters at the site particularly suited to their needs as well. Also in the area are many aquatic species that depend on a healthy, delicate balance in the marsh environment to survive. Unfortunately for the plant and animal species at the site, the environmental conditions of both land and water have been in decline for years. Immediate action became necessary in order to halt the continuing damage and begin restoring the area to sustainable and suitable levels of natural well-being.

In 1990, the Nature Conservancy partnered with Ducks Unlimited to produce a comprehensive restoration and conservation program for Mad Island Marsh Preserve. The Web site for the preserve is hosted by the conservancy and describes four central programs aimed at accomplishing the difficult reestablishment of the marsh and its surrounding lands. The first goal is to increase freshwater flow into the area, which will help produce the recreation of marsh habitat. Second, rice fields that function as feeding and roosting areas for native waterfowl need to be improved for the use of wintering populations. Past drainage efforts have also left their imprint on the wetlands, and now their freshwater foundations must be restored. Finally, grazing and burning must be controlled in the uplands to encourage the regrowth of the coastal prairie environments. Many of the local bird as well as other animal populations use these lands for foraging and nesting. Within 10 years, the conservancy shows that 650 acres of freshwater wetlands were either created or improved and 3,000 acres of coastal prairieland had been restored. Twenty five hundred acres of tidal wetlands and 1,200 acres of rice field habitat had been dramatically improved as well. The success of this partnership proves what can be accomplished in a relatively short amount of time when money, resources, and dedication are directed in a concerted conservation effort. As the last opportunity for migrating bird populations to get much-needed rest and valuable food stores, the restoration and preservation of Mad Island Marsh Preserve affects more than just local communities and native environments. Avian elements of ecosystems from all over North America depend on this stretch of land for their survival. Matagorda County and Mad Island Marsh have taken top honors in the annual National Audubon Society's Christmas Bird Count every year between 1997 and 2005. This clearly demonstrates the sheer numbers the preserve must host on a yearly basis.

Further Reading

Hatch, Stephan. *Texas Range Plants*. College Station: Texas A&M University Press, 1993.

Johnsgard, Paul A. *Prairie Birds: Fragile Splendor in the Great Plains*. Lawrence: University Press of Kansas, 2001.

PIERCE MARSH PRESERVE

Pierce Marsh was once a rich salt marsh environment. Groundwater withdrawal, though, transformed the area into an open water expanse and severely degraded the natural environmental conditions. Eventually, it was not possible to extract any more groundwater. This allowed for the gradual reestablishment of the basic conditions necessary to begin restoration of the original salt marsh environs. Many state, federal, and private organizations combined their collective knowledge and experience to begin rejuvenating the area. The Nature Conservancy of Texas is the largest stakeholder, managing two-thirds of Pierce Marsh since 1987. The restoration complex, though, after a series of land exchanges and purchases, would come to be managed by the Galveston Bay Foundation in cooperation with the conservancy. The result is a 4,600-acre block of permanently protected wetlands and uplands. The controlling partnership employed innovative techniques that included constructing 153 long terraces on open water that was close to the existing shoreline. The idea was to replace intertidal marsh and wetland vegetation that had been lost. After being arranged in open square patterns, volunteers planted vegetation bred by the Reliant Energy Natural Resource Center. Once the terraces are established and the water clarity improves, sea grass will be added to the shallow pools between the terraces. Eventually, more terraces will be constructed to add bends and curves that mimic the natural structure of marshes. These are just the first steps in a full restoration process that should eventually result in mature marshlands. Even though the project is in its relatively early stages, signs of success already show promising signs of permanent recovery.

Unlike many environmental restoration and preservation projects across the continent, the Pierce Marsh Preserve's mission is almost solely focused on re-creating necessary habitat for the more than 300 avian species that depend on the area each year. Many sites combine protection of rare plant and animal species, but in this case, the goal is to support and maintain a natural cycle that occurs every year: cross-continent bird migration. What this means is the managing partners are free to focus on what is necessary to sustain this necessary migratory pattern and not divide their efforts between a variety of interests and projects. Their whole focus is on the restoration of Pierce Marsh. What complicates the issue somewhat is the variety of habitats that comprise the totality of the preserve. Open water marine and estuarine areas, brackish prairie grasslands, tidal marshes, coastal uplands, barrier island traits, and riparian wooded bayou characteristics create an interplay of needs and resources that, if properly considered and used, greatly increase the chances of successful restoration. All of the pieces are important elements in the environmental health of the region, and understanding their individual roles and needs is a continual effort of the invested stakeholders. Duck, egret, curlew, sandpiper, and sparrow species are just a handful of the transitory and permanent residents of these coastal lands. Foundational efforts have resulted in seven acres of emergent marsh, but the goal is to expand the marsh to over 40 acres and protect an additional 1,600 acres of adjacent habitats, creating a necessary sustainable buffer for the marsh system. As one of the most difficult, work-intensive, and delicate types of environmental rebuilding efforts, the successful results of this program will help establish proven methods for use in other imperiled coastal areas.

Further Reading

Chabreck, Robert H. *Coastal Marshes: Ecology and Wildlife Management*. Minneapolis: University of Minnesota Press, 1998.

O'Brien, Michael, Richard Crossley, and Kevin Karlson. *The Shorebird Guide*. Boston, MA: Houghton Mifflin, 2006.

SHAMROCK ISLAND PRESERVE AND FRANCINE COHN PRESERVE

Shamrock Island Preserve and Francine Cohn Preserve are adjacent to each other, and the Nature Conservancy manages the two as one unit. Shamrock Island is what remains of a recurved barrier spit. The island was formed when Hurricane Celia hit the area in 1970. The change in the land's topography has resulted in the island becoming one of the major waterbird rookeries in the northwestern portion of the Gulf of Mexico.

The adjoining Cohn Preserve is an interdependent system of sea grass meadows, shell beaches, high marsh, open water, intertidal marshlands, and freshwater ponds. The biological connection between the two preserves is that birds nesting on the island often forage in the Cohn Preserve. Shamrock Island was acquired in 1995, but it was not until 2000 that the combination of land donation and purchase completed the partnership. The opportunity to explore the interacting systems of these two areas and to observe and learn about this rare habitat brings students and scientists to the site from Texas A&M University, the University of Texas, and other organizations around the state. To get to this point, though, quite of bit of restoration was necessary. Before the Conservancy owned the sites, they partnered with Bristol Resources, an oil and gas operator, to clean up the damage and debris left behind by previous oil and gas extraction activities. Steel tanks and collecting equipment needed to be removed, and a major sludge pit needed restoration. While the conservancy and Chapparal Energy, the new controlling interest of Bristol Resources, continue to work together toward responsible management and land use practices, a private third party controls the mineral rights. Also, the conservancy closes the island between February and August to protect nesting bird populations. Boaters and fishers can cause a great deal of disturbance and damage during these critical months. Additionally, debris from the nearby bay must be continually removed to improve the conditions around the island and the preserve. The ultimate goal is to find the balance between private interests, industry practices, and environmental concerns.

Surrounding the island and preserve is an important aquatic habitat, so the site is a crucial area for marine conservation. Many commercial and recreational species call these waters home, and maintaining the health of these waters is of utmost importance to their survival and promulgation. Without a strong marine habitat, the income from recreational and business use would be in jeopardy. While staunch conservationists often balk at the idea of compromising preservation with commercial interests, the reality is that cooperation is often necessary for long-term successful maintenance and sustainability. People are part of the landscape, and they use that landscape in their everyday lives and livelihoods. Shamrock Island and the Cohn Preserve provide one functioning example of how nonprofit, business, and private interests can meet in the middle to help each other be more successful in their goals and activities involving both literal and figurative common ground.

Further Reading

Perry, M. Cameron and Daniel J. Heilman. Planning and Construction of Shore Protection at Shamrock Island, Texas: Project Update. Shiner Mosesley & Associates, Inc. Report http://www.fsbpa.com/06Proceedings/11-Cameron%20Perry.pdf.

GLOSSARY

ACCLIMATIZATION The adaptations plants and animals undergo to adjust to environmental changes.

AERATION A process that facilitates the degradation of organic matter when submerged in water.

ALLUVIAL Sand that has been deposited by flowing water.

ASSIMILATION A body of water's capability to self-purify and rid itself of pollution.

BEST MANAGEMENT PRACTICES General methods of environmental management that have been identified and accepted as the most effective means of reducing or preventing pollution.

BIODIVERSITY The variety of natural organisms residing in an environment. Biological diversity can be discussed in a variety of contexts, such as addressing a complete ecosystem and all of its components or the smallest of biochemical elements that make up the basic structure of an organism and every size and scope in between.

BIOLOGICAL INTEGRITY The ability to support and sustain natural habitat in a defined region.

BIOLOGICAL STRESSORS Plants or animals that are accidentally or intentionally placed in environments where they do not natively belong.

BIOME A comprehensive community of living organisms residing in a single defined ecological area.

BIOTIC COMMUNITY A naturally occurring collection of plants and animals living in a collective, interdependent environment.

161

BLOOM   A sudden and widespread growth of algae or other aquatic plants that are not characteristic of the water environment in which they are found. Often seen in highly polluted areas where contaminants have changed natural nutrient levels.

BOTTOMLAND HARDWOODS   Freshwater wetlands that are adjacent to river systems across the south and southeast United States. These naturally heavily forested areas, when healthy, are ideal habitats for the nesting, breeding, and sheltering of many different wildlife species.

BRACKISH   Aquatic environment of mixed fresh and salt water.

CHEMICAL STRESSORS   Chemicals introduced into natural environments by human activity that can have negative impacts on local plant and animal species.

CHLOROSIS   Green plant discoloration caused by nutrient deficiency, disease, or pollution.

CHRONIC EFFECT   A negative effect that occurs in a wildlife population, the symptoms of which are characterized as frequently reoccurring or slowly, but consistently developing.

CHRONIC EXPOSURE   Multiple exposures to damaging substances that occur over a long period of time or over a significant portion of an organism's lifetime.

CLEAR CUT   The practice of cutting down every tree in one geographical place all at once. This practice often results in erosion, runoff, flooding, sedimentation, and habitat degradation.

COASTAL ZONE   Coastal land and bodies of water that either affect the adjacent sea and its ecology or are affected by the sea.

COMMUNITY   A collection of different species that live together in a defined ecological space.

CONSERVATION   Focusing on preserving and protecting resources but also restoring when possible. Conservation practices are guided by the effort to ensure economic, social, and environmental benefits.

CONSERVATION EASEMENT   An easement, or right of way, that limits private property use to practices that work toward conservation and environmental goals.

DESALINATION   The removal of salt from ocean or brackish water or from soil by artificial means.

DIVERSION   The process of utilizing stream flow as a water supply.

DRAINAGE BASIN   A singular outlet area along a river or stream where water and sediment drain.

ECOLOGICAL INDICATOR   A characteristic of an ecosystem that demonstrates information on that ecosystem's function and structure. Indicators help determine environmental stability and sustainability.

ECOSYSTEM   A system view of a region that includes its living communities as well as its nonliving components.

ENVIRONMENTAL INDICATOR   A characteristic, value, or measurement that provides evidence for the positive, negative, or neutral results of environmental management programs or the overall condition of a defined environment.

ESTUARY   When fresh water and shoreline ocean water mix as a result of tidal forces. Taking the form of bays, marshes, and lagoons, these specialized environments house a wide variety of marine animals, bird varieties, and wildlife species.

EXOTIC SPECIES   Nonnative species.

FEN   Wetlands that accumulate peat, or decaying vegetable matter. These are less acidic than bogs because they get water from nutrient-rich groundwater sources.

FLOODPLAIN   Relatively flat land along rivers and streams in tidal areas that occasionally flood.

GAME FISH   Any species of fish that is caught for sport. These varieties tend to be more sensitive to environmental changes and threats.

GROUND COVER   Plant growth encouraged specifically to prevent or slow erosion.

GROUNDWATER   Water found below ground, usually flowing through rock formations. It functions as the main water source for wells and springs.

HABITAT   The space in which a community lives, including all elements, both living and nonliving.

HABITAT INDICATOR   A physical characteristic of an environment that provides evidence for the conditions necessary to support life in the absence of pollutants.

HYDROGEOLOGY   The geological study of groundwater, focusing on its chemistry and movement.

HYDROLOGY   The science and study of water quality, properties, distribution, and flow.

INDICATOR   A characteristic that demonstrates specific environmental conditions in a defined area.

KARST   Limestone deposit geologic formations that host characteristic sinks, caverns, and underground streams.

LANDSCAPE ECOLOGY   The science and study of ecosystem distribution patterns, the processes that affect those patterns, and the changes in both processes and patterns.

MARSH   Wetlands that are dominated by herbaceous, or nonwoody, leafy plant life. Marshes can be brackish, fresh water based, or salt water based.

MORBIDITY   Rate and frequency of disease occurrence.

MUTAGENICITY   Chemical properties that cause the genetic profile of an organism to permanently change or mutate.

NECROSIS   Death of the cells or tissues that constitute a plant or animal.

NONPOINT SOURCES   Diffused sources of pollution from which the pollutants are usually carried away from the land by storm water.

PEAT   Organic material composed of decaying vegetation.

PLUME   A concentration of pollutants that radiate from a specific source.

POINT SOURCES   Specific locations from which pollutants enter the environment.

PUBLIC COMMENT PERIOD   The time given for public comment and discussion concerning proposed action by the Environmental Protection Agency.

RECLAMATION   The process of restoring resources to beneficial uses, which may or may not mirror the original condition of the resource.

RESTORATION   The process of restoring a natural site to preuse, alteration, or damage conditions.

RIPARIAN HABITAT   Areas near rivers and streams that host different densities and diversities of plant and animal organisms than the adjacent uplands.

RIVER BASIN   Lands drained by a river and its tributary system.

SALINITY   Percentage of salt in a body of water.

SALTWATER INTRUSION   The incursion of fresh water by saltwater sources.

SEDIMENT   Topsoil and sand washed from land into water.

SILT   Sediment composed of mineral particles.

SILVICULTURE   Forest land management

SURFACE WATER   Any body of water open to the atmosphere.

SWAMP   Wetlands dominated by woody plants but no significant peat deposits that can be brackish, fresh water based, or salt water based.

TERRACING   The construction of dikes built on sloping farmland to prevent runoff and hold sediment in the effort to control erosion.

WATERSHED   An area of land that drains into a stream or river.

WETLANDS   Lands that are either saturated or flooded by surface water or groundwater frequently or for significant time periods. Swamps, bogs, marshes, and estuaries, along with other inland and coastal water-soaked lands are examples of typical wetland environments, and they are characterized by plant and animal species specially adapted to these aquatic conditions.

WILDLIFE REFUGE   An area of wildlife protection where hunting and fishing are either forbidden or strictly controlled.

BIBLIOGRAPHY

Alden, Peter, and Gil Nelson. *National Audubon Society Field Guide to the Southeastern States*. New York: Alfred A. Knopf, 1999.

This is the Audubon Society's field guide to the geology, fossils, wildlife habitats, weather, and ecology of the southeastern states, as well as the region's trees, mushrooms, insects, mammals, reptiles, and fish species.

Andrews, Richard N. L. *Managing the Environment, Managing Ourselves: A History of American Environmental Policy*. New Haven, CT: Yale University Press, 2006.

Andrews explores environmental policy and action in North America over the last 400 years and looks at how that policy and action history affects today's actions. The book also discusses the potential for future policy changes and action plans.

Bailey, H. A., and A. W. Bailey. *Fire Ecology: United States and Southern Canada*. New York: John Wiley, 1982.

Fire Ecology provides an in-depth look at the essential role fire plays in ecological maintenance and sustainability in a wide variety of natural environments across North America. It explores the process by which scientists came to understand fire's role in the environment as well as representative efforts to institute prescribed burning and the results of the burning programs.

Baskin, J. M., and C. C. Baskin. *Cedar Glades of the Southeastern United States*. Cambridge, England: Cambridge University Press, 1999.

This is a concise look at the rocky outcrops and hardwood forests that characterize much of the southeast United States landscape. Biological needs, preservation methods, and evolving threats are explored through examined case studies.

Benke, Arthur C., and Colbert E. Cushing. *Rivers of North America*. New York: Academic Press, 2005.

Benke and Cushing offer a thorough examination of the ecology and role of the major rivers of North America. This book is an accessible scientific reference that includes valuable biological and hydrological information and maps and photographs to reference each river system.

Campbell, Linda. *Endangered and Threatened Animals of Texas*. Austin: Texas Parks and Wildlife Resource Protection Division, 1995.

Texas Parks and Wildlife Department (TPWD), through its Endangered Resources Branch of the Resource Protection Division, provides current and useful information to landowners, educators, and the public concerning endangered and threatened species. This book is an important part of the vast amount of information the TPWD compiles and disseminates concerning threatened and imperiled species in Texas.

Chabreck, Robert H. *Coastal Marshes: Ecology and Wildlife Management*. Minneapolis: University of Minnesota Press, 1998.

This book describes coastal marshes in terms of form, function, ecology, wildlife value, and management. The emphasis in on marshes of the northern coast of the Gulf of Mexico, but the book also deals with marshes on the Atlantic and Pacific coasts. Plant and animal communities are each given a chapter, and the work ends with a discussion of future uses and needs.

Chafin, Linda G. *Field Guide to the Rare Plants of Georgia*. Athens: University of Georgia Press, 2007.

This guide contains an abundance of photographs and illustrations of Georgia's rare and endangered species. More than 200 species are included in the guide, and it is designed to be easily accessible and understandable to make it convenient to use in the field. In addition to the plants that are examined, the entries also offer detailed information about the local environments that support the individual species.

Culver, David. *The Biology of Caves and Other Subterranean Habitats*. New York: Oxford University Press, 2009.

The work is a comprehensive but relatively concise introduction to cave ecology. The emphasis of the work is on the organisms native to these unique environments, but there is some discussion of conservation and management also. Both cave and noncave subterranean examples are used from all over the world, and clear, precise definitions of field-specific terminology are offered.

Davis, Donald Edward. *Where There Are Mountains: An Environmental History of the Southern Appalachians*. Athens: University of Georgia Press, 2005.

This book explores the historical relationship between the human inhabitants of the southern Appalachians and their environment over 400 years. This parallel exploration looks at a history of environmental degradation in conjunction with the local struggle to survive in one of the poorest regions of the country.

Davis, Jack E., and Raymond Arsenault, eds. *Paradise Lost? The Environmental History of Florida*. Gainesville: University Press of Florida, 2005.

This collection of essays surveys the environmental history of Florida, beginning with Spanish exploration and continuing through to the present. Four thematic sections—explorers and naturalists; science, technology, and public policy; despoliation; and conservationists and environmentalists—explore the constantly evolving policies and practices that have taken place over the last few centuries of Florida's natural history.

Davis, Mary Byrd, ed. *Eastern Old-Growth Forests: Prospects for Rediscovery and Recovery*. Washington, DC: Island Press, 1996.

As stated on the first page of the book, this "is a compilation of writings by a group of distinguished scientists, naturalists, and environmentalists about an exceedingly rare part of the natural world—the scattered remnants of the original Eastern forests." Exhaustingly researched, this volume offers a wealth of information on the natural ecology of old-growth forests, the historical and present-day environmental dangers, and the possibilities of reestablishment, regrowth, and sustainability.

Davis, S. M., and J. C. Ogden, eds. *Everglades: The Ecosystem and Its Restoration*. Delray Beach, FL: St. Lucie Press, 1994.

This thorough exploration of Everglades ecology offers a wealth of information on a wide range of ecological issues. The physical forces that shape the Everglades are examined, as well as their effects on the flora and fauna of the region. The volume is the product of collaboration between 58 authors who are experts in their fields. The focus of the book is the suggestion that a systemwide restoration process could be applied to the Everglades, increasing the overall health and sustainability of the region. The idea is that the only way to save the Everglades may be through this comprehensive, all-encompassing approach.

Dennis, John V. *The Great Cypress Swamps*. Baton Rouge: Louisiana State University Press, 1988.

This work discusses the central role cypress swamps play in the ecology of the southern United States, as well as exploring the history of human use of and interaction with the swamps and the damage that often resulted. The major cypress swamps that remain today are used as examples throughout the book, and each chapter offers a detailed exploration of the swamps' environmental health and condition, along with the native flora and fauna that characterize each site.

Dickson, James. *Wildlife of Southern Forests: Habitat and Management*. Blaine, WA: Hancock House, 2001.

This examination of the history of southern forests and their native wildlife populations includes detailed discussion concerning the habitat needs of plant and animal communities and offers guideline considerations for habitat management on a broad scale.

DiSilvestro, Roger P. *The Endangered Kingdom: The Struggle to Save America's Wildlife.* Hoboken, NJ: Wiley, 1991.

This works looks at the situation and fate of North American wildlife from the arrival of European settlers to the present. In the fates of the species DiSilvestro chooses as representative examples, he finds reoccurring patterns: abundance followed by decimation; recovery through conservation movements; and, now, in a world faced with the possibility of total ecological collapse, an uncertain future.

Eastman, John. *The Book of Swamp and Bog: Trees, Shrubs, and Wildflowers of the Eastern Freshwater Wetlands.* Mechanicsburg, PA: Stackpole Books, 1995.

This is a basic but comprehensively detailed guide to over 80 native North American wetland plants.

Frankenberg, Dirk. *The Nature of North Carolina's Southern Coast: Barrier Islands, Coastal Waters, and Wetlands.* Chapel Hill: University of North Carolina Press, 1997.

The work is formulated as an ecotourist's guide to the North Carolina coast, from Portsmouth Island to Calabash. It addresses current environmental threats to fragile coastal areas and discusses ways the issues could be addressed while facilitating responsible visitor enjoyment of the area.

Frankenberg, Dirk. *The Nature of the Outer Banks: A Guide the Dynamic Barrier Island Ecosystem from Corolla to Ocracoke.* Chapel Hill: University of North Carolina Press, 1995.

Frankenberg describes the dynamic natural forces that shape the barrier islands of North Carolina's Outer Banks. Included in the discussion about the barrier islands and the constant forces of change they experience is a visitation guide for readers focused on the viewing accessibility of these forces in action.

Gillieson, David. *Caves: Processes, Development and Management.* Hoboken, NJ: Wiley-Blackwell, 1996.

Caves provides a thorough exploration of karst management—the first, at its date of publication, to be published in 20 years on cave management. The information is accessible and useful for everyone from cave enthusiasts and spelunkers to karstologists and experts.

Gomez, Gay M. *A Wetland Biography: Seasons on Louisiana's Chenier Plain.* Austin: University of Texas Press, 1998.

Gomez first explores the geography and history of the Chenier Plain and then combines that history with the lifeways of its peoples, creating a portrait of a "working wetland" in which wildlife use and appreciation have produced a stewardship aimed to balance biological, economic, and cultural concerns in the process of species and habitat preservation.

Grunwald, Michael. *The Swamp: The Everglades, Florida, and the Politics of Paradise.* New York: Simon & Schuster, 2006.

The Swamp explores how a recent political and environmental movement has transformed Everglades politics and produced a major rescue plan that is now functioning as a blueprint for wetlands ecosystem restoration.

Hatch, Stephan L., Joseph L. Schuster, and Dale Lynn Drawe. *Grasses of the Texas Gulf Prairies and Marshes*. College Station: Texas A&M University Press, 1999.

This work functions as an identification manual for the study of grasses of the prairies and marshes that are adjacent to the Gulf of Mexico in prairies from northern Mexico to Louisiana. Some attention is paid to the ecosystems and the environmental needs of the grasses.

Helferich, Gerard. *High Cotton: Four Seasons in the Mississippi Delta*. Berkeley, CA: Counterpoint, 2008.

This work, while not directly referencing the ecology or environmental nature of the Mississippi River Delta, explores a full year in the life of a cotton farm in the Mississippi Delta. What the book does, from an environmental point of view, is sets up a physical context for discussion about the Delta region and its environmental concerns.

Howell, Benita, J. *Culture, Environment, and Conservation in the Appalachian South*. Urbana-Champaign: University of Illinois Press, 2002.

This volume explores the historic and contemporary connections between culture and environment in a region that has suffered from land misuse on the environmental side and disparaging stereotypes of its society members. The focus of the book is debunking the idea that nature and culture exist in separate spheres, and it explores the integral ties between Appalachian peoples and their environment as a single, intertwined manifestation rather than two separate entities.

Jose, Shibu, Eric J. Jokela, and Deborah L. Miller, eds. *The Longleaf Pine Ecosystem: Ecology, Silviculture, and Restoration*. New York: Springer, 2007.

This work looks at what used to be one of the most expansive ecosystems in the United States. Land clearing logging, fire suppression, and nonnative species invasion have all taken their toll, and this book looks at each of these threats, discusses the damages caused, and explores restoration and preservation options that could help negate some of the injury incurred through long years of natural resource use and abuse.

Kavanagh, James, and Raymond Leung. *Arkansas Trees and Wildflowers: An Introduction to Familiar Species*. Guilford, CT: Globe Pequot Press, 2008.

This is a reference work that covers the common and familiar tress and wildflowers found across Arkansas. Set up to facilitate exploration and identification of different species, this work provides valuable information on the ideal habitats and environments for each species.

Kemper, Karin E., Ariel Dinar, and William Blomquist. *Integrated River Basin Management through Decentralization*. New York: Springer, 2006.

Using major river basins from around the planet, this work examines how management of water resources at the river-basin level have been designed and implemented, what the inspiration for the plans has been, and what types of management systems tend to be more or less successful in the long run.

Kirkman, L. Katherine, Claud L. Brown, and Donald Joseph Leopold. *Native Trees of the Southeast*. Portland, OR: Timber Press, 2007.

This practical field guide facilitates the identification of more than 200 trees across the Southeast from North and South Carolina and Tennessee through Georgia, Florida, and Alabama, to Mississippi, Louisiana, and Arkansas all the way to Texas. With over 600 photographs and full descriptions for each tree species, the compact format of the book makes for a useful, easily accessible guide.

Kunz, Thomas H., and M. Brock Fenton, eds. *Bat Ecology*. Chicago: University of Chicago Press, 2006.

In *Bat Ecology*, the authors present an up-to-date, comprehensive, and authoritative review of ongoing research involving the ecological and evolutionary diversity of bats. Life history and behavioral ecology, functional ecology, macroecological issues, and conservation challenges are all thoroughly addressed.

Linzey, Donald W. *A Natural History Guide: Great Smoky Mountains National Park*. Knoxville: University of Tennessee Press, 2008.

This park guide is a somewhat lengthy, extremely informative look at the Great Smoky Mountains National Park from a natural history perspective. There is a great deal of information concerning the ecosystems of the park as well as their plant and animal inhabitants. The book also discusses management and access issues common to the park and addresses conservation and restoration activities.

Little, Charles. *The Dying of the Trees: The Pandemic in America's Forests*. New York: Penguin, 1997.

The argument of this book revolves around the idea that the best explanation for the degradation of North American forests is the combination of effects caused by human use, habitation, and abuse. The list of culprits includes acid rain, heavy metal contamination, smog, ozone depletion, and misguided forest management practices.

Lockwood, Mark, Brad McKinney, Jim Paton, and Barry Zimmer, eds. *A Birder's Guide to the Rio Grande Valley*. Colorado Springs, CO: American Birding Association, 1999.

This is a well-researched, well-illustrated guide to the birds that inhabit the Rio Grande Valley. Not only are the individual species detailed in their behavior and identifying characteristics, their environmental needs are explored as well.

Mara, W. P. *Racers, Whipsnakes, and Indigos (Herpetology Series)*. Neptune, NJ: TFH Publications, 1996.

This is a short but informative look at three breeds of snake. Written to be accessible to high school students, the book provides useful information on the habitats necessary for the support of these species as well as the threats they face in different environments across the South and Southeast.

Markham, Doug. *Boxes, Rockets, and Pens: A History of Wildlife Recovery in Tennessee*. Knoxville: University of Tennessee Press, 1997.

The title of this work references the equipment used to help restore wildlife populations across the wilderness areas of Tennessee. It explores the history of animal population declines and recovery efforts, discusses the importance of and reasoning behind wildlife restoration, and examines issues that pertain to the species' future stability.

Mitsch, William J., and James G. Gosselink. *Wetlands*. Hoboken, NJ: Wiley, 2007.

This is the most recent edition of a classic text on the scientific details of wetland ecology. It is one of the mainstays for reference on wetland science, management, and restoration knowledge and practices. This edition revises and updates the previously covered topics concerning wetlands worldwide, including recent developments and practices involving restoration and conservation activities.

Mohlenbrock, Robert. *This Land: A Guide to Eastern National Forests*. Berkeley: University of California Press, 2006.

This book is one in a series of three regional volumes that takes readers through all 155 national forests of the United States. The volumes are comprehensive field guides that describe natural features, campgrounds, scenic drives, hiking trails, and basic ecological characteristics of each forest.

Muller-Schwarze, Dietland, and Lixing Sun. *The Beaver: Natural History of a Wetlands Engineer*. Ithaca, NY: Cornell University Press, 2003.

This is a very well-illustrated exploration of the beaver's role in wetland systems. It provides a detailed look at biology and management issues of both North American and European species. The information is designed to be accessible; although it presents a good amount of scientific information, it is communicated at the reading and understanding level of high school readers and above.

The Nature Conservancy. www.nature.org.

This Web site is the gateway to the most comprehensive collection of information on current preservation efforts taking place across the country. Each state has its own chapter and its own site, with individual pages for each conservation site under the management of the Nature Conservancy. The Web pages provide the foundation for many of the sites chosen for inclusion in this book. The Nature Conservancy is now or has been involved in many conservation efforts that have taken place over the last four decades.

Odum, Howard T., Elisabeth C. Odum, and Mark T. Brown. *Environment and Society in Florida*. Philadelphia: Taylor & Francis, 1997.

Using Florida as a model of study, *Environment and Society* offers a total systems approach to understanding the environment. The focus is the interactions between human society and natural systems. Population, resources, economics, and environment are all explored. The work concludes with suggestions on how such issues might be addressed in the future to obtain more favorable results.

Peacock, Evan, and Timothy Schauwecker, eds. *Blackland Prairies of the Gulf Coastal Plain: Nature, Culture, and Sustainability.* Tuscaloosa: University of Alabama Press, 2003.

This book shows that the Black Belt of Mississippi and Alabama has always been an important refuge for a wide variety of species, both plant and animal. This study integrates ecological, historical, and archaeological information to create a comprehensive portrayal of recent changes in the Gulf Coast blackland prairies.

Porter, John Jr. *A Birder's Guide to Alabama.* Birmingham: University of Alabama, 2001.

This comprehensive guide to bird species of Alabama covers physical characteristics and identifying traits, typical habitats, and threats to population stability and habitat health.

Randolph, John N. *The Battle for Alabama's Wilderness: Saving the Great Gymnasiums of Nature.* Tuscaloosa: University of Alabama Press, 2005.

This book covers the political history of Alabama's three national forest wilderness areas from recognition of the sites as places of environmental significance through the fights for funding and protection to the current conditions of the three areas today.

Ripple, Jeffrey S. *Southwest Florida's Wetland Wilderness: Big Cypress Swamp and the Ten Thousand Islands.* Gainesville: University Press of Florida, 1996.

This book examines the natural history of Florida's Big Cypress Swamp watershed. It looks in detail at the ecological processes that keep the watershed and the Ten Thousand Islands estuarine system functioning. Included in the work is an important section on the threats to these valuable habits and the possible solutions that can reduce environmental damage and degradation.

Ruckdeschel, Carol, and C. Robert Shoop. *Sea Turtles of the Atlantic and Gulf Coasts of the United States.* Athens: University of Georgia Press, 2006.

This guide is a complete introduction to the biology, ecology, habitats, and threats concerning sea turtle species that inhabit the Atlantic and Gulf coasts. Evolution, life stages, nesting, feeding, disease, predators, and conservation issues are all given detailed treatment. Provided for each species is a description of its distribution, habitats, general appearance, life history, behavior, and conservation concerns.

Rydin, Hakan, and John K. Jeglum. *The Biology of Peatlands.* New York: Oxford University Press, 2006.

Included in this comprehensive overview of peatland ecosystems are descriptions of peatland systems and their characteristics, the common challenges peatlands face in maintaining their ecological health, and conservation and restoration activities that have historically proven to work best in rejuvenating damaged or devastated systems.

Samson, Fred B., and Fritz L. Knopf, eds. *Prairie Conservation: Preserving North America's Most Endangered Ecosystem*. Washington, DC: Island Press, 1996.

Prairie Conservation is an examination of the history, ecology, and current status of North American grasslands. It presents in a single volume information on the historical, economic, and cultural significance of prairies, their natural history and ecology, threats, and conservation and restoration programs currently underway.

Sanders, Albert E., and William D. Anderson. *Natural History Investigations in South Carolina from Colonial Times to the Present*. Columbia: University of South Carolina, 1999.

This book explores the natural history investigations that have taken place in South Carolina from the colonial time period in North America to the present. It describes the state's diverse flora and fauna; the impact of social, political, and economic events on natural history; and the role Charleston played in the state's scientific heritage.

Seale, Jan E., and Land Fund Valley. *Creatures on the Edge: Wildlife along the Lower Rio Grande*. McAllen, TX: Chachalaca Press, 1997.

Creatures on the Edge provides an in-depth look at the vast array of wildlife along the lower Rio Grande. Behavioral characteristics are explored, but the focus of the work is on the connections between resident wildlife and the larger ecological environmental of the lower Rio Grande region.

Silliman, Brian R., Mark D. Bertness, and Edwin D. Grosholz. *Human Impacts on Salt Marshes: A Global Perspective*. Berkeley: University of California Press, 2009.

For a long time, it was believed that salt marshes were uniquely resistant to ecological changes and upset, but now scientists understand that these marshes are highly sensitive indicators of environmental change and impact. This work looks at how human society has modified and affected salt marshes around the planet and why these valuable systems desperately need protection now in order to assure their survival for the future. The book also explores what can be done to remedy damage that has already occurred in order to begin the process of restoring the natural functions of salt marsh systems.

Streever, Bill. *Saving Louisiana? The Battle for Coastal Wetlands*. Jackson: University Press of Mississippi, 2001.

Saving Louisiana focuses on the issue that large influxes of salt water are disturbing the brackish and freshwater environments of coastal Louisiana wetlands. The suggested program for restoration carries a huge price tag and would require tremendous management and logistical efforts. This work asks whether restoration is the best path based on a variety of concerns, including societal preference, economic health, environmental interests, and scientific feasibility. This is an in-depth look at an "ecological uproar" with scientists, industry, and citizens in the center of the conflict.

Tennant, Alan. *The Guadalupe Mountains of Texas*. Denton: University of Texas Press, 1997.

Natural and social history of the area from prehistoric times to the present are covered, with 60 color photographs illustrating some of the most striking and characteristic scenery of the Guadalupe Mountains.

Tidwell, Mike. *Bayou Farewell: The Rich Life and Tragic Death of Louisiana's Cajun Coast.* London: Vintage, 2004.

This work is a travelogue-styled look at Louisiana's vanishing coast and its diminishing natural health. It examines both natural forces and human interactions that are causing the disappearance of the coast as well as the human communities that live and work along its length. Environment, economy, and culture are all suffering in the face of these seemingly unstoppable changes, and Tidwell explores the effects in depth.

Weidensaul, Scott. *Mountains of the Heart: A Natural History of the Appalachians.* Golden, CO: Fulcrum, 1994.

Mountains of the Heart explores how geology, climate, evolution, and 500 years of history have shaped the Appalachian region. Weidensaul's portrait of the Appalachians looks at both the natural history and the effects of human presence.

Williams, Joy, and Robert Carawan. *The Florida Keys: A History & Guide.* New York: Random House Trade Paperbacks, 2003.

While mainly a historical recount intended for visitors to the Florida Keys, Williams's guide offers valuable information on the role of the natural environment in the daily life of the keys and what it could mean to residents, visitors, and the local economy should environmental protection issues be ignored.

Yahner, Richard. *Eastern Deciduous Forest: Ecology and Wildlife Conservation.* Chicago: University of Chicago Press, 2000.

This is a thoroughly researched, meticulous presentation of the ecology context of eastern deciduous forests and an examination of the historical and present-day actions taken toward ensuring successful wildlife conservation.

Yaffee, Steven, Ali Phillips, Irene Frentz, Paul Hardy, Sussane Maleki, and Barbara Thorpe. *Ecosystem Management in the United States: An Assessment of Current Experience.* Washington, DC: Island Press, 1996.

The authors explore ecosystem management in the United States from both a physical and policy-based perspective. This book offers a thorough look at the many approaches to habitat management across the country as well as a discussion of each system's strengths and successes.

INDEX

About the Author

Stacy Kowtko, a tenured history professor at Spokane Community College, holds an all-but-dissertation specialty in American history with a research focus on 20th-century U.S. environmental history. She teaches undergraduate courses and learning communities on the theme of environmental history as well. As a native of Louisiana, she has a particular affinity for and connection to the South and Southeast. Additionally, she serves as the faculty liaison for service learning, helping place students in local and international volunteer opportunities aimed at improving and preserving community and environment through active engagement in service opportunities.